T0331419

The Struggle Over Work

Since the 1980s, there have been repeated warnings that post-industrial societies face the 'end of work' – job numbers are declining, work is less important in people's lives, and labour movements are losing their power. Wilson argues that this scenario is misleading and distracts us from the problems confronting societies still dependent on paid employment.

The Struggle Over Work examines the theoretical origins and contemporary versions of this scenario, criticising the arguments of leading thinkers Claus Offe, André Gorz, Alain Touraine, and Jürgen Habermas. These thinkers advocate a basic income to cope with falling employment. Wilson contrasts this proposal with employment-centred alternatives: the 'US model' of work and welfare advocated by business and policy-making elites, and a full-employment model advocated by revived labour movements.

The Struggle Over Work challenges the pervasive pessimism about work and argues for a new engagement with the pressing problems of employment. This book will interest students and academics in labour economics and the politics and sociology of work as well as public policy specialists.

Shaun Wilson is Research Fellow in the Research School of Social Sciences at the Australian National University.

Routledge frontiers of political economy

To Mohsen Rezaie and a free Iran

The Struggle Over Work

The 'end of work' and employment alternatives for post-industrial societies

Shaun Wilson
with the assistance of Peter McCarthy

Routledge
Taylor & Francis Group

LONDON AND NEW YORK

First published 2004
by Routledge
11 New Fetter Lane, London EC4P 4EE

Simultaneously published in the USA and Canada
by Routledge
29 West 35th Street, New York, NY 10001

Routledge is an imprint of the Taylor & Francis Group

© 2004 Shaun Wilson

Typeset in Sabon by Wearset Ltd, Boldon, Tyne and Wear

British Library Cataloguing in Publication Data
A catalogue record for this book is available from the British Library

Library of Congress Cataloging in Publication Data
A catalog record for this book has been requested

ISBN 0-415-30550-0

Contents

Illustrations

Figures

Tables

Acknowledgements

In writing this book, I have been inspired by the humour and wisdom of others. Three people stand out. The first, Jocelyn Pixley of the School of Sociology at the University of New South Wales, was my doctoral supervisor from 1995 to 2000, and guided the thesis that led to this book. Jocelyn is not only an ideal supervisor but also a very able and thoughtful sociologist whose work I admire. The second is Gabrielle Meagher of the School of Economics and Political Science at the University of Sydney. Gabrielle offers perfect editorial advice, the kind that is often tough but always sensible. The third is Peter McCarthy of the Political Science Program in the Research School of Social Sciences at the Australian National University. Peter read the entire draft, and commented meticulously on style and content. His attention to detail and commitment to the project made a much better book than it would otherwise have been. I have learnt a great deal about writing from my three friends.

At the School of Sociology at the University of New South Wales, my thanks go to my teachers, Maria Markus, Michael Pusey, and Clive Kessler for their encouragement and dedication to the social sciences. At the University of Sydney, my appreciation goes to the staff of Political Economy, particularly Joseph Halevi, Dick Bryan, and Evan Jones. At the Australian National University, where I currently work, I have enjoyed the support and encouragement of my colleagues in the Centre for Social Research in the Research School of Social Sciences. I have benefited from the generous conditions provided by the School, and the high level of intellectual engagement there. I thank Sophie Holloway and Rachelle Graham in particular for data assistance and layout work. At Routledge, I am very grateful to Economics editor, Robert Langham, for both his patience and confidence in this project. I am also grateful to Terry Clague for his hard work and support.

I appreciatively recognise the love and support of Martin Heusel and Sally McManus during the years I worked on my thesis and wrote this book. I acknowledge the warm and sustaining friendships of Selene Alcock, Yane Svetiev, Charron Hannah, Didi Ratno, Loren Fykes, Amanda Perkins, Javier Mera, Yann Savy, Laurence D'Ambrosio, Sonia

Hoffman, Denise Mimmocchi, Nick Turnbull, Toby Fattore, Robin Walton, Sally Auld, Fiona Moore, Jerry Scharen, Adam Voits, and Lisa More. And a special thanks to Xena ('Ween') who we just adore.

I dedicate this book to Mohsen Rezaie. Mohsen has struggled so hard for his freedom, and taught us a lesson about the virtues of humility and inner strength when our lives are threatened by forces we cannot control. May he have the same peace and love that he has brought to the lives of others.

Introduction

When Jeremy Rifkin published *The End of Work* in 1995,[1] the *US News and World Report* claimed that more Americans were working than at any other time in the country's history.[2] With working hours fast approaching an annual average of 2,000 hours per person, the article concluded that the United States was 'addicted' to work. These two developments seemed at odds: a high profile book forecasting the 'end of work' published during one of the stronger periods of employment growth in American history. The strengthening prospects for employment during the Clinton years justified a major shift in social policy that favoured getting people off welfare and into paid work. Other advanced countries, led by the market-embracing Blair Labour Government, followed the American model of promoting employment and workfare. Even those European countries usually most resistant to American social and economic policy solutions looked to the American experience as they searched for ways out of long-term unemployment. Clinton left Washington, recession came and the employment boom slowed remarkably. Yet the policy experience of the United States during the 1990s has had a lasting impact on policy-makers and politicians, especially those who support deregulated labour markets as an alternative to extensive employment and welfare protections.

Strengthening employment trends in the English-speaking world at the end of 1990s contrasted starkly with the pessimism about the future of work prevailing elsewhere. Like Rifkin, various major European social scientists (following in a long line of distinguished writers) have made their reputations by forecasting the decline of a work-based society. They have argued that technological change leads to irreversible job loss, and employment no longer sharply defines contemporary social structures. While many thinkers have proposed different versions of the 'end of work' argument, the most important recent advocates belong to the European 'post-industrial left' and, in this book, I shall devote particular attention to their claims. Inspired by new social movements and pessimistic about class-based change, the post-industrial left has looked not to employment and the class structure but to civil society for alternative ways of organising a diverse society. The post-industrial left's key thinkers – Claus Offe, André

Gorz, and Alain Touraine – have not claimed that work will disappear in any literal sense. But they abandon their Marxist past when they claim that work has lost its central function in the social structure and its driving force in politics and society. Jürgen Habermas even wrote of the 'exhaustion of utopian energies' attached to work when he dissected the shortcomings of a society based on full employment.[3]

Given the employment situation there, European pessimism is understandable. If we take the employment-to-population ratio over time, which measures the number of people in paid employment within the working-age population, major continental European countries have experienced decline. However, in other parts of Europe, and in the English-speaking world, employment levels measured this way have been steady or have even risen.[4] These divergent employment trends make it timely to ask two questions, which I hope this book will help us answer. The first question is: what are the sources and propositions for the 'end of work' argument we encounter among writers on the post-industrial left? And the second is: what alternatives can societies ponder in considering how work might be transformed in the coming decades? In helping to answer these questions, my contribution seeks to challenge the 'end of work' argument. My challenge proceeds in two stages, forming the respective parts of this book. The rationale for Part I is to establish the sociological sources and main arguments of this pessimistic view about work, revealing its widespread influence. The rationale for Part II is to use my critique of the arguments proposed by the post-industrial left to evaluate three alternative models for transforming work that seek to solve the current impasse: one that relies on deregulated labour markets, one that relies on a basic income scheme, and one that relies on renewed labour movements to drive full employment objectives.

Part I: the sociological sources of contemporary pessimism

Part I traces the sociological sources of contemporary pessimism. By this I refer to the pessimistic arguments about work that have had a lasting impact in sociology. For now, I will sketch out just a few points of departure. In Chapter 1, I take up the insights of Karl Marx, Max Weber, and Emile Durkheim. Despite his early attempts at building a social theory around the idea of production, Marx went on to present a dramatic version of a post-work society arising out of technological change and the passing of scarcity. When Marx foresees the emergence of a 'collective labourer', he assumes that, by virtue of capitalist development, labour becomes so abstract it almost ceases to depend on meaningful human input. While Weber did not directly anticipate a post-work society, he shares common ground with Marx. Both writers envisage a severe rationalisation of work which strips it of its human qualities. Taken together, Marx and Weber set a pessimistic stage for understanding the relationship between work and modernisation. This pessimism has cast a long shadow.

Throughout the twentieth century, writers have drawn attention to work's apparent waning importance. In the 1950s, Herbert Marcuse and Hannah Arendt represented these efforts in social theory. Marcuse attempted to realise Marx's 'liberation from work' argument. Arendt attempted to slay the idea that the foundations of democracy could ever rely on a work-centred social theory. Inspired by the social revolts of the 1960s and 1970s, a new generation of social thinkers returned once again to these themes. Intellectuals, including Habermas, Touraine, and Offe, have attempted to go beyond a sociology founded on work and social classes, looking to other concepts and social forces to explain contemporary change.

Chapter 2 examines the contributions of the three most prominent theorists for our purposes: Habermas, Touraine, and Offe. Taken together, these thinkers offer a distinctive and plausible account of post-industrial social change, which describes in dramatic fashion the declining importance of a work-centred industrial society. They have tried to draw out the implications of the decline of work for social theory, for welfare and for social movement contention. Because their arguments are important in their own right, and provide a lynchpin between the two parts of this book, I'll spend a moment outlining each author's contribution.

Influenced by Marcuse and Arendt, Habermas attempts to find a better foundation for a general social theory. But in laying down new foundations, he ends up suggesting that work is closer to a kind of 'instrumental action' than a social practice, as Weber had implied before him. In doing so, Habermas's challenge to traditional Marxism went much further than his Frankfurt School predecessors. Confining work to instrumental action gave Habermas room to develop a new and durable concept of communicative action that would allow him to better explain the forces that drive social rationalisation. For Habermas, our communicative achievements, and not our work activities or the things we produce, determine 'social rationality'. Work no longer provides a clear reference point for explaining social transformation. But Habermas pays a price for this achievement. As even his sympathetic critics point out, Habermas's recourse to systems theory means that he obscures an ongoing understanding of the impact work has on social identities, conflicts, and social structure.

While Habermas concentrated his efforts on moving social theory away from work-centred categories, Alain Touraine's theory of social change pointed to the displacement of labour movements from their central role as social movements with the advent of post-industrial society. For Touraine, labour's role was quickly being replaced by other social movements engaged in new social struggles such as for the rights of women, the environment, and for the recognition of social identity. Declining social activity in the sphere of work is consistent with a post-industrial society that has simply 'moved on' into new areas of contention and conflict. This leads Touraine to a gloomy forecast: 'the role of trade unionism is not over ... the history of the workers' movement is.'[5] But we must ask: does Touraine adopt an overly pessimistic view of unions by insisting that they cannot maintain or return to a social movement-style of activism and politics?

Post-industrial thinkers responded to rising unemployment in the 1970s and 1980s by doubting the prospects for full employment, and searching for a new model of welfare and redistribution that could cope with permanent joblessness. Claus Offe's contribution addresses these declining prospects most thoroughly, and I will use his insights to help establish some basic parameters of the employment debate, the subject of this book. Offe argues that welfare states can no longer operate on the prospect of full employment, and that the most viable, progressive alternative is now a basic income scheme. This scheme, which I shall examine in detail in Chapter 4, proposes to guarantee a *universal* minimum income with few or no work obligations on the part of citizens. Because a basic income scheme promises to break the nexus between work and income, it has naturally received support from post-industrial thinkers who see it as a viable exit route from a work-based industrial society. But are the prospects for employment growth as dim as post-industrial critics like Offe assume?

When the ideas of the post-industrial left are stripped of their nuances, we can see that they depend on a pessimistic scenario of permanent joblessness, declining skill and attachment to work, weak labour movements, and hopeless prospects for full employment. But this scenario depends on a number of assumptions that we must scrutinise. Five brief points are sufficient here to get at the argument I'll develop throughout the book. First, if we take objective measures of employment rates in advanced societies (like employment-to-population ratios), we find no clear trends to lower employment levels. Second, evidence suggests workforce skills are generally increasing, and, in some instances, skill differences are actually narrowing. Third, survey evidence suggests that workers still prefer paid employment – *even* when presented with the alternative of a living income without having to work. Fourth, while in many countries unions face serious problems (decreasing membership, strikes, and reduced political power), their problems are not necessarily irreversible. Finally, full employment policies may still be possible if they are politically 'reinvented' and find new public support, bolstered by strengthened labour movements.

Part II: post-industrial pessimism and three options for work and society

The post-industrial 'end of work' scenario is a compelling reading of change. If its assumptions hold, and employment levels continue to decline, then it would point clearly to policy solutions, like a basic income, that would distribute income in a way less dependent on participation in employment. But if the assumption that work will inevitably decline does not hold, then at least two other scenarios and some quite different policy solutions come into view. Each of these alternative scenarios is examined in Part II. The first model is a deregulated market approach such as we find in the United States which claims to have restored employment levels through competitive labour markets and pro-work social policies. The second is a social-democratic alternative, closer to what we find in contemporary Scandinavia, which would attempt to re-establish full employment, presumably with the support of revived labour movements. Taken together, it is these three approaches – a deregulated labour market model, a basic income model, and a new full employment model – whose prospects and desirability we evaluate in Chapters 3 to 5. Table I.1 summarises some key features of these alternative models.

The recent American employment experience is our point of reference for the deregulated market approach. As I mentioned in the opening paragraphs to this book, the 'US model', as Lawrence Mishel and John Schmitt and others call it,[6] has received unprecedented attention for its apparent ability to marry deregulated labour markets with tough new 'workfare' policies, and thus to stimulate jobs. Although employment and growth in the United States dropped sharply after President George W. Bush assumed power, America's success during the 1990s made it a source of 'policy

Table I.1 Three alternative paths for work and society

Model	Diagnosis of the problem	Proposed solution	Main advocates	Main opponents
'US model': deregulated labour market	Over-regulation; welfare state disincentives	Deregulation; pro-work social policy; institutional and legal limits on unions	Business; market-oriented think tanks; conservative and liberal parties; some mainstream social democratic parties	Organised labour; welfare groups
Basic income	Permanent employment deficit; over-emphasis on work in social policy	Basic income (universal minimum income)	Some post-industrial left and green parties; some liberal parties; some liberal economists; social movements	Taxpayers
Full employment social democracy	Public policy ignores unemployment	Regulation of labour market; employment creation	Labour movements; traditional social democratic or socialist parties; pro-labour think tanks	Business

transfer' for other countries looking to lower unemployment without increasing spending. We shall start with the US model because the American approach is clearly dominant, finding support among political, bureaucratic, business, and media elites, and because its claims of employment success comprehensively challenge the 'end of work' scenario. These two facts make it a sensible vantage point from which to compare apparently less probable alternatives: the basic income and social democratic models.

What are the claims made for the US model? Advocates say that the US model produces higher employment rates because of its business-friendly labour market, and lower welfare 'dependence' because of its tough welfare policies. In the eyes of its supporters, these two strengths make the US model the most likely to maintain a high level of employment, especially when America is compared with more regulated economies elsewhere. Chapter 3 tests these claims by offering a detailed assessment of the policies and problems of the American path to higher employment. Although the USA has experienced higher employment growth, it is misleading to assume that this is simply the result of its pro-market policies. We also find high levels of inequality in the labour market, abetted by a difficult, if not hostile, environment for unions and collective bargaining. The US model makes it harder for workers to 'find a voice' through union activity and contention so that they might better shape their working lives. A wealth of evidence, some anecdotal, some psychological and some sociological, points to the pressures faced by an over-worked, under-paid workforce. Still, we explore the reasons for the US model's international reputation and ask: is it a viable model for international policy transfer to other advanced countries looking to solve the problems of work and welfare?

The inequality problems of the US model make the exploration of alternatives desirable or even necessary. In Chapter 4, I take up the basic income model preferred by the post-industrial left who argue that employment gains in a tough, market-driven work and welfare regime are not worth the costs. For them, it is better to forsake the employment goals of modern societies if these heavily compromise the goal of equality. Emboldened by a belief in the impossibility or undesirability of full employment, basic income advocates propose to restructure work and welfare regimes so that an adequate minimum income is provided universally, regardless of people's employment status. For this reason, basic income schemes are sometimes called citizens' income schemes.

Chapter 4 looks at the assumptions that underlie basic income proposals and tests some of their arguments empirically. I foreshadow here three problems with basic income. First, as I have suggested already, basic income ideas frequently depend on the 'end of work' scenario. Continuing employment growth undermines the rationale for basic income reform. Second, basic income advocates often assume that people have only weak attachments to their work, or, in economists' language, find work to be a 'disutility'. But when the British Social Attitudes Survey of 2000 asked employees, 'if without having to work, you had what you would regard as a reasonable living income, would you still prefer to have a job or wouldn't you bother?', a large majority responded that they would prefer to work. And when we analyse these findings further, we discover that disengaged attitudes towards work are more a product of *poor working experiences* than a lack of interest in working as the post-industrial left would have it. The third problem for basic income proposals lies in their political feasibility. Finding a supportive political coalition would be essential for such root-and-branch reform. Business would object to the costs, and to the possible disincentives to work. Taxpayers would resist what conservatives would easily misrepresent as 'subsidising the lazy'. And the public may not be satisfied, given they, for better or worse, still expect government to create jobs.

Does a basic income scheme face better prospects if it is taken up in a more modest form, either by reducing the benefit level or restricting coverage? Recently, basic income advocates have begun to take seriously the option of partial implementation. And in a hard-edged policy environment, policy-makers have been developing income support policies that could arguably be seen as the first steps towards a basic income scheme. The Earned Income Tax Credit scheme in the United States or the Working Families Tax Credit in the United Kingdom are two obvious examples of this kind of policy, providing income support to low-wage working individuals and families. Some basic income supporters see these policies as the institutional foundations for building a basic income-style scheme in the form of a universal negative income tax.

But it is not clear whether negative income tax policies or tax credit schemes would weaken the link between employment and income, as post-industrial supporters of a basic income seek, or actually reinforce it. Certainly, for pro-market advocates, the appeal of these kind of measures comes in their design: these policies deal with the problems of inequality not through raising wages, which critics claim costs jobs, but through tax-based redistribution. Writing of North American policies, John Myles and Paul Pierson refer to such schemes as 'Friedman's Revenge', reflecting the growing influence of the Chicago School economist's original negative income tax proposal.[7] One consistent criticism of these policies is their potential to entrench low-wage employment. So we must ask: do these policies offer a building block for a basic income scheme that breaks with employment, or do they compromise basic income ideals too greatly?

If the dynamic performance of the US model suggests a quite different transformation path than that envisaged by the post-industrial left, one that remains centred on employment and job creation, are there still hopes for committing to employment expansion of a more social-democratic kind? Certainly this has been the long-term mission of labour movements, and labour parties committed to the goals of full employment. If a 'jobs with inequality' model remains viable, is it possible to aspire to a 'jobs with equality' alternative? Critics would say no. Pro-market critics would say the model is a proven failure because it depends on sclerotic regulations that make jobs growth too costly. Post-industrial critics would claim that technological and social change, and an 'exhaustion' of the forces that built full employment make this goal undesirable and not feasible.

Chapter 5 argues that the prospects of a 'jobs with equality' approach will depend critically on the capacity of labour movements to offer an alternative model for labour market regulation. But I shall argue that for this alternative to emerge, presently weak union movements would need to revive their influence in the workplace and in politics. How likely is this prospect? Chapter 5 attempts to answer this question by considering the factors that have led to union weakness in the advanced industrial economies. We find that there are good grounds to challenge the view that labour movements, especially in countries like Australia, the United Kingdom, and the United States, are weak because of 'post-industrial social change' that deprives unions of their social relevance and power. Instead, we find that national labour institutions, historical factors, and internal organisation of unions matter more in the union decline story. By highlighting these factors, and studying recent developments in national labour movements more carefully, we can identify the difficulties unions face in their efforts to assert workplace influence and increase their political power. We conclude the chapter by considering how unions could, once again, become a driving influence on politics and policy. I shall argue that a revived union movement is the most important institutional influence for a new full employment policy designed to suit the times.

Methodology of the book

Before proceeding further, I shall declare some of my guiding instincts and methodological influences. I am not proposing to make a specialist contribution to the sociology of work. There is already plenty of other writing making this kind of contribution. Rather, I wish to raise some general arguments about prospects for work and confront them in a debate about directions and ideas. For some, my contribution will not deliver the specialist or country-specific insights that now tend to dominate this area and set the terms of reference for further research. Instead, my efforts are argument-driven, and I am eager to find empirical evidence that helps sort fact from fiction, as well as drawing out the socio-political implications of alternatives.

My comparative, empirical analysis includes ten advanced nations: Australia, Canada, France, Germany, Italy, Japan, the Netherlands, Sweden, the United Kingdom, and the United States. These comparisons are not intended to be exhaustive; rather, they are largely used to develop relevant contrasts between national outcomes and approaches. Readers may find this book has greater purchase for the English-speaking countries that I examine than for the other countries included in this research. This is partly because the English-speaking countries have travelled further down the road to 'employment reform' than many of their European counterparts. In the coming decade, European economies and societies may increasingly follow a similar path of reform. Others could plausibly argue that the most exciting developments at the moment are occurring elsewhere, in countries like South Korea, South Africa, and Brazil. While these developments have greater importance for advanced democracies than ever before, they are the subject of a different book. Mine is about comparing countries with broadly similar profiles and levels of development so that we can meaningfully assess their performance, policies, and institutional development.

Either sympathetic or critical, no book about the general direction of work in advanced societies can sidestep the Marxist tradition. Within Marxism, work has a special, universal significance, a kind of 'meta-category' status as Axel Honneth puts it.[8] I do not seek to defend work as a universal category that, either by clever or outmoded extrapolation, is used to explain all human action. As Habermas has demonstrated over the past four decades, this approach has definite limits. My motivation is a more pragmatic defence of the place of work in social identities and structures, and in political life. My view is there is a real risk of the social sciences neglecting the interactions between work, society, and politics.

Understanding social trends depends on what we assume about social change. I contrast two views. A 'thin' approach assumes that the technical accomplishments of ever-more complex systems will displace the institutional foundations of work. 'Formal' macro-sociology tends to talk about systems, structures, and technically driven transformations. Habermas, for example, adopts a 'formal' approach to understanding large-scale organisations even as he searches out the links between systems and what he calls the lifeworld. Such approaches sometimes neglect or cannot explain persistent social institutions within technical systems and organisations. By this I mean that the web of social relationships disappears from view in this type of theorising, even though these relationships matter in understanding change. How institutions conform to and mould social structures is an important part of the 'micro–macro' problem in sociology.[9] When we talk about work environments, I think the micro-social processes that motivate action, and particularly collective action, help us understand the broader dynamics of work and social change. Formalistic macro-sociology assumes away the institutional role of work in social structures, and it also assumes away the role micro-processes play in social change. Chicago School sociologist, Everett Hughes, brought concrete attention to this kind of problem several generations ago. He stated:

> We are ... alerted to the value of work situations as posts for observing the formation of groups and the generation of social rules and

sanctions. I am not sure that we are using the findings of such observation vigorously enough in building our theories of social control and of the larger legal and political processes.[10]

Finally, some qualifications about my use of the term 'work'. Feminists rightly point out that identifying 'work' with paid employment implicitly excludes unpaid domestic work. Reducing work to *paid employment* does not recognise the traditionally defined contribution of women to work. I agree with this. Unfortunately, since most sociological theory (such as Habermas's distinction between 'work' and 'interaction') refers to work when the authors mean paid employment, I shall persist with the term 'work' for purposes of convenience while recognising the traditional, implicit bias it maintains against household labour. Also, a number of writers like Hannah Arendt, for example, distinguish between 'work' and 'labour' to distinguish between self-directed craft work and labour that is more externally directed and more menial. I refer simply to 'work' in the present project, aware of the practical importance of Arendt's distinction.

Part I

The sociological sources
of contemporary
pessimism

1 Pessimistic origins
Work in classical sociology

In my introductory comments, I suggested that classical ideas cast a long shadow over the ways we think about the future of work. This chapter highlights the most salient of these ideas for understanding contemporary pessimism about work. Claus Offe rightly points out that work is a 'key sociological category' in the classical tradition,[1] serving as a springboard for more ambitious claims about social change. My purpose in this chapter is to present some of the most important insights in the writings of Marx, Weber, and Durkheim that helped to shape later understanding of the relationship between work and society, and which contributed to a pessimistic mindset in social thought. In the next chapter I will show how these ideas resurface in the writings of European post-industrial social thinkers. Here, I shall try to show why classical sociology did not leave us with a strong sense of the social foundations of work, constituted by relationships that would prove to be a source of social change, of contention, and of significance for social understanding.

Our point of reference is Karl Marx because he was so influential for later critical thinkers as well as for Weber and Durkheim. Most people today associate Marx with the utopia of a 'worker's paradise', or with trade unions and socialist parties. But we should not assume Marx held a consistent view about how work, the mainstay of his theory of human action, would evolve in a post-capitalist society. His earlier philosophical anthropology treats work as a universal category for understanding human action. However, his later writings provide a strong hint of the 'end of work' scenario we find in subsequent thinkers. The move Marx made was away from hopes for 'humanising work', and towards the view that work can, and should be, minimised in a rational society. Marx's pessimism about work, if I can call it that, is a precursor of Weber's later contribution. Despite efforts by some commentators to draw their theories into sharp contrast, Marx's description of the evolution in the labour process overlaps with Weber's depiction of rationalised work organisation. Like Marx, Weber recognised the advances of both bureaucratic and technical organisation, and he expressed ambivalence about them. But he had little faith in the democratising potential of the workplace's social institutions, built up through the labour movement, to limit the dehumanising impact of a rationalising society. Durkheim's contribution in his *The Division of Labour in Society* does not attend to all the new forms of solidarity we find in industrial societies. I shall argue that he recognises only a limited kind of solidarity, one that provides the inspiration for later 'integrationist' sociology. But for an understanding of the connection between work and social change, Durkheim's theory is limited, failing to fully appreciate a deeper kind of solidarity produced in work that continues to shape industrial development and social conflicts.

Marx and the 'end of work'

Marx's contribution to nineteenth-century social thought is the key point of reference for looking at classical sociological ideas about work, and thus for our discussion here. Work or labour (I use the terms interchangeably) is at the heart of Marx's understanding of modern economies and societies. Building on the contributions of Adam Smith and the classical economists, as well as Hegel's philosophy, Marx's understanding of the labour process establishes the dynamic foundation for his theory as a whole. Work is both an encompassing element in his philosophical framework, and the basis for his analysis of capitalism. Marx's earlier writing, his philosophical anthropology which some scholars call the 'paradigm of production', conceives of work as the basic building block for human action. By transforming work, we transform ourselves, our social relations, and our society. However, Marx's later analysis of capitalist development leads him to a different scenario, one in which capitalism eliminates work, rendering it an increasingly minor part of a technical machine. And Marx sees something rational in this: he envisages that human freedom will depend not on 'humanising' existing work, but on rationalising it, and making way for an enlarged realm of freedom in which humans may develop.

There is something tidy about how Marx sees the 'abolition of work' as part of a rational process, driven in essence by the technological and organisational conquests of mature capitalism. But does Marx pay a price for this conceptual economy and for assuming that work can be rationalised in this way? Is the later Marx actually forced to argue that, in order to reclaim our freely producing spirit, work must be abolished? French sociologist, Georges Friedmann, addresses this tension in the following terms:

> For a long time Marx thought that the citizens of a socialist society could become 'fully developed individuals' in and through their work; individuals, for whom, as he wrote in his *Critique of the Gotha Programme*, productive labour is the 'first necessity of life'.... By the end of his life, when he was revising the third volume of *Das Kapital* ...,

[however], his attitude had changed and his whole emphasis was upon the 'realm of freedom', which, so he declares, 'only begins, in fact, where that labour which is determined by need and external purposes, ceases'.[2]

My main interest is in seeing how Marx goes about developing the 'end of work' scenario we identified in the Introduction, and which influenced so many later thinkers. I must make a strong qualification before going any further. My investigation into Marx's views about the course of work under capitalism does not assume that Marx can only be interpreted in this way.[3] Indeed, seeing Marx as the primary intellectual source for 'humanising work' is quite tenable. But the vision of a society without workers inspired many, and it is worth understanding how others came to view Marx in this way.

We must begin with a brief outline of the general ideas Marx develops about work. In early writings, the *Economic and Philosophic Manuscripts* and his commentary on James Mill, Marx develops an expressive concept of work, which he uses as a foundation stone for his critique of philosophy, and that captures the full sense in which he believes society is practically and historically *produced* by real human beings (i.e. human praxis).[4] The prominence of work in both English political economy and German idealism, particularly in Hegel's philosophy, presented Marx with a brilliant opportunity for synthesis.[5] For him, work becomes a needs-directed activity that drives social action, and the key means through which economic value is created in the capitalist system.

Marx contends that we work to meet needs that arise out of our interchange with the natural and social worlds. By producing things, we transform our social relations and our relationship to the external world.[6] He declares that: 'the first historical act is ... the production of the means to satisfy these needs, the production of material life itself'.[7] Through its transforming force, production starts to change the balance between humans and nature. As Agnes Heller notes:

> According to Marx, ... industrial production makes it possible to resolve the opposition between 'natural' needs and 'socially produced' needs, even if in capitalist society this takes place in a contradictory way, and even if this society – temporarily – reproduces the contradiction. The overcoming of the contradiction between 'natural' and 'socially produced' needs is thus a result of the pushing back of the natural limits. The pushing back of the objective and subjective natural limits is interrelated: Marx does not distinguish between internal and external nature.... External nature exists for man only in reciprocal interaction with society, in the process of socialisation, in the organic exchange between man and nature.[8]

Clearly, as human needs develop, so do society's productive capabilities. And as this process of development gathers pace, people no longer express the raw needs they have in scarce natural environments; instead they express the much more complex needs that emerge out of society itself. Heller cites Marx's *Capital*:

> 'necessary' needs *develop*, historically, they are not dictated by mere survival; the cultural element in such needs, the moral element and custom, are decisive, and their satisfaction is an organic part of the 'normal' life of people belonging to a particular class in a given society.[9]

So if expressing new, more complex needs drives human development, then work provides the engine for progress.

When Marx turns to a more scientific study of capitalism, he remains committed to the philosophy of praxis developed in his earlier writings. Work provides the bridge between Marx's overall theory of society and his rigorous attempt to uncover the laws of capitalism. Marx's point of departure is obvious. While work is, in essence, a 'needs-directed' enterprise, the capitalist system organises labour for its own purposes, extracting value from the productive labour of the working class, which it is able to organise more rationally and technologically. Rather than expressing our species being, the form and content of work are subsumed under the capitalist order. Use values are produced for the purposes of exchange, and the craft of work is transformed into the abstract labour demanded for capitalist production. The great gap between the capitalist search for exchange values and human needs gives rise to humanity's alienation.

Marx thinks our species being can be recovered by transcending the capitalist system, with its ever-developing and ever-more abstract division of labour. We are interested in understanding how Marx envisages the process of change that would lead this to happen. As Friedmann suggested, the early Marx leads us to believe that somehow work could be humanised, in a manner consistent with his praxis philosophy. However, as Marx's thinking about capitalism matures, he increasingly turns his attention away from the sphere of work in his search for sources of freedom. Some of this shift belongs to a larger development in Marx's thinking, with many scholars identifying 'discontinuities' between Marx's praxis philosophy and his later scientific study of capitalism as a process of 'law-like' development. Of course, Marxists like Louis Althusser see a distinct virtue in Marx's unromantic 'systems' depiction of capitalist development. But others see real difficulties. Hans Joas outlines the problem in the following terms:

> His seminal work, *Capital*, is a fundamental restructuring of his critique of capitalism. Whereas in his [earlier] writings . . . the impossi-

bility of self-realization through labour under conditions of private ownership was the central tenet of Marx's theoretical construction, in *Capital* itself ... the idea of a self-positing mind is taken up in a completely different form. It is no longer the individual producer but rather capital upon which he now bestows the predicates of the 'mind' and its development.... The predicates of subjectivity and creativity are now no longer based in anthropology but, in imitation of Hegel's dialectical logic, are transposed onto a subject, namely capital, that positively destroys the subjectivity of the individuals subsumed under capitalist relations.[10]

Joas goes on to trace the most important implication of this shifting focus, one that takes Marx from the reality of producers to the laws of the capitalist system. Joas claims that 'the fact that [in Marx] social processes become independent of the intentions and wishes of the actors, makes it conceptually difficult, if not impossible, to grasp the sources of a subjectivity that is directed against capital'.[11] It is precisely this shift, I shall argue, that makes it possible for Marx to envisage an 'end of work' scenario in some future society.

Marx offers an ingenious account of capitalist development.[12] Capitalists struggle over profit by transforming the labour process. Their struggles drive the economy forward, increasing its technological sophistication at the expense of the labour force: workers are displaced, organisation becomes more rationalised, and the 'human qualities' of work are increasing stripped away. Of course, Marx understood the process of capitalist development as one of profound contradictions, manifesting in periodic crises, and providing the dynamics for further change. Technology plays a critical role in this story of contradictions. While profits are boosted by new technologies that lower labour costs and by rational organisation, fierce competition eventually reduces profit margins. While the mass of profits tend to grow in the expanding system, they do so at a declining rate as the 'organic composition' of capital rises, displacing labour, which is the source of economic value. And the periodic crises of capitalist development, an inherently unstable process, produce economic and social tensions. Marx argues with all his political and scientific passion that capitalism is a process of both rational development and social destruction. The system's fundamental weaknesses do not lie in its ability to create wealth, but rather in the way it undermines the conditions and status of the workers who produce that wealth.

Two assumptions in this scenario about the transformation of work under capitalism are particularly relevant to Marx's understanding of change. He assumes that labour is increasingly transformed by technological change, and that work in the factories of the capitalist system is more and more reduced to simple units of 'abstract labour'. While capitalism still depends on general labourers, and workers still compete for jobs, the endpoint Marx anticipates for all these changes leads him famously to state that, 'labour no longer appears so much to be included within the production process; rather, the human being comes to relate more as watchman and regulator to the production process itself'.[13] Marx captures the growing marginality of labour in an increasingly system-like productive process. The dynamics Marx describes would limit any prospects for humanising work, and lead him to a new understanding of the prospects for social change.

As Marx's emphasis shifts, we get a new picture of how society would function in post-capitalist form. As the astute dialectician he was, Marx, of course, is always searching for the positive in the negative. He thus sees a clear virtue in labour's subsumption under capital. As Herbert Marcuse later explains, Marx thought the remaining economic system, defined by its efficiency and its use of abstract labour, would develop the character of a 'collective labourer'.[14] Echoing Hegel, Marx starts to locate work within rational society as part of a 'realm of necessity' he contrasts with a 'realm of freedom'. The latter realm would greatly expand as the system progressed, allowing for humans to engage in their free activity. The following passage from *Capital* expresses the larger picture Marx envisages:

> In fact, the realm of freedom actually begins only where labour which is determined by necessity and mundane considerations ceases; thus in the very nature of things it lies beyond the sphere of actual material production. Just as the savage must wrestle with Nature to satisfy his wants, to maintain and reproduce life, so must civilized man, and he must do so in all social formations and under all possible modes of production. With his development this realm of physical necessity expands as a result of his wants; but, at the same time, the forces of production which satisfy these wants also increase. Freedom in this field can only consist in socialized man, the associated producers, rationally regulating their interchange with Nature, bringing it under their common control, instead of being ruled by it as by the blind forces of Nature; and achieving this with the least expenditure of energy and under conditions most favourable to, and worthy of, their human nature. But it nonetheless still remains a realm of necessity. Beyond it begins that development of human energy which is an end in itself, the true realm of freedom, which, however, can blossom forth only with the realm of necessity as its basis. The shortening of the working day is its basic prerequisite.[15]

Marx is not suggesting that work would literally disappear. But by confining it to the realm of necessity and juxtaposing it with activities in the realm of freedom, work no longer seems to capture his hope for human praxis. For later writers, like Marcuse and André Gorz, Marx's scenario of greater freedom from work is a wellspring of insight and inspiration. But is seeing work in these pessimistic terms a realistic model from which to build hopes for a future society?

We might first address this question by wondering about the plausibility of such a pessimistic description. A couple of doubts must surely be countenanced. If we accept that the form and content of work activities ultimately depend on the progress of human needs, then to assume that work, under whatever socio-economic system, diminishes in its volume and complexity, requires us to assume also that needs cease developing or that they can be met increasingly through technology. Agnes Heller argues that Marx comes close to the latter position when she says:

> The idea of unlimited progress in material production is a clear characteristic of Marx's thought; his ideas on the *rate* of increase of production are, however, contradictory on more than one occasion. On the one hand, he assumes that capitalism arrives at a point where the development of the forces of production (and in particular the increase in fixed capital) ceases, and that therefore the rate of material production in the society of associated producers would have to be more rapid, at least in comparison with the situation in latter-day capitalism. On the other hand, the increased rate of material production ... is determined by the needs of the associated producers. However, in parallel with the growing wealth, these needs will be less and less directed towards material consumer goods. This already suggests a new structure of needs which is of decisive importance. In the new structure of needs, Marx uses a sort of 'saturation model': material consumer goods ... would play an increasingly limited role in the structure of needs of individuals, or at any rate their proportion would be less.[16]

But, clearly, even under advanced capitalism, the complexity of human needs has generated an enormous increase in employment and an increasingly complex and sophisticated workforce to meet these needs. We might then ask whether locating work within the realm of necessity in the way Marx does would conceptually accommodate any increase in the complexity and skill involved in work. Heller is doubtful. She suggests Marx's overall picture assumes a trend towards simple labour, interchangeable by its nature, measured in time rather than by the type of task, and consistent with the idea of a collective labourer.[17] If it is fair to say that Marx thought work would tend towards simple, abstract labour in a realm of necessity, it would be difficult for us to place complex work within this realm. These activities involve technical, human, and social skill, complicated interactions between people, and forms of learning and dedication that are incompatible with the mundane activities that belong to a realm of necessity. Many forms of work, because they are complex, involve skill, or are pleasurable, would slip between these two realms of necessity and freedom. This problem, among others, leads Heller to conclude that it is 'inconceivable that there should be such a huge abyss between the activity of labour and the activity of free time'.[18] Heller further observes: 'We ourselves cannot imagine any social order in which the need for material goods can become saturated relatively easily and where the individuality of needs develops exclusively through non-material needs.'[19] There is an alternative to Marx's vision that would avoid such assumptions. As society develops, so do the variety and complexity of needs that find expression. To meet this development, complex work tasks, requiring specialisation and skill, emerge alongside advancing technology.[20]

Developments in work and employment levels in advanced capitalist societies subsequent to Marx's time do not provide clear support for the image of work increasingly confined to a 'realm of necessity'. Skilled work continues to grow in service occupations, and skilled jobs remain in manufacturing despite the predictions of pessimists. Moreover, technological change has not eliminated skilled work. Even though technical change deskills or eliminates employment, technologies also enhance and develop skills and complex work-tasks. Certainly, Harry Braverman demonstrated the fundamental forms of deskilling that occurred in the job types he studied in his classic, *Labor and Monopoly Capital*.[21] But macro-studies of skill changes have highlighted a complicated trend, pointing to the growth of new and different kinds of skill within the workforce.[22] We might recall Georges Friedmann's comments during the 1950s when fears about the employment costs of automation abounded. He states that:

> new techniques require new resources, resources in money and materials ... and resources in human beings, specialists, skilled foremen, executives and technicians. In no country can we hope to build up either of these at any given speed, nor can the adoption of the new techniques be imposed upon producers and administrators at all levels, or upon the trade unions either, without arousing forces of inertia, or even actual resistances, commensurate with the magnitude of such a technical transformation.[23]

The production and destruction of skilled work are part of a complex pattern of economic, technological, and social change. Many factors militate against any universal trend towards simple labour. These include the increasing technological, social, and economic costs of meeting needs, the value of skilled work to enterprises, the activities of unions and the effects of organisational change, and training and education.

Marx gives us a strong hint that he sees a way out of capitalism and alienation in the very forces that create a technologically complex 'realm of necessity' which requires minimal labour input. In a rational society, technology and organisation would reduce work to a minimum. But the pattern of development of work under capitalism has not reduced labour's role in production except in specific jobs and circumstances. While working hours have generally reduced over time, neither the number of people working nor the number of skilled jobs in advanced economies have dropped away sharply. By assuming that work in the realm of necessity would require minimum skill and input, that it would become unimportant, Marx finds a way of sidestepping the problem of how to humanise or democratise the workplace, or in other words, resolving the problem of alienation.

However, if we cannot easily reduce society's reliance on work, how do we deal with what Marx would see as its persistent alienating effects? Margaret Radin develops an alternative way of understanding this problem. She claims that, for many workers, 'work is understood not as separate from life and self, but rather as a part of the worker, and indeed constitutive of her. Nor is work understood as separate from relations with other people.'[24] Radin argues that, in even the most degraded forms of factory work, 'many people can express their humanity in their relationships with co-workers; humanity is hard to suppress completely. Yet I think that basically we agree with Marx that these jobs involve inhumane commodification of people.'[25] In using their skills, and maintaining all kinds of social interaction at work, most workers avoid the extremes of alienation Marx envisaged under capitalism. Radin is also right when she points out that 'complete commodification of work – pure labor – does violence to our notion of what it is to be a well-developed person'.[26] In fact, it is the simple labour of a realm of necessity that would come closest to this description. By contrast, if we accept that employment of different types and complexity continues to develop within advanced capitalist societies and that many people identify with the skills and activities they perform at work, we arrive at a quite different problem than the one Marx tried to resolve. Alienating work environments persist – the problem is how to organise often fragile social forces to change this reality.

As I briefly mentioned earlier, fears about automation in the period following the Second World War led many writers to speculate about the imminent decline of work, and to imagine a 'society without work'. Hannah Arendt spends a good part of *The Human Condition* criticising the 'work-oriented' foundations of Marx's social theory because, as she pointed out, this was contradicted by Marx's prediction that work would disappear. In the age of automation, Arendt contends, Marx's vision of emancipation loses its main social actors. She adds: 'what we are confronted with is the prospect of a society of laborers without labor, that is, without the only activity left to them.'[27] For Marcuse, the same scenario that Arendt uses to criticise Marx offers the foundations for a substantial and sympathetic reinterpretation. Automation would lead to the 'end of work'. Marx foreshadows and Marcuse believes it would also free society from the moral constraints imposed by work. Like the young Marx, Marcuse's earliest writing on labour enthusiastically identified with the 'praxis' that was common to all work. And like the later Marx, he linked truly *authentic* praxis with the kinds of emancipation that would be found in the realm of necessity.[28]

In his *Eros and Civilization*, Marcuse draws on the distinction between the realms of necessity and freedom in a way similar to Marx. He identifies a major point of convergence between Marx and Sigmund Freud, reconciling the distinction between work and freedom that appears in the later Marx with Freud's distinction between work and play. For Marcuse, both thinkers see work as an effort in overcoming scarcity. For Marx, work under capitalism represents alienation. For Freud, work represents the repression demanded by scarcity. Marcuse finds Freud's concept of scarcity deficient because: 'the brute fact of scarcity ... is the consequence of a specific organization of scarcity, and ... a specific existential attitude enforced by this organization.'[29] However, Freud's insights enrich a critique of capitalism because they capture the specifically repressive psychological elements bound up in work, and present us with an alternative organising principle in Eros.

Overcoming the repressive elements of capitalist society thus involves abolishing the system of work it perpetrates, to free individuals and society from the 'performance principle' of wage labour. Marcuse argues:

> The performance principle, which is that of an acquisitive and antagonistic society in the process of constant expansion, presupposes a long development during which domination has been increasingly rationalized: control over social labor now reproduces society on an enlarged scale and under improving conditions. For a long way, the interests of domination and the interests of the whole coincide: the profitable utilization of the productive apparatus fulfils the needs and faculties of the individuals. For the vast majority of the population, the scope and mode of satisfaction are determined by their own labor; but their labor is work for an apparatus they do not control ... And it becomes the more alien the more specialized the division of labor becomes. While they work, they do not fulfil their own needs and faculties but work in alienation. Work has now become general, and so have the restrictions placed on the libido: labor time, which is the largest part of an individual's life time is painful time, for alienated labor is absence of gratification, negation of the pleasure principle.[30]

Marcuse rejects the idea of taming capitalist society by creating 'new and durable work relations',[31] a view he attributes to Charles Fourier who had tried to develop a utopia of work and administration. Instead, Marcuse makes the strong claim that:

> no matter how justly and rationally the material production may be organized, it can never be a realm of freedom and gratification ... The

more complete the alienation of labor, the greater the potential of freedom: *total automation would be the optimum*. [my emphasis][32]

Marcuse's vision offers a powerful reading of the 'end of work' scenario we detect in Marx, presented anew with Freudian overtones. Marcuse's influence on later thinkers that came to be associated with the post-industrial left like Jürgen Habermas and André Gorz is unmistakable.[33] For them, he represented a Marxism committed to liberation. It is revealing (as Douglas Kellner observes) that later in his life, Marcuse stopped distinguishing between the realms of freedom and necessity, speaking instead of 'letting the realm of freedom appear within the realm of necessity – in labor and not only beyond labor'.[34] In shifting ground, Marcuse was no doubt influenced by the re-emergence of labour struggles in Europe and the United States during the 1960s.

In examining the 'end of work' ideas of Marx, and then Marcuse, I have questioned the view that the endpoint of capitalist development would be the worker as 'watchman' over a totally automated system. The development of work has been more complicated: many jobs have become more skilled and work has been humanised. However, Marx and his followers were certainly not the only thinkers to offer a pessimistic scenario for the transformation of work. A second strain of pessimism emerges in the thought of Max Weber whose writings about work and rationalisation point, with some ambivalence, to increasing technical control.

Weber on work and rationalisation

Andrew Feenberg says 'a great deal of 20th century social thought has been based on a pessimistic view of modernity that achieved its classical expression in Max Weber's theory of rationalization'.[35] Weber's pessimism is a moral panic about the future of a technically controlled society, expressing an uncertainty people feel when they lose sight of a better or more convincing alternative. Unlike Marx, Weber does not appear to think work would disappear as technological forces gathered strength. But he certainly conveys the strong impression that work would be rationalised by advances in organisation and technology. His is a pessimistic view of work because he sees it as subject to forces of rationalisation. Given the strength of these forces, he believed there was little prospect for democratising work and most of Weber's objections to both union demands and socialist politics emerge from his strongly held belief that rational organisations could not be democratised 'from within'. In this section, I shall draw out the impression Weber's thoughts give us about work, arguing that he gives technical rationalisation in all its guises the status of an independent force. But, as we shall see, the advancing economic rationality that Weber describes remains dependent on social and historical factors that are actually contingent and open to contest.

Weber's contributions to the social sciences are labyrinthine. He developed many of modern sociology's 'formal' foundations while undertaking vast historical and theoretical studies. The sum of his contributions does not add up to a completely unified theory. But Weber gives us a strong depiction of the dynamics of organisational change in modern economic and political life. In *The Protestant Ethic and the Spirit of Capitalism*, Weber pursues what he calls the 'elective affinity' between the inner-rationalising effects of Puritan religious strictures and the rise of a capitalist rationality in production.[36] Weber's point here is not merely historical: he seeks to challenge a shallow materialist account of change he attributes to Marxism, one that falsely understands economic forces as driving social change. By contrast, Weber cautiously underlines the role of cultural, religious, and social practices in driving change. In the particular case of capitalism, these practices constituted a powerful motivating force for economic rationality.[37] As Weber put it: 'the origins of economic rationalism depend, not only on rational technology and rational law, but also in general on the capacity and disposition which men have for certain kinds of practical rationality in the conduct of their lives'.[38]

Contrary to interpretations made by some, Weber did not explain the origins of capitalism through the singular insights he made into Protestant motivations.[39] The rise of capitalism depended on a complex of specific developments including democratic change, the emerging capacity of bureaucracy, and technological innovation as well as the peculiar ascent of the acquisitive ethic. But, over time, Weber increasingly gives the impression that he sees technical rationalisation as an independent force, breaking free of specific cultural motivations. In his never completed *Economy and Society*, Weber develops his formal definitions that provide a sense of the architecture of a rational economy: narrowly calculative economic conduct, capital accounting, and the rational organisation of the workforce,[40] and the impression Weber conveys is of a technical order in which rational organisation with its managers, bureaucrats, and technicians forces out 'substantive' values from the sphere of economic life. The traditional forces that once steered economic, political, and social life are overrun by a new rational order. This leaves us in a predicament: while a rational system brings with it enormous advantages of organisation, it forces substantive values out of decision-making and social life. As Roger Brubaker puts it:

> in the technical idiom of *Economy and Society*, it is not conflict between different forms of *wertrational* [substantively rational] action that Weber emphasizes, but conflict between the purely *zweckrational* [instrumentally rational] action required in the economic and political realms and the *wertrational* action demanded by every commitment to ultimate values.[41]

Weber was aware of the advances and threats presented by the forces of rationalisation. Take his often-cited remarks about wage-labour:

> The upshot of all these considerations is that the maximum of formal rationality in capital accounting is possible only where the workers are subjected to the authority of business management. This is a further specific element of substantive irrationality in the modern economic order ... free labour and the complete appropriation of the means of production create the most favourable conditions for discipline.[42]

In setting down the technical conditions for managerial–capitalist control of work, Weber describes the modern workplace in formalistic terms.[43] Here, Weber importantly acknowledges the 'substantive irrationality' produced by formal rationalisation. As Robert Holton and Bryan Turner point out, 'the conflict between optimal economic rationality and the substantive rationality of protesting classes or disprivileged status groups striving for justice [Weber regards] as endemic'.[44] But as I shall argue, this substantive rationality, which provides both the resources for institutionalising formal systems and also contending with those systems, never attains the same categorical status in Weber's theory as does formal rationality. The ongoing inner-organisational importance of substantial rationality is still largely implicit. The contemporary sociology of work makes these factors more explicit: the contest between employers and workers over technology, working hours, autonomy, and for equal pay reminds us that often the 'formal organisation' of work is in fact value-laden, contingent, and contestable.

If we accept that the technical, technological, and organisational factors involved in workplace change continue to contend with a whole range of institutional and social factors, then we understand the workplace to be the institutional domain in which capitalists, managers, and workers mobilise different resources to achieve their ends. Dieter Rueschemeyer reworks Weber's position, improving it as follows:

> While the formal rationality of the market, bureaucratic administration and the formal justice of modern law are peculiarly characteristic of modern Western societies and have tremendous staying power, they do not reign absolute. It is not merely due to historical accident, but to structural reasons inherent in modern social formations that they are counteracted by effective substantive demands and supporting ideological orientations asserted by workers, farmers, professionals and many other groups. As the relative power of different groups and social classes shifts, the formalist social order becomes increasingly shot through with substantive elements at odds with its formal automatism.[45]

I would agree with Rueschemeyer. But Weber's legacy, if not his own thinking, leads us to see the contest over rationalisation as a losing battle between the ever-encroaching technical order and the weakening traditions and values of social actors forced to deal with technical systems. Instead the battle in the modern workplace involves more than a technical struggle to ensure profitability and a rational order; specifically, it has involved employers and states attempting to socially regulate their workforces. But we do not find much of an idea of this in Weber. As Göran Therborn suggests, Weber 'analyzed the variant forms of the organization of domination, but not the means whereby subordination was ensured'.[46] He further claims that 'Weber's political writings paid more attention to the utilization and satisfaction of material interests than to processes of legitimation in the exercise of domination'.[47]

Weber's hostility towards socialist proposals for work-council-based industry reveals one motive he might have had for failing to give greater conceptual priority to substantive rationality within work. Doing so would have led Weber to a different scenario of social change, one less inclined to a pessimistic view of technical domination, and one more inclined to understand change as a struggle between technical and social imperatives. Even though Weber objected to socialist demands for a democratic organisation of industry, these demands serve to remind us of the social energies of the workplace, which must be conceptually recognised in a theory of organisation. Rueschemeyer is right in saying that formal rationality 'does not reign absolute', so we are obliged to account for the forces that compete with it, both outside and within organisations.

Historical research suggests that the workplace was indeed a battle between substantive and technical interests. Certainly, the interests that lay behind the legal regulation of work highlight the divergent organisational imperatives of unions and employers. Karl Polanyi's *The Great Transformation* reminds us that nineteenth-century capitalism was hardly a self-regulating affair: it was sustained by a contradictory and one-sided application of law, contradictory because the market was supposed to be self-regulating, and one-sided because the law was motivated as much to weaken collective activity as it was to reinforce individual interests.[48] Labour historian, David Montgomery reaches a similar conclusion, revealing the substantive interests behind the laws of nineteenth-century America. According to Montgomery, laws regulated every area of social life, attempting to rein in popular organising, undermine poor relief programmes, and promote, somewhat unsuccessfully, a free market in real estate.[49] Montgomery writes that

> [the] combined effect of these changes was both to strengthen the coercive capacity of government and to narrow the sphere of its authority, so as to insulate the economy from democratic government while exercising a more systematic discipline over the behavior of working people.[50]

Comparing his own insights with Weber's description of the rational state, Montgomery observes: 'Weber's clear statement disguises ... the way in which class rule was exercised both through governmental machinery and in opposition to it – through business institutions and private associations that kept elected government at arm's length.'[51]

When Weber describes Taylorist work practices, the larger contest between labour and capital is left implicit. Quite understandably, Weber holds up Taylorism as evidence of encroaching formal rationality. He observes that:

> Practice, and the resulting skill, can only be perfected by rational and continuous specialization. To-day, it is worked out on a basis which is largely empirical, guided by considerations of minimizing costs in the interest of profitability and limited by these interests.[52]

However, Montgomery's discussion of Taylorist techniques gives us a 'thicker' account of their overall purpose. He points out that early American unions had developed their own 'rationality' to regulate work, one that stressed egalitarian values. Work rules achieved a number of goals: they protected worker and craft autonomy, they embodied a form of collective power, which was defended and advanced through strikes, and, as Montgomery emphasises, they 'repudiated important elements of acquisitive individualism'.[53] Montgomery stresses the wider point to the Taylorist experiment:

> the appeal of the new managerial techniques to manufacturers involved more than simply a response to new technology and a new scale of business organization. It also implied a conscious endeavor to uproot those work practices which had been the taproot of whatever strength organized labor enjoyed in the late nineteenth century. A purely technological explanation of the spread of Taylorism is every bit as inadequate as a purely technological explanation of craftsmen's autonomy.... the apostles of scientific management needed not only to abolish older industrial work practices, but also to discredit them in the public eye. Thus Taylor roundly denied that even 'the high class mechanic' could 'ever thoroughly understand the science of doing his work'.[54]

Although Taylorist techniques became widespread in industry, Montgomery highlights the initial controversy over their apparent efficiency and the 'control strikes' that some unions mounted in an attempt to defeat them.[55] In the end, Taylorism failed to repress social conflicts in the workplace or to eliminate worker organisation. Taylorist management techniques did not prevent new types of workplace organising across the United States. This, in turn, prompted further industry efforts at promoting 'open shops', and passive consumption as well greater efforts aimed at understanding 'human relations' in the workplace.[56] And, elsewhere, Taylorist techniques were successfully limited by organised labour. In his comparative study of Sweden and the United States, Johansson shows that Swedish workers were able to limit the introduction of Taylorist methods.[57] Johansson's study has a clear message: organised labour was able to resist Taylorism, and that alternative organisational forms in industry remained viable.

Weber was not an apologist for a tough and mean capitalism. However, by strongly emphasising the emergence of a technically rational order, Weber leads us to think that workplaces would become iron cages, that organisational imperatives would overwhelm the social foundations of work. Historical evidence suggests otherwise, confirming an alternative view that understands workplaces to involve competing forces and tensions, and in which challenges to formal rationality are recognised. In suggesting this, I am not asserting that social forces, by which I mean collective action and the creation of social institutions by workers, has anything like the same impact as managerial and economic imperatives on the workplace. And I do not claim that an alternative form of democratic work organisation is readily available. But, to give a firmer footing to the substantive, social constitution of the workplace, we do not need either a symmetrical emphasis on democratic rationality to balance technical rationality or a comprehensive theory of self-management.

Feenberg gives greater theoretical substance to what I have in mind when he refers to *democratic* or *subversive rationalisation*. He offers it in a clear contrast to the one-sided emphasis on technical or formal rationalisation that we find in Weberian sociology. Such democratic rationalisation, he claims, uses:

> new technology ... to undermine the existing social hierarchy or to force it to meet the needs it has ignored. This principle explains the technical initiatives that often accompany the strategies of structural reform pursued by union, environment, and other social movements.[58]

And Feenberg is correct to claim that:

> 'subversive' rationalization is a contradiction in Weberian terms. On those terms, once tradition has been defeated by modernity, radical struggle for freedom and individuality degenerates into an affirmation of irrational life forces against the routine and drab predictability of a bureaucratic order.[59]

Weber recognised labour's contribution to a civilised, liberal society but he roundly criticised the 'substantive' goals of trade unionism. David Kettler and Volker Meja note that Weber:

worried especially about [union] inclinations towards *legislative challenges to the formal rationality of law*, their weakness for *substantively rational* renderings of the law of contract, in the vain hope of using *law to provide 'fair' wages or guarantee against exploitation* of superior bargaining power. [my emphasis][60]

These substantive union goals no doubt conform to Feenberg's description of democratic or subversive rationality. Neither his understanding of social groups and classes[61] nor his deep appreciation of historical change lead Weber to formulate an integrated theory that could attend to the struggle over rationality by competing classes and social forces. Instead, Weber's legacy is more pessimistic, in places hostile to anything that challenges what he sees as economic rationality.

Durkheim, *The Division of Labour* and modern solidarity

If we find in Weber's writings a failure to fully integrate the substantive dimension of modern workplaces into his theory of social change, we also find a similar problem in Emile Durkheim's *The Division of Labour in Society*. *The Division of Labour* is concerned with describing what sharply distinguishes modern from pre-modern societies.[62] As for Marx, the division of labour is Durkheim's point of reference. He uses it to describe real changes in work and industry, and as a springboard for his larger description of modernity. And, in doing so, Durkheim seeks to settle debates about the implications of social change that had pre-occupied his predecessors. Steven Lukes explains:

> [*The Division of Labour*] sought to develop an explanation of social solidarity in industrial or 'organized' societies that was consistent with Durkheim's objections to Comte, Spencer, and Tönnies: that is, an explanation which did not, like Comte, exaggerate the role of consensus and conformity, of shared beliefs and sentiments, and of uniform patterns imposed on individual behaviour, and which allowed for increasing differentiation of occupation, beliefs and behaviour; an explanation, secondly, which did not, like Spencer, assume a harmony of interests, but postulated a complex social regulation of individual behaviour; and an explanation, finally, which unlike Tönnies and also Comte, detached such regulation from the State, linking it rather to the 'internal' functioning of society, and to the processes of social differentiation.[63]

For our purposes, the key concept we must take from Durkheim is *solidarity*. How close does he come to using this concept to describe modern work relations? I shall argue that Durkheim does not come very close, missing an opportunity to fully account for conflicts arising out of the division of labour. His idea of modern solidarity remains too close to Herbert Spencer's earlier vision of a self-integrating social order emerging out of large-scale change, even though he makes a more serious attempt to understand social breakdown and conflict. Durkheim's preoccupation with 'order' and 'integration' is, of course, an important cue for later functionalist theories of society which were criticised for their failure to understand social conflict and dissent.

Following Spencer and others, Durkheim argues that the modern division of labour generates a new form of solidarity.[64] In *The Division of Labour*, Durkheim distinguishes specifically modern societies from premodern ones by contrasting the 'organic solidarity' he locates in the former with the 'mechanical solidarity' he locates in the latter. Pre-modern societies are regulated by holistic social exchange, which Durkheim describes as mechanical: a powerful *conscience collective* regulates the different roles within group relations.[65] In modern industrial societies, a complex, everchanging division of labour forces a new type of organic solidarity to the fore. The regulating centre of society, which in pre-modern society is governed by a set of binding roles and institutions, is emptied out. Modern society 'leaves open a part of the individual conscience in order that special functions may be established there, functions it cannot regulate'.[66]

Like Marx and Weber, Durkheim emphasises the unstoppable forces of change that produce industrial society, but unlike them, he draws an optimistic conclusion: 'far from the progress of specialisation whittling away the individual personality, this develops with the division of labour'.[67] In some respects, Durkheim frees us from the view that all forms of specialisation in the advancing division of labour undermine our humanity. Instead, he recognises the prospects for greater individual recognition in a more complex and differentiated society.

Durkheim asserts that a society with differentiating roles, occupations, and moral values no longer needs a legal and moral system that performs a repressive, integrating function across society.[68] Instead, law and morality perform a different, more 'harmonising' rather than controlling, role.[69] Like Spencer, Durkheim tends to *naturalise* this new form of social integration, seeing it as a functional component of a complex, differentiated society. Unlike Spencer, Durkheim does not think that this emerges spontaneously out of markets or from contracts. It is a 'thin' set of social relations that drives this change. Durkheim states:

> If the division of labour produces solidarity, it is not only because it makes each individual an agent of exchange, to use the language of economists. It is because it creates between men a whole system of rights and laws joining them in a lasting way to one another.[70]

Durkheim stops well short of implying harmonious interchange between the ever-more complex division of labour and the social relations that institutionalise it. In fact, he is particularly interested in moments of discord between the division of labour and social institutions. Durkheim considers the modern division of labour to be a 'normal' development except where it is either *anomic* or *forced*. He attributes the emerging division of labour to numerous sources, including increased social density, transport and communication changes, and population growth. But he examines the instances where the division of labour develops too quickly, producing rapid change that impinges on a settled moral order. Durkheim describes this unsettled world as anomic.[71] Durkheim's concepts of anomie and the anomic division of labour allow him to brilliantly describe the personal and social alienation resulting out of breakdown in the moral capacities of social order.

Durkheim identifies one other form of conflict between the division of labour and social institutions, which is directly relevant to us here. While he argues that the division of labour develops in correspondence with the pre-given diversity of capacities among the population,[72] he also raises the prospect of rapid economic development within the capitalist system producing a *forced* division of labour that enforces an intolerable degree of specialisation in the workforce. Durkheim is clearly trying to account for Marxian ideas about work routinisation and alienation, but rather than seeing these as all-encompassing, he sees the forced division of labour as a special case within overall, capitalist development. In seeing the forced division of labour in this way, Durkheim risks downplaying the conflict between capitalist organisation and labour. By stressing the 'normality' of industrial society, Durkheim marginalises problems that are *endemic* to capitalism. Referring to this problem, Jeffrey Alexander remarks: 'national markets, great concentration, and the inequality of conditions must be seen as a part of the "capitalist" system or "industrial" form of differentiated society rather than a phase in "interdependent" society itself.'[73]

By identifying organic solidarity with the integrative functions of industrial society, Durkheim forfeits any capacity to fully explain conflict. Robert Perrin makes this clear:

> One of the prescriptions for the alleviation of an 'abnormal' variety (where those involved experience friction and conflict) is to cause workers to realize that they are mutually dependent parts of one great body or whole. But this [solidarity] is the very thing that the division of labor is supposed to produce, not that on which its ultimate success must depend.[74]

Equally, Durkheim is forced to see conflicts as impediments to solidarity. If we accept conflicts which arise out of the division of labour, particularly conflicts between employers and workers, are 'normal' in industrial society, we cannot assume the division of labour simply produces solidarity. Moreover, we would be forced to consider whether conflicts themselves produce solidarity, by opening up substantive contests about social organisation. Georges Friedmann highlights this problem for Durkheim, claiming that the type of solidarity produced by struggling workers is similar to Durkheim's mechanical variant, and the one supposed to have faded away.[75] Friedmann argues:

> social solidarity, uniting the workers and making them feel indispensable to one another, bound together by common interests and a common aim, is quite another matter and much more than such interdependence. Here we must distinguish between two kinds of solidarity, both found in real life to-day. There is the firm's unity, which brings together all the personnel of a business or a factory, ... and so causes a group solidarity *within* the firm. And there is the unity of the workers as wage-earners, linking them to other wage earners *outside* the firm ... The powerful 'industrial relations' movement, which has continued to-day under the name of the 'human relations movement', aimed precisely at increasing this spirit of co-operation ... by introducing more and more considerations of a psychological kind into the scientific management of labour. ... [Workers'] solidarity has clearly nothing to do with the division of labour itself ...[76]

Alvin Gouldner identifies other reasons for Durkheim's failure to fully recognise the problems raised by his own account of the division of labour. Gouldner states that:

> Durkheim backed away from the problem of the forced division of labor and, instead, concentrated on anomie, which is to say on the *moral* conditions necessary for social order. If Durkheim had followed up his own lead on the forced division of labor, it would have blurred the very difference between Academic Sociology and socialism on which he was then polemically insisting; it would have been difficult to tell the difference between Durkheim and Jaurès.[77]

Later social scientists did attend to the role of solidarity in the workplace, recognising that it was more than the remnants of a traditional outlook or stubborn resistance to inevitable change. Conservative elements within 'human relations' sociology, in particular, realised that understanding group interactions within the workplace were central. At the same time, they realised that challenging these social networks was critical to limiting the power of organised labour.[78]

Kenneth Thompson challenges critics that accuse Durkheim of anticipating the conservative 'human relations' school. Thompson argues that 'this interpretation ignores the context in which Durkheim made his remarks about workers' anomie, and it distorts Durkheim's political position',[79] and, further, that Durkheim 'made it clear anomie could only be dispelled by policies based on equality and justice'.[80] Thompson is justified in defending Durkheim – he was clearly committed to reformist social policies.[81] But Durkheim's theory forces us to view conflicts as breakdowns that require greater efforts at social integration. If conflicts are not understood as potentially substantive challenges to social organisation, it is hard to see social integration in other than coercive terms. Moreover, later Durkheim-inspired 'mass society' theories of social change persist in understanding challenges to the status quo as 'breakdowns' in the integrative capacity of the social order, and not as legitimate alternatives in themselves.[82]

Durkheim's emphasis on social integration is transferred across into Parsons's influential brand of functionalism. By Parsons's time, work – or the division of labour – had begun to lose its metaphoric grip on the general warrants of social theory. Today, we speak of 'social systems' and 'social structures'. But Durkheim's concept of solidarity was important to Parsons when the latter thinker set out his theory in *The Structure of Social Action*.[83] Indeed, the strongly integrative concept of solidarity is evident throughout Parsons's work. Take the following example from *Economy and Society*, where Parsons and Smelser write:

> solidarity is the generalized capacity of agencies in the society to 'bring into line' the behaviour of system units in accordance with the integrative needs of the system, to check or reverse disruptive tendencies to deviant behaviour, and to promote the conditions of harmonious co-operation.[84]

When Parsons and Smelser apply functional analysis to the economy, we clearly see the continuity with Durkheim's approach, and the way its problems are repeated. The authors do not focus on conflicts in the workplace or the alternatives that emerge out of them. My point is best illustrated by Parsons and Smelser's explanation of trade unions, attributing their purpose to 'role imbalances', and describing their role as 'semi-ritual':

> Such imbalances in role systems usually give rise to compensatory mechanisms in the social structure ... Some of the union's functions are thus semi-ritual rather than bargaining. They integrate the individual worker and his household into a larger collectivity, membership in which enhances his self-respect ... [S]uch enhanced self-respect and confidence can stimulate management, ... to give a larger output of contingent support and moral approval of the labour role to the household.[85]

Nicos Mouzelis successfully criticises Parsons, and by implication, Durkheim, when he states that, 'in Parsonian theory, incompatibilities between institutionalised parts cannot be articulated with actors' strategies and struggles. Therefore, whenever institutional incompatibilities lead to transformation, ... this transformation is either explained not at all, or it is explained in teleological terms.'[86] In the same vein, Durkheim-inspired social theories could not fully grasp the productive contribution and challenge labour made to social organisation. A concept of solidarity, recognising substantive interests that Weber marginalises alongside the productive function of conflict Durkheim does not see, enables us to represent the underdogs of social change. As we shall see in my next chapter, when later social theorists like Jürgen Habermas and Alain Touraine attempt to rebalance social theory to better reflect the role of social actors and social rationality, the tide had turned against organised labour on many fronts, and so labour's place is once again obscured.

Conclusions: Classical themes and the 'end of work'

This chapter presents insights from Marx, Weber, and Durkheim into the problems of work and social change. I have argued that these thinkers, especially Marx and Weber, provide a pessimistic view, which doubts the possibility of democratising work by building on its social foundations. Each thinker makes a distinct contribution to this pessimistic view, and I shall summarise the most prominent of these contributions below:

1   From Marx, we get the idea that technological change reduces the complexity and skill of work. Capital displaces labour in its search for profits and efficiency. These two facts combined lead Marx away from finding social liberation through 'humanising work'. Instead, we find speculative fragments that suggest the later Marx saw liberation beyond the sphere of work, in a realm of freedom that would flank a technical, rational economic system. Marxism leaves us with two ways of thinking about work and social change: the first would involve 'humanising work' by creating greater democracy at work, and the second would involve 'abolishing work' by encouraging economic and technical efficiency.

2   From Weber, we get the idea that work is increasingly rationalised by technical and managerial organisation. Although Weber recognises that formal rationality must be socially institutionalised, these institutions are not important to his understanding of change and rationalisation. Weber thought substantive challenges to formal rationality were irrational, frequently criticising demands for workers' control and legislative changes that would favour workers' interests.

3   From Durkheim, we get the idea that work (or the division of labour) generates solidarity in modern society. But this solidarity refers to 'thin' social relations that support social integration. Solidarity in the form of collective action in the workplace is not satisfactorily integrated into his overall studies of the division of labour.

I shall argue that this pessimistic legacy, especially in the combined contribution of Marx and Weber, provides an important foundation for the 'end of work' scenario embraced by the post-industrial social thinkers whose contributions we shall consider in the next chapter. These thinkers identify a contemporary scenario of declining numbers of paid jobs, increasingly rationalised employment, and declining social attachment to work. They respond to this scenario by asking us to look beyond the social relations of work and the policies that have supported full employment.

2 Work and the post-industrial pessimists

As we saw in Chapter 1, there is a distinctly pessimistic streak in the writings of Marx, Weber, and Durkheim about work. When later social thinkers develop a more concrete vision of a post-work society, we can see the influences of those forebears. Marx saw a possible 'end of work'-based society, which could be achieved through technology, Weber envisaged increasing rationalisation, and Durkheim pointed to a complex division of labour that would lack a defining centre. These writers leave a lasting impression on sociology: an impression that modern work would be transformed by organisation and technology; organisational imperatives would overlay social relations with technical ones; and technology would eliminate huge numbers of jobs, deskilling others. In a modern, rationalised world, a utopia of labour that inspired many social thinkers and labour movements would not survive the forces of rationalisation. So hopes for a democratic workplace would remain sterile, doomed by the greater forces of organisation, technology, money, and power. Despite a century of organisational and technological change, I shall argue that the pessimistic forecasts made about work have not transpired. Societies remain alive and vibrant in the face of apparent technocracy. And vast numbers of people still do skilled work, go on strike, and express attachment to their jobs. In short, we see the resilience of employment structures and the social institutions that regulate them.

This chapter presents the most forceful set of arguments from three post-industrial social thinkers that draw on this pessimistic legacy: Jürgen Habermas, Alain Touraine, and Claus Offe. Anyone familiar with these thinkers would recognise that they are much more than theorists of post-industrial society. If we really wanted to look at post-industrial social thought, why wouldn't we look instead at the writings of Daniel Bell, for example? My reasons for pursuing the arguments of these thinkers are twofold. First and foremost, they offer the most coherent and plausible efforts at understanding a post-industrial social structure that is less dependent on work, industry, and class. Second, they attempt to build this 'end of work' scenario into both the structures and normative orientations of social theory. As I made clear in the Introduction, the 'end of work' scenario does not involve the disappearance of work in any literal sense. It involves the argument that industrial rationalisation and changing social values combine to make work less 'central' to social life, that labour movements are no longer the dominant social movement, and that full employment is neither realistic nor desirable from a normative standpoint.

Although the contributions of Habermas, Touraine, and Offe overlap, this chapter itself depends on a division of labour allowing us to familiarise ourselves with the distinct contributions of each thinker to the 'end of work' scenario. First, to Habermas. In challenging the grandiose place of work in Marxist theory, Habermas searches for new foundations for a social theory that remains true to the hopes of liberation expressed in the Marxist tradition. He finally 'unburdens' work from the role classical praxis philosophy accredited to it – work was never, and could never be, the sole foundation for a social theory. However, in emphasising the fundamental difference between working and communicating, Habermas commits to an approach that surrenders the institutional domain of work to systems theory. In doing so, he leaves us with only an implicit sense that work remains socially constituted. I shall argue that Habermas needlessly downplays the connections between work and society, the influence of work on individual and social identities, and the influence of those identities that shape, and even contend, organisational forms.

Second, to Touraine. Alain Touraine's theory of society develops out of his analysis of social movements. Touraine strongly links his idea of social movements to the highest kind of social conflict possible for a given 'societal type'. In the societal type Touraine calls post-industrial society, new social movements are the chief social movements: the labour movement is relegated to a lesser role as the conflicts of industrial society fade. I shall argue that Touraine's approach commits us to an inflexible and overly pessimistic view about the future of labour movements and about their continuing capacity to influence society and politics.

Third, to Offe. Like his colleague Habermas, Offe continues a pessimistic view of work in his diagnosis of problems facing welfare states and in considering solutions to these problems. Offe assumes that full employment is no longer economically feasible, and is an unrealistic policy goal for advanced societies rapidly losing their attachment to work. He offers an admirable proposal for a basic income that would redesign the welfare state, achieving equality without relying on full employment. I shall bring this chapter to a close by summarising my main misgivings about the 'end of work' scenario. Doing this sets up the terms for the second part of this book, which explores anew the options for employment in advanced societies.

Habermas on work and social theory

A leading European intellectual, Habermas is now better known for his views on law, rights, and democracy than his earlier reworking of social theory. However, these earlier efforts are of central importance to us. More than anyone else, Habermas can claim to have successfully tackled the grand problems of modernity we find in Marx and Weber, and to have addressed their theoretical weaknesses. For our purposes here, we are primarily interested in the way Habermas deals with the Marxian idea of work, which he rejects, and what this implies for understanding contemporary society. Habermas does not believe a paradigm built around work provides an adequate basis for social theory. For him, work is closer to what Weber described as instrumental action. Instead, Habermas argues that societies depend on social interactions, and that these interactions follow fundamentally different rules and dynamics.

Habermas opens a new chapter in social theory by drawing into sharp contrast the concepts of work and social interaction, developing the latter into a robust theory of communicative action. But what does this achievement hold for our understanding of work? I shall argue, as others have, that Habermas clarifies the rules governing social interaction but at a price. While his theory is able to explain something often lost in classical sociology – the dynamic place of social interaction in social change – he still follows Weber in suggesting that social relationships inside technical systems are marginalised by rationalisation. And when Habermas finally adopts a 'systems' approach to explain bureaucracy and the economy, he loses sight of the durable, social institutions of work almost completely.

Habermas first distinguished between 'work' and 'interaction' in response to Marcuse's criticism of the apparently neutral idea of technical or instrumental rationality, an idea Marcuse finds in Weber.[1] Habermas distances himself from Marcuse's criticism and takes the opportunity to lay the groundwork for his own contribution. *Contra* Marcuse, Habermas believes that technical rationality is, in itself, neutral. So, when Marcuse attacks this neutrality, he is really attacking the way it is institutionalised in a set of *distorted* social relations. Habermas echoes Weber's own ambivalent attitude towards rational economic, bureaucratic, and legal development: he does not accept the implication of Marcuse's view – that rational systems are intrinsically dominating – and is not as pessimistic as Weber about their development. In later writings, Habermas stops using the terms work and interaction, preferring instead the terms 'system' and 'lifeworld' to understand the structures that cradle social evolution. But Habermas has been forced to defend himself against critics who argue that he has overlooked the social aspects of work when he equates it with instrumental action. Let us take up some of those criticisms.

When Habermas rejects Marx's idea of work, he does so sympathetically and critically: sympathetically because he appreciates Marx's attempt to explain technical and social change, and critically because he thinks Marx cannot realise his own normative convictions through the idea of work. Habermas thinks that Marx's idea of work in fact conflates two distinct processes.[2] He writes that:

> If Marx had not thrown together interaction and work under the label of social practice (*Praxis*), and he had instead related the materialist concept of synthesis likewise to the accomplishments of instrumental action and the nexuses of communicative action, then the idea of a science of man would not have been obscured by identification with natural science.[3]

By understanding social change through developments of work, Habermas believes Marx ends up tying his model for explaining social development too closely to the technical achievements of an ever-more complex system. This is a problem we encountered earlier when we looked at the drawbacks of confining work to the realm of necessity: the complex, social interactions of work were increasingly understood from the standpoint of pure technical rationality. Even Habermas's critics, like Gyorgy Márkus, concede that Marx's own logic points to this.[4] But Markus goes on to argue:

> When he [Habermas] describes the Marxian paradigm of production in terms of labour as merely goal-rational, instrumental activity, he himself accomplishes a technicist reduction that cannot be attributed to Marx, not even on the level of conceptual analysis. For the Marxian paradigm of production rests on the unity of processes of interaction between men and nature *and* between men and men. It can even be argued that the Habermasian critique (at least in its early and most elaborated variants) rests on a philological misunderstanding. It is not true that the paradigm of production necessarily reduces the concept of historical development to the sole dimension of growth in the technical mastery of man over nature.[5]

Márkus argues that work constitutes a set of social relationships: rules, technical knowledge, and tasks are interpreted and acted on by flesh-and-blood subjects. Márkus is right. But Habermas is also right to claim that even if work is understood as a social activity, not all social activity can be understood as work.[6] However, by insisting on a clear separation of work and social interaction, we shall see that Habermas has trouble explaining work as a social institution that does in fact combine technical and social interactions. In separate contributions, Andrew Feenberg and Axel Honneth underline this point.[7]

Habermas had good reason to replace the categories of work and interaction with more comprehensive terms to describe social structure and evolution. He initially tried to map the concepts of work (instrumental action) and interaction (communicative action) onto distinct parts of society. In his 'Science and Technology as "Ideology"', he had stated:

> In terms of the two types of action we can distinguish between social systems according to whether purposive-rational action or interaction predominates ... [T]here are subsystems such as (to keep to Weber's examples) the economic systems or the state apparatus, in which primarily sets of purposive-rational action are institutionalized.[8]

This approach has an obvious weakness, as Habermas recognises. Economic and bureaucratic systems do not merely rely on technical accomplishments or formal rationality. To deal with the problem, and following his engagement with Niklas Luhmann's systems theory as well as Parsonian sociology, Habermas adopts what he calls a 'two-level' model of society that operates between the system and lifeworld. He accepts that complex economic and bureaucratic systems are 'steered' by resources of money and power, and they do not rely, in the first instance, on our communicative achievements to function.

Habermas's use of systems ideas does not mean he succumbs to a 'systems worldview'. After all, he is primarily interested in explaining social interaction and evolution, not how technology and organisation combine to build complex systems. Habermas maintains that systems cannot explain society, a determinist logic he finds creeping through the writings of Marx, Weber, his Frankfurt School predecessors, and in some forms of system theory. Systems are institutionalised in the social world, what Habermas calls the lifeworld, which maintains and reproduces the fragile structures of our society, culture, and social identities. Here, his idea of communicative action is central. He argues that underlying human communication is an attempt to reach a consensus found in our norms and values. Over time, our ability to communicate becomes less constrained by traditions, and drives us to a progressively more open form of moral consciousness. Thus our capacity for communicating directs our social evolution, challenging the ways we are socialised, the influence of culture on us, and the ways we interrelate.

Habermas's overall aim becomes clear. Although Habermas accepts that the technical rationalisation that Weber describes most powerfully in his 'iron cage' metaphor continues apace, social theory must also attend to social rationalisation which he understands through his insights into communication. He states that, 'through his basic action-theoretic assumptions Weber prejudiced this question in such a way that processes of societal rationalization could only come into view from the standpoint of purposive rationality'.[9]

In raising the status of social rationalisation so that it parallels technical rationalisation, Habermas is obliged to establish how these two processes develop together. To do this, he proposes a new thesis in the second volume of *The Theory of Communicative Action*: that the system and life-world are 'uncoupled' from each other as modernity progresses. Here, he draws heavily on his earlier insights about Weber's theory of rationalisation, reworking key ideas of Durkheim and George Herbert Mead as well.[10] It is a complicated argument we cannot hope to develop here and I'll mention only what we need to understand Habermas's treatment of work. He believes that as modernity progresses, rational organisations are forced out of their lifeworld contexts; in other words, as the economy, technology, and bureaucracy develop in their technical sophistication, they do so by breaking free of norms and other social constraints. This process depends on the complicated interaction of cause and effect. Following Weber, Habermas also believes that for technical systems to expand, there must be a shift in law and morality that encourages this form of rationality. Complex systems, in turn, create an environment that cradles greater rationality within social life. Of course, these changes do not proceed altogether harmoniously. Following both Marx and Weber, Habermas argues that systems threaten to 'colonise the lifeworld' as bureaucracies and markets encroach on more and more parts of social life. In turn, for systems to remain legitimate, societies demand that they are appropriately institutionalised in laws and regulations that are consistent with norms.

Habermas's uncoupling thesis allows him to explain the dynamics of social change. But does it (like his earlier work) rely on the assumption that systems develop an ever-greater technical rationality that inevitably forces out their social institutions? Even quite a few of Habermas's sympathetic critics think he does make such an assumption.[11] Let's first deal with some of the concepts Habermas uses to develop his systems approach. Habermas follows both Parsons and Luhmann in claiming that abstract media steer the system.[12] The two most important media are money, which steers the economy, and power, which steers politics and bureaucracy. In fact, Habermas thinks the growing capacity of money and power to steer systems is direct evidence of the uncoupling of system and lifeworld.[13] Adopting this concept of steering allows Habermas to avoid assuming (as he did earlier) that action types neatly correspond to parts of society like the economy or bureaucracy. By arguing that money and power steer the economy and bureaucracy respectively, Habermas does not claim that social institutions within the bureaucracy, law, and the economy are irrelevant to system functioning. Rather, he argues, that money and power steer systems *in the final instance*.

Habermas's refashioned approach is only partly successful, at least for understanding the social role of work. We shall consider three problems with this approach: his concept of steering media, his understanding of 'inner-organisational' action (Axel Honneth's term), and his neglect of the relationship between work and social identity. Turning first to the problem of steering media, while Habermas understands the role of money in steering the economy, he neglects the role of economic power. Power, in the form of market dominance, technical capacity or managerial control, does obviously play a role in steering the economy, and, of course, in the organisation of work. Equally, a form of countervailing power emerges in the contending activities of unions. Even Parsons, who developed the idea of steering media in his own theory, recognises the role of organisational power in the economy, suggesting that free market economics fails to fully grasp this role.[14] At the same time, politics and bureaucracy are not only responsive to power: the advent of 'money politics' reminds us of the impact of money on both.

The second problem concerns the place of inner-organisational institutions within Habermas's account of systems, which self-evidently include the working environment. Habermas still gives us the impression that the social foundations of systems are increasingly marginal to their functions. He states:

> that tendencies towards bureaucratization are represented from the internal perspective of organizations as a growing *independence* from elements of the lifeworld that have been shoved out into system environments. From the opposite perspective of the lifeworld, the same process presents itself as one of increasing *autonomization*, for areas of action converted over to communication media and systemically integrated are *withdrawn* from the institutional orders of the lifeworld.[15]

Habermas's summary is, however, qualified by the following observation:

> the externalization of lifeworld contexts cannot be carried through without remainder, as the informal organization upon which all formal organization relies amply demonstrates. Informal organization covers those legitimately regulated, inner-organizational relations that, notwithstanding the juridification of the framework, may be moralized. The lifeworld of members, never completely husked away, penetrates here into the reality of organizations.[16]

Despite this, Habermas does not pursue the dynamics of inner-organisational life much further. His protégé, Axel Honneth, thinks this leaves Habermas in the same camp as Max Weber.[17] Honneth suggests an alternative, one that sees an ongoing struggle between the lifeworld and systems over what he calls the 'organisational form'. Referring back to Habermas's earlier criticism of Marcuse's view of technical reason, Honneth argues:

> Habermas is so wedded to the basic convictions of the technocracy thesis that he attempts to conceive the domain of material reproduction as a norm-free, purely technically organized sphere of action.

Hence, he excludes it from the ultimate definitions of his own theory of communication.... But therefore Habermas ... abandons within his social theory the normative orientation to another domain, namely the communicative organization of material production which, under the title of 'self-administration', belongs to the productive part of the tradition of critical Marxism.[18]

I would agree with Honneth. Moreover, we need not assume that workers' self-management is the only viable alternative to modern capitalism to acknowledge that ongoing social interaction and power contests shape the workplace, and thus systems generally. Alternative accounts of the workplace recognise this quite clearly. Take the 'social rules' systems theory developed by Tom Burns and his colleagues. Burns and Flam remind us of the endemic function of social institutions in the workplace when they state:

> sociological studies of factories and other workplaces show that workers set up and conform to group norms restricting production – work quotas – at the expense of their own higher earnings or the satisfaction of their supervisors. In addition, informal status hierarchies and leadership patterns develop, countervailing and providing a basis for challenge to those formally designed and supervised by management.[19]

The third problem stems from Habermas's failure to adequately recognise the impact of work experiences on individuals and their social identities. Honneth draws out the consequences of this failure for social theory when he argues that:

> in Habermas's recent theory of society, the concept of 'instrumental action' into which he formerly transformed the Marxist concept of labor no longer plays a systematic role; the central distinctions he makes today in the praxis of human beings are no longer categorized according to differences in the coordination of actions conceived as teleological in principle. However, this conceptual strategy brings it about that the experience of labor no longer appears systematically in the categorial framework of the theory; the question of what experiences we have in dealing with external nature plays an equally insignificant role in Habermas's concept of personal identity formation as the role played in his theory of society by the question of how societal labor is distributed, organized, and evaluated. But if individual identity formation is also dependent upon the social esteem enjoyed by one's labor within society, then the concept of labor may not be constituted such that it categorially suppresses this psycho-social connection; the dangerous consequence of this would be that any effort to

develop a theory of society that strives to re-evaluate or reshape particular forms of labor might remain incomprehensible, indeed indiscernible.[20]

Honneth worries that Habermas's theory of society loses a comprehensive view about the effects work has on individual and social life (the life-world). Other research in the social sciences, especially in social psychology, provides empirical support for Honneth's argument. Melvin Kohn and his colleagues stress the role work plays in learning and moral development. High levels of autonomy and complexity in work have an *independent* influence on adult socialisation of children, on communication, on positive risk-taking, and on moral development. Kohn argues that there is a strong link between the lack of complexity and autonomy in an individual's work and feelings of powerlessness and moral conformity.[21] Other research indicates that richer working experiences also contribute to more effective communication between parents and children.[22]

Work is not only important to social identity, it also provides resources for expressing solidarity. Solidarity and contention are more than products of communicative action, they draw on the technical and social resources of the workplace to find expression; for example, the withdrawal of labour during strikes, and the subversive use of technology. Chris Tilly and Charles Tilly make this point, one long recognised by social movement theorists, when they observe, 'the deep grounding of collective contention in *existing social organization*, for example the crucial part played by pre-disposing network ties in recruitment to social-movement activism [my emphasis]'.[23] These activities might be best understood as a form of strategic action, combining social and organisational resources, and one that we do not find in Habermas's theory. Andrew Feenberg offers us a way of understanding these types of activities when he writes of 'democratic' or 'subversive' rationalisation.[24]

Habermas's more recent scholarship presents us with a model of more wide-ranging democratisation than the one he envisaged in *The Theory of Communication Action*.[25] Key to democratisation is law. Michael Power suggests that Habermas now sees the law as a kind of functional counterpart of communicative action, transmitting the norms of civil society into rights and legislation.[26] Habermas's theory of law and democracy opens up at least the prospect of democratising economic institutions but he does not pursue this prospect.[27]

Does Habermas envisage new opportunities to democratise the economy? It would seem not. He still argues against succumbing to the illusions that follow from understanding society as a single 'macro-subject'.[28] To do so, he believes, only returns to the unrealistic aim of self-management once taken up in Marxism. But systems theory also risks conceiving of society in this way. Arguing that Habermas draws on a 'more elaborate version of the idea of a self-regulating market system',[29]

Forbath responds that critical legal scholars have effectively challenged the idea of such apparently neutral concepts as contracts and property rights. His view is that 'all markets ... are political artefacts, based on and constituted by highly plastic legal norms and rules'.[30] Here, we can identify a parallel with the political content of laws regulating work: labour laws that define a 'right to manage' or a right to 'hard bargaining' are equally not incontrovertible legal translations of neutral organisational imperatives. Given this is indeed the case, regulating the economic system will continue to be driven by organisational conflicts, with all the potential this holds for greater workplace democracy.

By challenging the all-encompassing praxis idea of work, Habermas opens up a new path for social theory, and one that has inspired other sociologists to think beyond the frame of work. He is surely right to argue that the concept of work cannot explain all human action. His own approach stresses the place of communication in human evolution, and overcomes the failure of the classical tradition to recognise the place of *social* rationality in the dynamics of change. But Habermas's adoption of systems theory to explain large-scale technical and organisational change leaves him exposed to the same kind of biases that prejudiced Marx, Weber, and Durkheim. To overcome these, his account of the modern system requires a better empirical foundation, one that does not unduly sterilise richly contested, social institutions, making them neutral organisational imperatives. Treating work from a systems standpoint can only lead to such a problem. Indeed, when Habermas has discussed the changing role of work in contemporary societies, he echoes the broader post-industrial 'end of work' sentiment, something best reflected in his phrase the 'exhaustion of utopian energies'.[31] Indeed, one has to assume that his ambition to restructure social theory is reinforced by their pessimism.

Touraine's post-industrial society: the demise of labour as a social movement

Like Habermas, Alain Touraine recognises the central role of social interaction in social change.[32] Unlike Habermas, who writes at a higher level of abstraction, Touraine identifies social movements as critical forces of social change. Touraine's early research in the area of industrial sociology had demonstrated the decisive role the labour movement played in the workplace. In his later research, however, Touraine stakes out a larger theoretical position in which the workplace and labour movements are no longer central. One thing does stay the same. He criticises functionalism, Marxism, and organisational sociology because they all concentrate on institutions and social structure, failing to recognise the dynamic place of social actors.[33] Touraine insists we cannot understand society through stale concepts such as 'shared values' and 'norms'. For him, social action is more creative and open, often undermining norms and institutions.[34] And social movements give the most powerful expression of what it is to be a social actor.

Touraine understands social change as the dynamic interaction between social movements and their corresponding *societal types*. When societal types change, so do their constitutive social movements. So when Touraine argues we are undergoing a transformation from industrial to post-industrial society, he insists that only new social actors can now represent the 'highest level' of social conflict. Touraine claims that new social movements, which include environmental, anti-nuclear, and women's movements, have replaced the labour movement as central social actors. This argument, very popular in the 1980s, is less prominent now. New social movements have lost their novelty and labour movements have continued to show vitality. Yet even in the face of a major strike-wave in France during 1995, Touraine remained adamant that labour was no longer a social movement.

Why does Touraine believe that unions are no longer a viable social movement? I shall argue that Touraine holds to this pessimistic view of labour because he believes there are only a limited number of social movements within any given societal type. However, in arguing this, Touraine depends on a somewhat arbitrary and unstable distinction between industrial and post-industrial society. My view is that social movement action is more open, and less directly tied to apparent shifts in overarching societal types. Even if we accept that societies are now more 'post-industrial' in their organisation, activities, and social identities, it seems hasty to exclude union movements from the definition of social movements.

We shall begin by examining Touraine's definition of social movements. His most theoretical study, *The Self-Production of Society*, published in the late 1970s, gives an elaborate account of social change, much of which we do not need to rehearse here.[35] Touraine's main argument is that societies are defined by what he calls their 'historicity', that is, the evolving forms of cultural, social, and economic organisation that define a particular social period. For Touraine, social movements are defined by their challenge to historicity; these movements are no longer merely acting collectively, they are engaged in a fundamental struggle over the shape of progress in society. As societies become more modern, centred on innovation, they also become more open to challenge and redefinition. Social movements increasingly intervene in what Touraine calls the system of historical action, attempting to influence culture.[36] At the same time, the state becomes more involved in managing these conflicts.[37]

Like many social thinkers in the 1960s and 1970s, Touraine exploited the idea of a post-industrial society to capture the increasing role of government, greater use of information in work and production, and new forms of social and cultural expression.[38] Unlike other writers including Daniel Bell, Touraine did not think post-industrial society would bring with it an 'end of ideology'.[39] For Touraine, post-industrial society signalled new and diversifying conflicts, as more parts of society were open to challenge, redefinition, and the incursion of technocracy. Industrial societies had been structured around the logic of production and consumption. Post-industrial societies are structured around the struggles between a diverse public and a growing technocracy.

New conflicts in Europe and the United States led by women, anti-nuclear protesters, and environmentalists seemed to represent a decisive break in social contention, prompting many scholars, including Touraine, to abandon class analysis. Touraine seized this opportunity to replace class-centred theory with one focused on new social movements.[40] Touraine and his fellow researchers conducted several innovative studies into these new movements developing a method they called *intervention*. Touraine and his colleagues engaged in a dialogue with activists of these new movements, to discover the 'highest level of meaning' in their activities and protests.[41] The point of the interventions was to test Touraine's larger thesis – that new social movements were involved in a novel and fundamental challenge to the historicity of post-industrial society. Their approach attracted criticism. Alan Scott argues these interventions were somewhat self-confirming because Touraine had decided in advance on the central social conflicts of post-industrial society. Scott argues that, 'Touraine's researchers lack[ed] an objective and theory-independent criterion of "highest level of meaning" which could give their analysis absolute writ over any interpretation which the actor might proffer.'[42]

This criticism could equally be directed at the study of the French labour movement that Touraine conducted with Michel Wieviorka and François Dubet, and published as *The Workers' Movement*. The research was conducted among demoralised activists in the French union movement (from the CGT, the CFDT, and the FO) during the early 1980s.[43] The authors argued that the French union movement's decline could be put down to the passing of industrial society.[44] Their study breaks with the once influential 'new working class' thesis articulated by Serge Mallet and André Gorz that had assumed 'system technicians' would emerge as labour's new militants.[45] Touraine's intervention finds that the labour movement had lost its critical resource, a strong class consciousness, which they argue belongs to industrial society.[46] The authors argue that class consciousness is

> not – or at least not solely – consciousness of a social and cultural identity, nor is it a subjective expression of the experience of exploitation. It is consciousness of conflict, and develops in situations where the conflict between wage-earning workers and those who control the organization of work can be directly perceived.[47]

For them, class consciousness reached its historical peak when mass production replaced craft-based production. At that point, class expectations of work differed enough from the emerging experiences of industrial labour to generate the central conflict of industrial society.[48] However, Taylorist work practices, deskilling, and the uprooting of class traditions all eventually weaken this awareness among workers.

Post-industrial society presents more dilemmas for organised labour. The new workforce, Touraine *et al.* argue, exists at the margins of employment, failing to develop class consciousness.[49] Equally, organisational changes, such as greater state intervention, renewed economic nationalism, and regionalism, all conspire to complicate the struggle between labour and capital.[50] Touraine insists that globalisation forces anew the redefinition of the old class conflicts of industrial society when he claims that:

> L'entreprise n'est plus la cellule de base d'une société qui a cessé d'être une société industrielle.... Le succès de l'entreprise ne tient plus à son éthique, protestante ou autre, mais à sa capacité d'élaborer une stratégie et de mobiliser des ressources d'abord financières, ensuite techniques et humaines. Il se creé ainsi une distance immense entre ces deux acteurs de la société industrielle, si proches l'un de l'autre qu'ils étaient presque entièrement définis par leurs relations et leur conflits, le travailleur et l'entreprise. Le travailleur s'est transformé en consommateur, et ce qui était une organisation au sens sociologique du terme est redevenu vraiment une entreprise, définie par sa position sur le marché des capitaux et celui des biens et des services.[51]

Touraine's pessimism about the capacity of unions to act like social movements does not lead him to deny a role for unions. Instead, unions retreat from their place as central social actors into a host of other contentious roles, some defensive of their industrial gains and others more political. But their place in post-industrial society is confused and awkward. In particular, labour's 'productivism' is at loggerheads with the green consciousness of post-industrial social movements.[52] Touraine *et al.* end on a doubtful note, stating:

> Trade-union action is not doomed to a future of retreat and demobilization ... It may no longer be a social movement but it does not have to become locked into purely defensive demands; it can try to link past and future struggles, it can appeal to socialism to show its desire to safeguard the heritage of the workers' movement ... [The trade union] can take a more open attitude towards new social movements, knowing that they are the only force who have ... the sort of ability to inspire conviction and mobilize people which the workers' movement once had.... [I]ts highest role is as a political actor, and it can pursue this in a minor way if it simply remains an agent in the elaboration of social and economic policy, as it will always be less important than the political parties ...[53]

In heralding the rise of new social movements in post-industrial society, and the corresponding decline of the labour movement Touraine is, according to Jeffrey Alexander and Maria Pia Lara, the intellectual to most closely identify his sociology with the fate of new social movements.[54] Yet Touraine's position relies on the fundamental assumption that societal types define the type and range of social movement activity. This means that Touraine must show that societal types, like industrial or post-industrial societies, in fact produce distinct and quite different forms of social movement activity. To establish the central importance of new social movements, we need a clear definition of *post-industrial* society. But Touraine's definitions vary over time and are never sufficiently specific to reveal the distinct role societal types give to social movements. Take the definition Touraine offered in 1985:

> post-industrial society must be defined more strictly by the techno-logical production of symbolic goods which shape or transform our representation of human nature and of the external world. For these reasons, research and development, information processing, biomed-ical science and techniques, and mass media are the four main com-ponents of post-industrial society, while bureaucratic activities or production of electrical and electronic equipment are just growing sectors of an industrial society defined by production of goods more than by new channels of communications and the creation of artificial languages.[55]

This definition is frustratingly general. It is not clear why new social move-ments would articulate the most important conflicts if society is defined in this way. Could it be that anti-nuclear protests are part of a struggle over industrial society defined more widely than Touraine considers? At the same time, what we call new social movements have long and complex his-tories, suggesting their recent prominence is conditioned as much by historical and institutional factors as it is by any particular societal type. For instance, we cannot adequately explain the feminist movement, which has a long history, in this way. Surely growing awareness of gender inequalities, and of other inequalities for that matter, emerges out of a long process of social redefinition that has its own logic, one not easily traced back to societal types. Take Michael Hanagan's study of the women's and peace movements. Hanagan not only demonstrates that these movements have long, independent histories but they have close and complex links to the labour movement.[56] He suggests that:

> Too much attention has been given to the success or failure of indi-vidual social movements, too little to the interrelationships among social movements and their social contexts. An examination of Euro-pean social movements over the long haul shows that one way in

which changing configurations within families of social movements affect outcomes is by reorienting the goals of social protestors.[57]

If we cannot necessarily ascribe the rise of new social movements to the concrete structure of a post-industrial society, we equally cannot use this same model to disclaim the ongoing social movement capacities of labour movements. Indeed, Touraine was confronted with this problem in a practical sense when, in 1995, the French labour movement launched a strike-wave whose impact no new social movement could easily match. He persisted with his pessimistic view, referring to the protests and strikes as a 'shadow' of a movement.[58] Perhaps Touraine is right to point out that the strikes were only political in scope, a defence of pension rights and employment against an incompetent government. But social movements contest political as well as social territory, something Touraine seldom recognises. Alan Scott criticises Touraine on this score, pointing out that all social movements enter both social and political arenas of conflict:

> [Touraine] underestimates not only the political character of new movements but also the cultural character of the old. Cultural elements in labour movement activity, the broader demands of even the most corporate of unions, for example, for a social wage, and the diversity existing within and between trade unions are played down in order to play up the uniqueness of new social movements. We can only understand this polarization and the tendency to reduce the activities of the workers' movement to their more 'labourist' and corporatist manifestations against the background, once more, of the functionalism and teleology of the theory of post-industrial society.[59]

Scott believes that, by emphasising societal types so strongly in his definition, Touraine treats relationship between post-industrial society and new social movements in a deterministic fashion. He claims that Touraine's argument 'ascribes the causes of social change to changes within the *forces of production*'.[60] Social movement activity is broader, less dependent on societal types, and more conditional on historical, institutional, and political factors. As we shall see in Chapter 5, if we explore these historical and institutional factors, as well as the internal state of unions, we arrive at a more compelling account of labour movement weakness than Touraine does. Touraine's position certainly contributes to an 'end of work' social vision, assuming that labour is inevitably weakened. But even if we return to Touraine's own definition of class consciousness – a consciousness of conflict between workers and those who organise work – these are precisely the terms in which we should view today's significant labour conflicts. Indeed, recent innovative labour struggles, like the 'Justice for Janitors' campaigns in the United States during the 1990s, show this is true. New social movements have emerged powerful, labour movements have weakened. But their strengths and weaknesses as movements do not tell us as much about beginnings and ends as they do about the tempests of social change.

Claus Offe on the end of full employment and the basic income alternative

In assuming that labour movements are no longer capable of generating major social conflicts Touraine makes a claim that resonates powerfully with the 'end of work' scenario. One further claim stands out in this scenario: that full employment is no longer a realistic or desirable goal for advanced societies.[61] A whole range of post-industrial thinkers have also reached this conclusion, looking to alternative ways of organising a 'post-work' society which would be less dependent on a full employment objective to achieve the goals of social equality. Claus Offe gives the most comprehensive and thoughtful account of the problems raised for advanced societies by the apparent waning of employment. In this section, I shall show why Offe adopts an 'end of work' argument and considers the employment options facing welfare states to have narrowed. For Offe, welfare states cannot sensibly aim to realise full employment, a goal too conservative and economically infeasible for a diverse post-industrial society. In its current 'disorganised' form, post-industrial society requires a new policy framework less dependent on work.

To understand why Offe gives up on the full employment objective, it is first necessary to consider his views about the choices facing welfare states. During the 1970s and 1980s, Offe made a consistent and straightforward claim: capitalism cannot live *with or without* the welfare state. Contrary to conventional wisdom, he maintained that 'the embarrassing secret of the welfare state is that, while its impact upon capitalist accumulation may well become destructive ..., its abolition would be plainly disruptive'.[62] How does Offe arrive at this claim? According to him, welfare states must balance two contradictory forces: the push by capitalists for efficiency and profits, and the pressures from the public for social reforms.[63] The crises of liberal capitalism greatly accelerated pressures for intervention to restore both economic and social stability, and where these interventions occurred, they greatly expanded the role of the state.[64]

Until recently, the promise of the welfare state was to reconcile market efficiency with political democracy by implementing expansionary fiscal policies that primed demand in the market and provided income support across society. But, according to Offe, welfare states can only reconcile the competing demands of private economic interests with social interests by keeping latent some inevitable contradictions. How do these contradictions present themselves? Offe argues that welfare states are increasingly unable to reconcile economic and social interests, and their attempts to do so further encumber state functions. Clearly, the employment problem is at the root of these contradictions. In his earlier writings, Offe adopts the straightforward two-sector 'monopoly capital' common among Marxists in the 1960s and 1970s.[65] As the monopoly sector produces greater efficiencies, and absorbs smaller capital, it increasingly introduces labour-saving technology that ends up displacing workers.[66] Endemic problems of economic development force the state to compensate for falling aggregate employment through demand management, a policy that becomes impotent when overtaxed, and when unemployment creates too much pressure on the fiscal position of governments. To compensate for falling profits and unemployment, governments increasingly intervene in markets, attempting to regulate private economic activity or even to replace it altogether with public sector activity.[67] But these efforts create serious problems, increasing bureaucratic burdens on business and lowering private investment (i.e. 'crowding out'). At the same time, the state is forced to expand its role to meet the rising pressures for income support and social reform from an activated public. The two pressures combined dramatically during the 1970s in a period of strikes, stagflation, and growing government. Right-wing theorists and commentators captured the essence of the crisis when they spoke of an 'overburdened state' and a 'crisis of democracy'.[68]

Offe puts the problems facing the welfare state in the following terms: 'the substantive, temporal and social expansion of administrative action is necessarily accompanied by an internal irrationalization of the organizational structure of the state administration'.[69] He adopts the concept of the overburdened state to explore afresh alternatives to faltering welfare state capitalism. While he accepted that welfare states had become dysfunctional, he rejects the New Right recipe for dealing with this by reducing democratic pressures on state structures and deregulating the economy to revive profits. This option, he thought, would compromise legitimate government, limiting labour rights, increasing regressive taxes and obliging 'surplus labour' to work.[70] It would also limit democratic involvement in decision-making.[71] Moreover, Offe believed this option would only cause a whole series of new problems and legitimacy pressures for governments. This assessment has essentially proved correct: nowhere have welfare states been comprehensively dismantled. But, as we shall see in the second part of this book, some welfare states have fared worse than others, especially among the English-speaking countries I shall survey then.

The obvious way out of welfare state dilemmas for the Left was to attempt to guarantee employment through state intervention and legislating a right to work. But Offe is too influenced by the view that employment cannot be restored to see this as a credible option. Moreover, he opens up a larger question about the desirability of full employment,[72] and this question remained an underlying theme in his work when he later considers the various employment options for the state in *Disorganized Capitalism*.[73] This book of essays, published in the mid-1980s, deals with the coordination and policy problems that emerge with the breakdown of organised interests in capitalist society.[74] One of its most important themes, and the one relevant to our purposes, is the fragmentation of the structures and organised interests of *Arbeitsgesellschaft* or 'work-society'.

In *Disorganized Capitalism*, Offe provides the best overall account of labour market fragmentation, which he thinks has a disorganising effect on collective interests and the state. He sums up the fundamental problem as follows: 'labour markets will continue to exhibit a declining absorption potential, thus removing or excluding increasing numbers of potential workers from direct and full-time contact with the supposedly central power mechanism of capitalist society.'[75] He describes the disaggregation of interests within the workforce, the weakness of unions, and the socio-cultural shift away from a work-centred society, driven by both changes in employment and in values and social identities.

At the time he wrote *Disorganized Capitalism*, Offe did not think the rise of a post-industrial service employment would compensate for job losses in the industrial economy or help to organise the interests of the workforce.[76] He believed that service-sector employment would remain prohibitively expensive, an argument that perhaps applies slightly more to Germany than it would to the United States or Sweden.[77] Because service work involved different skills and employment arrangements, Offe did not think the interests of service-sector and industrial workers could be so easily harmonised.

A new service employment stratum, high unemployment, and an increase in the number of marginalised workers all contribute to 'interest disaggregation' within the workforce. This poses the greatest problem for the central social actor of industrial society – the labour movement. This would affect labour movements in at least two ways. First, Hinrichs, Offe, and Wiesenthal. believe that disorganised work environments made labour's objective of full employment more difficult to defend. They claim that the view that:

> all workers are equally and strongly interested in promoting the collective interest in steps toward full employment would therefore mean ignoring those sharp differences of employment risks ..., or to rely on a sense of class solidarity which can hardly be expected to prevail under conditions of a deep and lasting economic recession.[78]

Second, the labour movement's weakened presence in the labour market would mean that its formal influence in the system of industrial relations would eventually come under threat. Offe and Helmut Wiesenthal argue that, unlike business, which has the resource of money, labour movements depend on their capacity to mobilise collective interests.[79] During periods of strength, organised labour is increasingly able to exercise *formal power* through law and through decision-making bodies. But by relying on formal power, labour movements are at risk if their capacity to organise the workforce or mobilise collectively is undermined, either by their own strategies or by adverse changes in the labour market. And without a strong capacity to mobilise, Offe and Wiesenthal warn that: 'the [union] organization is most likely to experience a reversal of the process of institutionalization that has taken place ... as soon as the political and/or economic conditions are favourable.'[80] Offe and Wiesenthal's depiction of the dilemmas facing labour movements in contemporary societies is a compelling reading of the problem, one that is more soundly constructed than Touraine's, and one we shall revisit when we look at the prospects for labour movements and full employment again in Chapter 5.

For Offe, declining employment and greater disorganisation in the labour market signal a larger social trend away from organising society around work. He claims that socio-cultural trends now assert themselves in a different direction, one increasingly divorced from the work ethic. In the face of these changes, Offe wonders whether work remains a 'key sociological category', as he puts it, endorsing Habermas's concepts of system and lifeworld.[81] He writes:

> the convincing power of the idea of work as an ethical human duty is probably disintegrating not only because of the erosion of religious or secularized cultural traditions. Nor is it weakened solely because of the growth of a consumer-centred hedonism, whose propagation ruins the moral infrastructure of industrial capitalist societies. The obligatory power of the work ethic may have been additionally weakened by the fact that it can only function under conditions which (at least to some extent) allow workers to participate in their work as recognized, morally acting persons. It is quite uncertain whether, and in which areas of social labour, this precondition is today being satisfied.[82]

Of course, such a description does not allow for workers developing new work identities based on self-fulfilment that replace traditional attachments to work as duty.[83]

Like Touraine, Offe identified with the new social movements, especially those that challenged the technocratic organisation of society and prompted environmental and social goals of the New Left. But he goes further than Touraine, directly linking the experiences of new social movements to those groups newly 'decommodified' in disorganised capitalism, either by public spending or by the declining place of work in social life. He states that:

> By 'decommodified' groups I mean social categories whose members are not (presently) defined directly in their social situation by the labor market and whose time budget is, consequently, more flexible;

examples include middle class housewives, high school and university students, retired people, and unemployed or marginally employed youths. One common characteristic of these social categories is that their conditions of life and life chances are shaped by direct, highly visible and often highly authoritarian and restrictive mechanisms of supervision, exclusion and social control, as well as by the unavailability of even nominal 'exit' options. They are in this sense 'trapped', and this has often led them to engage in revolts against the bureaucratic or patriarchal regime of these institutions.[84]

In his most recent scholarship, Offe remains closely attached to the idea of disorganised capitalism, or the breakdown of a work-based society. He sees this process of interest fragmentation in the labour market, and in society more generally, to be a major factor in declining support for welfare states.[85] This is not entirely convincing because it assumes that support for welfare state policies has evaporated in the current environment. American and British evidence contradicts this.[86] For Offe, the challenge remains similar to one he identified in his earlier studies of welfare states: how to avoid disintegration and deregulation without returning to discredited bureaucratic solutions. He now formulates that problem in slightly different terms, drawing on the experiences of market deregulation in the West and state socialism in the East.[87] He states that reliance on any one sector – state, market or community – becomes insufficient to address the complex steering needs of modern societies.[88] Offe argues that states, markets, and communities all rely on different mechanisms for production and distribution, each with self-evident strengths and weaknesses. Over-taxing one sector to steer society for whatever reason, increases the likelihood of pathologies from its over-use, so Offe sees a viable solution in experimenting with a combination of the three sectors to do the job of social steering.[89]

Following post-industrial writers like André Gorz, Offe has strongly argued for a basic income as a viable model for overcoming the present work and welfare dilemmas. This, of course, means renouncing once and for all the goal of full employment. Offe sees the problem in these terms:

> The failure of a model of sociopolitical progress resting on full employment, economic growth, and social state security reveals its negative side all the more clearly: namely, wage labor as the focal means of leading a 'normal' life within industrial society; a gender-specific inequality of access to the labor market; the destruction of those traditional forms of life not regulated through the labour market or state administration; and the overburdening of infrastructure and environment. . . . A traditional strategy for full employment, be it through 'more growth through more market' or 'growth through state intervention', appears illusory. A return to the apparently 'normal'

model of a society of work and wage labor insulated by a welfare state is (a) economically undesirable, (b) ecologically indefensible, and (c) socially unacceptable.[90]

A basic income would deal with the three problems Offe identifies with full employment. It would not rely on employment growth to achieve a fairer distribution of income. Unlike full employment, it would not rely on economic growth, which has increasingly adverse environmental consequences. And it would recognise the social status – and fundamental right to an income – of citizens outside the labour market. A basic income policy also appears to fit well within Offe's proposal for balancing the steering mechanisms of state, market, and community. A basic income model of the welfare state would be administratively less complex than current welfare regimes, it would curb income inequality we find in markets, and it would provide income resources to individuals and social groups who perform socially useful activities outside the formal economy. Offe argues that additional policy offensives would be required:

> the two supplementary elements of a comprehensive solution are, a comprehensive reduction in working hours, promoted in all its variants; and second, the political stimulation and development of an 'informal sector', of organized independent labor, and all other forms of socially useful work.[91]

Offe presents a compelling alternative vision for organising a more complex society, one that is less dependent on social labour but still able to achieve social justice. He excludes employment-based alternatives – a deregulated labour market model to boost jobs or a social-democratic policy promoting full employment – on the assumption that neither are feasible or desirable. But, as I shall argue below, in the second part of the book, we can only confidently exclude these alternatives if we continue to believe that employment is destined to become less central to advanced societies.

The post-industrial 'end of work' scenario challenged

Offe presents us with the most comprehensive account of the 'end of work' scenario that I have developed over the course of this chapter. Of course, Offe, Touraine, and Habermas are not the only social thinkers who have contributed to this set of arguments. A more extensive treatment could also include André Gorz, and perhaps Ulrich Beck. Whatever the range of writers considered, there are four central propositions to the 'end of work' scenario: (i) that the number of jobs will only decline, largely because of labour-saving technological change; (ii) that work increasingly loses its central place in the social structure, reflected in declining social attachment to a 'work ethic' and the ongoing weakness of labour movements; (iii) that the reformist goal of full employment is now outmoded and unfeasible; and (iv) that a basic or guaranteed income offers a way of distributing income fairly in a post-work society. A fifth proposition finds its way into sociological thought: that work is, to use Offe's formulation, no longer unquestionably a key sociological category.

In this chapter, I have criticised the assumptions, arguments, and empirical foundations of the 'end of work' scenario. Work remains as important to contemporary advanced societies as it was in the past. I shall develop this point in greater depth in the second part of this book where we will investigate social attachment to paid employment (Chapter 4) and consider afresh the prospects for labour movements (Chapter 5). For now, I shall deal in detail with the fundamental assertion of the post-industrial left: that paid employment is diminishing across advanced societies.

In the Introduction to this book, I mentioned that one good measure of the 'work dependence' of advanced societies is the employment-to-population ratio (EPR), which tells us the proportion of individuals in the adult population who are in paid employment. Table 2.1 reports trends in the employment-to-population ratios (EPRs) in ten OECD countries using two different sources. The first source is the EPRs supplied by the US Bureau of Labor Statistics. The BLS statistics measure the proportion of people in work of the population aged 16 or over (or the lower boundary year in other countries). These ratios are included at ten-year intervals between 1960 and 2000. The second EPR measure comes from the OECD. This defines the EPR as the proportion of adults in paid employment in the population aged between 15 and 64. Here, Table 2.1 includes two data points, for 1973 and 2000.

When we examine the BLS results in Table 2.1, we notice divergent trends. In five of the ten countries, the EPRs either rose or stayed about the same. Four of these countries were Australia, Canada, the United Kingdom, and the United States, countries where we encounter higher levels of earnings inequality in the labour market. The Netherlands also recorded a higher employment to population ratio between 1980 and 2000; no doubt a baseline consequence of the 'Dutch miracle'. On these results, France, Germany, and Italy stand as poor performers.

Because the BLS statistics include all adults over the age of 16 in their calculation of the EPRs, we find that EPRs have fallen faster in societies with older or ageing demographic profiles such as many European nations. So this decline is not strictly the result of a dramatic reduction in the number of people working within the working-age population. The OECD statistics, which exclude adults 65 years and over from calculations, demonstrate my point. Again, these figures show a decline in the EPRs of France, Germany, and Italy, but these declines are much more modest in proportion. By contrast, all the EPRs in the English-speaking countries included in Table 2.1 rose between 1973 and 2000.

Table 2.1 Employment-to-population ratios, 1960–2000 (BLS) and 1973 and 2000 (OECD)

Year	Australia	Canada	France	Germany	Italy	Japan	Netherlands	Sweden	UK	USA
BLS										
1960	NA	52.6	58.6	59.2	54.0	66.7	NA	65.4	60.6	56.1
1970	61.1	54.5	56.0	56.6	47.4	63.8	NA	63.1	59.2	57.4
1980	58.3	60.2	53.8	53.1	46.1	61.3	52.1	65.6	58.1	59.2
1990	60.4	62.2	50.9	52.6	43.9	61.3	52.6	66.1	59.6	62.8
2000	60.6	62.1	51.1	52.8	42.9	59.0	61.6	60.1	59.8	64.5
Change	NA	9.5	-7.5	-6.4	-11.1	-7.7	NA	-5.3	-0.8	8.4
OECD										
1973	68.5	63.1	65.9	68.7	55.1	70.8	56.3	73.6	71.4	65.1
2000	69.1	71.1	61.1	66.3	53.9	68.6	72.9	74.2	72.4	74.1
Change	0.6	8.0	-4.8	-2.4	-1.2	-2.2	16.6	0.6	1.0	9.0

Source: OECD (2002, p. 304); OECD (1995, p. 291); Bureau of Labor Statistics (2002), available online at: http://www.bls.gov (accessed 23 October 2003).

What do these figures tell us? First, taken as an aggregate measure of society's attachment to, and dependence on paid-employment, there is no overall trend to falling employment levels measured either between 1960 and 2000 (BLS) or between 1973 and 2000 (OECD). In fact, using the OECD data, six countries actually have more people in paid work in 2000 than they did in 1973, a time when post-industrial thinkers started to challenge the place of employment in society. If we were to interpret these findings sociologically, we might reach a very different conclusion: that advanced societies are as dependent on, or even more dependent on, paid work now as they have been in the past. Second, these figures show the strongest supporters of the post-industrial 'end of work' scenario come from two countries where employment levels have fallen most on the OECD's figures – France and Germany. But even in Europe, the trends are not universally negative, being more mixed than the 'Eurosclerosis' image of a declining employment base suggests. Danish scholars, Jorgen Goul Andersen and Jan Bendix Jensen, point out that several smaller European countries have managed to improve their unemployment problem without sacrificing extensive labour and social protections.[92]

Critics might argue that looking at trends in national EPRs in this way does not tell us much about the hours worked by individual workers or about the number of workers only marginally attached to the labour market. They could argue that if we took into account these facts, then we would see a clearer trend towards declining employment. But this is not the case for the United States, which has increased its EPR over time without a corresponding fall in working hours, or a rise in the number of part-time workers. The trends in Table 2.1 actually do serve to provide a clear picture of post-industrial societies. Structurally at least, we are not experiencing a clear decline in work brought about by the inexorable forces of technology or anything else. The employment picture is more complicated: labour markets must meet the needs of more and more people, especially women, who seek employment opportunities. However the great virtue of the 'end of work' arguments put by post-industrial thinkers is that they open up an overdue debate about the employment alternatives facing advanced societies, a debate to which I shall now turn in the second part of this book.

Part II

Post-industrial pessimism and three alternatives for work and society

Introduction to Part II

The first part of the book surveyed classical and contemporary versions of the idea that work-based society is now in decline. The four major elements to this pessimistic scenario are that:

i   the number of jobs will continue to drop, especially due to labour-saving technological change;
ii work will continue to lose its central place in social structures: the work ethic will fade and, as new collective identities develop, unions will cease to be major social movements;
iii the goal of full employment is now outmoded and infeasible; and
iv the most equitable way of distributing income in post-industrial society is now a basic or guaranteed minimum income.

In Chapter 2, I criticised this scenario at a number of levels. If we take one objective measure – national employment-to-population ratios – we do not find a general decline in the number of people working in post-industrial societies. What we do find is considerable change in working life but within a larger, more stable scenario that still depends on paid employment. And what has changed is that women have entered the workforce in much greater numbers, and continue to do so, though at a slower rate; national employment structures in some countries are now more fragmented and unequal; many labour movements are weaker actors in the workplace and politics; and unemployment remains an endemic product of policy failure in some countries. We can expect employment growth into the future, that people will still find meaning in their jobs, and that labour movements will remain contentious actors in the workplace and politics.

The 'end of work' scenario presents a formidable challenge to the assumptions and polices of a work-based society. In envisaging a post-work society supported by a basic income, protagonists of this vision propose a clear alternative. However, if employment continues to grow, people continue to express attachment to work, and labour contention continues to foment, the 'end of work' alternative must be contrasted with other alternatives for organising work and society, ones which recognise the ongoing role of paid employment. In the chapters forming the second part of this book, we consider three alternatives in this light. These are:

i   a return to a tougher, work-driven capitalism represented by the 'US model'. In it, private markets are seen as the way of increasing dependence on employment and lowering welfare costs. The US model finds its strongest support among political and economic elites, while unions play only a marginal role in the workplace and politics;

ii   a basic income model, which would attempt to achieve economic justice without relying on a full employment policy, and which would guarantee citizens a right to a 'living income'. Promoted by the post-industrial left, this policy alternative hopes to build a 'post-industrial political coalition' that supports citizens outside labour markets and workers disaffected with working life; and,

iii   a revival of full employment policies through social democratic measures that depend on reviving the power of labour movements in workplaces and politics. This model would build a new 'full employment coalition', which would have strengthened unions and pro-labour social democratic forces at its heart.

We are interested in establishing the ways each alternative deals with the problems of employment, connects work and welfare, and accommodates the interests of organised labour. As I mentioned in the Introduction to this book, the US model stands out as the dominant alternative in restructuring work and welfare regimes, and is the natural starting point for this discussion in Chapter 3.

3 Work without limit?

Work and welfare in the US model

When we raise the prospect of examining alternatives in the future of work and welfare, the US model stands out as a major experiment in returning work to the centre of society. The US model promotes private sector employment, business control in the labour market, a lean system of employee protection, and a lean welfare state.[1] When policy analysts wrote about the American labour market or welfare policies a generation or two ago, none of them held up the American experiences of persistent unemployment and poverty amidst affluence as a success story. Times change. At the height of America's employment boom in the 1990s, politicians, business, and the mainstream media all proclaimed the triumph of the model; it had restored full employment and successfully wound back welfare dependence by allowing the private economy to once again take the lead. Here are some examples. Commenting on the 2000 Davos Economic Summit, the editor-in-chief of *The Sydney Morning Herald* told us that 'the primary message of Davos was that the US economic model … had triumphed over the regulated alternatives practised by continental Europe and Japan'.[2] *The Economist* magazine also asked: 'How far should Europe's social model be protected from the "mercilessness" of the American version, given that such protection carries an economic cost?'[3] The sense of triumph spread to American accomplishments in welfare reform. When President Clinton signed into law the Personal Responsibility and Work Opportunity Reconciliation Act in 1996, setting new limits on America's welfare programs, we can only wonder whether tough new laws were what he intended when he promised in 1992 to 'end welfare as we know it' or whether his words were a cruel prophecy.[4] The apparently recession-proof 'new economy' would now provide 'welfare to work' opportunities for millions outside the workforce and bring the era of 'welfare dependence' to a close.

Booming employment conditions and bold workfare policies attracted the attention of policy-makers outside the United States who, alongside big business, trumpeted deregulated labour markets as a solution to everything from unemployment to the social ills of runaway welfare. Blair's New Labour Government and European social democrats looked to Clinton's

America for the way forward. Although there is healthy dispute about the underlying reasons for America's success,[5] the unquestionably central appeal of the US model is its claimed capacity to generate jobs. For politicians, jobs mean growth, profits, and votes, and jobs also mean less welfare. As Lawrence Mishel and his colleagues confirm, 'supporters of the U.S. model have long argued that the U.S. ability to generate a greater volume of work, whether measured in terms of number of jobs or hours of work, is a major feature of the U.S. model'.[6] Certainly, as we shall see, the model achieved considerable employment growth and historically high employment levels during the 1990s. Claims about the 'end of work' seem alien in this picture even as the US unemployment rate started to betray the optimists.

Times change again. The economic downturn that followed the American employment boom has all but wiped out this display of enthusiasm. The US unemployment rate rose steadily from 2001 onwards, hitting new sectors of the economy and sectors dominated by low-paid workers with less marketable skills. Low-income parents, particularly mothers, it had been claimed, would be the key beneficiaries of the market-led employment boom. But they have been among the hardest hit by recessionary conditions, and left to face the tough labour market with a fragmented scheme of social protections seemingly designed for permanent good times.

Should the US model be the benchmark for dealing with employment and welfare reforms elsewhere? What does the apparent success of the American model in generating employment tell us about the direction of work and its place in society among the advanced countries? We cannot get very far in answering these questions without considering what led to 'American exceptionalism' in work and welfare, a subject which I explore in the first section of this chapter. One popular explanation is the apparently distinct culture of individualism that valorises markets and self-reliance. But taken alone, this argument ignores the long-term weaknesses of labour in the workplace and in politics. While labour's weaknesses cannot be offered as a single factor explanation for American exceptionalism, they surely have a place in explaining America's response to the economic problems that beset it in the 1970s – a response that placed the US model at the centre of international options for work and welfare reform. In the second section, I further analyse the post-1970s' consolidation of the US model that has attracted so much international attention. Much has been made about the job-creating capacity of the deregulated US labour market. But does it achieve the success that is claimed for it? I answer this question in the third section, examining: (i) the comparative performance of the US model in employment and unemployment, workforce poverty levels, and working hours; and (ii) the success of the United States in reforming its own welfare institutions and accommodating the needs of working families. Although my analysis leads us to be very wary of the US experience, there are good reasons for powerful interests – international business, and domestic elite politicians and policy-makers – to advance it as a template for national reforms elsewhere. Wary opponents – unions, economic nationalists, welfare constituents, and working families – are constituencies capable of keeping reforms in check. In the final section I ask whether the US model is likely to become the international template for reforming work and welfare. By considering the opportunities and obstacles in such a reform agenda, I will assess the place of the US model in future reforms of work and welfare and its broader significance for society.

Power, politics, and the labour market: sources of the US model

When we consider the 'US model', we describe a set of legacies, policies, policy priorities, and institutional arrangements that are born out of a distinctly *American* form of capitalism. But there is still some dispute about why the United States developed differently from other models of capitalism found in Europe, in Canada, and in Australia and New Zealand. Seymour Martin Lipset offered a definitive sociological statement about what he, and others, called 'American exceptionalism'.[7] Lipset thought the reasons that the United States did not follow a more social-democratic path in politics and in the labour market could be explained by the different cultural orientations of the United States produced out of a nineteenth-century social structure that had diverged from its European origins. Lipset makes the reasons clear: 'the major societal variables that reduced the potential for socialism and class-consciousness in pre-World War II America were the anti-statist value system, the socially more egalitarian social class structure, and the individualistic Protestant sectarian tradition.'[8] Although Lipset recognises the Europeanisation of American politics produced by the 1930s' labour struggles and the New Deal attempts to institutionalise welfare-state policies, he argues that 'statist proclivities ... gradually declined after World War II as a result of long-term prosperity that helped to refurbish traditional values'.[9]

The explanatory weight in Lipset's understanding of American exceptionalism rests with value-differences that he thinks are deep-rooted in American society and that permeate its political parties, driving ideologies, and defining policies. Although Lipset points to clear social sources for the individualist, pro-market, and anti-government attitudes that distinguish the United States from other advanced societies, he leaves us with the impression that it is these value-differences alone that determine politics and policies. But there are risks in assigning too great an authority to these values in accounting for the US model. Without a doubt, values shape politics and policy. But these values are themselves mediated by political and social institutions shaped – often by sharp conflicts – over long periods of time. And if we look at comparative empirical studies of the value-differences towards income inequality and welfare policies across the industrialised world, we can clearly see the impact of long-term institutions on these alternatives orientations.[10] Europeans, especially Scandinavians, hold highly redistributive and pro-government views – consistent with their past institutional experiences. Americans hold less redistributive and interventionist views – again, consistent with experience. Commenting on these attitude and value-differences, Stefan Svallfors claims that:

> What might be regarded as 'the feedback effect' of policies upon politics, or the sense in which 'policies produce politics', might then be regarded as one in which the baseline from which attitudes are formed is clearly affected by regime type, when it comes to attitudes towards redistribution among the populations of Western nations.[11]

If Svallfors is right in claiming that work and social policies help produce both politics and values, then it is difficult to accept the opposite argument that values produce politics, and policy, as Lipset believes. Clearly, the interaction between values, politics, and policy is complex and institutionally mediated. Recognising this forces us to confront the process through which policies become institutionalised over time, a process that in turn is conditioned by a complex array of political, social, and bureaucratic factors. Moreover, the development of an institutional framework provokes often intense political and social struggles, the outcomes of which may have a lasting impact on the future path of policy development. What does this mean for our understanding of American exceptionalism, at least as far as the US model of work and welfare is concerned? It means that political and social conflicts over policies should have a place in a social-scientific explanation of the US model. Below, I provide three facts that challenge the 'culture and values first' approach. These are: (i) the extraordinary struggle to resist unions encountered in the United States; (ii) the weakness of labour's representation in the political system; and (iii) the failure of national employment and welfare institutions to fully evolve in the post-war era.

The efforts to prevent unionisation in the United States

Resistance by business, the courts, and political figures to organised labour in the latter part of the nineteenth century was particularly fierce in the United States. In Europe, labour struggles combined with radical-democratic claims in favour of universal suffrage and the political representation of workers in politics. But in the United States, the extension of suffrage rights in an earlier period – particularly the era of Jacksonian democracy – largely divorced popular demands for political openness from labour struggle. Labour's weakness and exclusion, in turn, had a huge impact on organised labour's own political ideology. Samuel Gomper's famous phrase, 'unionism pure and simple',[12] was as much a concession to business and the dominant forces in American politics as it was an attempt to carve out an appealing ideology and viable strategy for American labour.[13] When a massive upswing in labour struggles took place across America during the Depression years, and after the savage defeats business inflicted on organised labour in the 1920s, Roosevelt's administration moved to enshrine collective bargaining rights in American labour law, securing the passage of the Wagner Act through Congress in 1935, and thus ensuring labour's support in the 1936 elections. But the pro-labour mood in politics quickly shattered. The Republicans won the first post-war Congressional elections, and the 1946 strike-wave provided the perfect backdrop to pass the anti-labour Taft–Hartley legislation the next year.[14] The anti-communist ideological offensive really mattered too, weakening hitherto strong unions and curtailing progressive policies like shorter working hours and the social control of industry.[15] Taking union density as a guide, labour's overall influence in the workforce peaked in the mid-1950s and weakened gradually over the next two decades, well before labour movements in other parts of the world started to lose numbers and influence. Fiercer attempts to de-unionise the workforce and avoid unions took hold again during the 1970s. Against this, unions have attempted to re-establish themselves through legislative avenues and in the workplace with few successes.

Labour's limited entry into politics

Although organised labour and working-class voters became central planks of Roosevelt's New Deal coalition, the party structure that had emerged in the previous century remained remarkably intact. By contrast, the entrance of labour, social-democratic, and communist parties into politics transformed the twentieth-century European party structure. In the United States, labour remained an element in a broader political coalition built around the Democratic Party. But other elements of the Democratic electoral coalition, rooted in the past, remained decisive in limiting organised labour's input. Theda Skocpol, Ann Shola Orloff, and Margaret Weir point to such weaknesses when they account for America's social politics, especially the two periods of progress in twentieth-century US politics: the New Deal and Great Society Democratic administrations.[16] On both occasions, the influence of the conservative Southern Democrats provided one brake on progressive, labour-initiated reforms.[17] The 1940s revealed the fragile basis of labour's political support: two years before the Taft–Hartley amendment was passed, labour-supported legislation for full employment, the Full Employment Bill of 1945 failed to pass Congress.[18] Later attempts to revive such legislation also failed. Labour remained a central element of the Democratic political coalition[19] but its influence fell, and it never came close to the influence unions have had over the British or Australian labour parties or the German Social Democrats.

The weakness of national employment and welfare policies

The weakness of organised labour and its political representation were two factors contributing to the emergence of a relatively weak Federal institutional framework for dealing with the employment and welfare needs of modern America.[20] And opportunities to build a powerful national policy capacity were also often thwarted by state, sectional, and local interests. The limits of progressive influence on the Kennedy administration were laid bare when it legislated for tax cuts to stimulate growth, and very targeted measures to deal with poverty, a framework extended with the Great Society programs.[21] A stronger influence would have led to a national full-employment policy (something that had been thwarted a generation before) and more universal welfare measures. Margaret Weir remarks that the failed attempts to build a national employment and welfare infrastructure in the 1960s contributed to business and conservative-led success in shifting the debate about unemployment and welfare back to 'individual responsibility'.[22] She remarks that, 'The failure to create strong national institutions to cope with unemployment also limited the possibilities for amassing political support for employment policies.'[23] Weir's point about employment serves a larger one: America did not develop the kind of policy infrastructure that would allow for different values to become institutionalised, to create a redistributive and pro-welfare policy coalition, and the reasons for this are rooted in significant resistance to any social-democratic alternative.

Consolidating the US model of work and welfare

Employment

The restructured American economy with fewer manufacturing jobs and more service industry employment emerged out of the changing world economic conditions that hit the United States in the 1970s. But the new employment structure was in turn determined by labour's weak presence in the workplace and in politics, and the fragile Federal employment and welfare system. While European states, as well as Japan and Australia, experimented with variants of corporatism, reflecting labour's greater influence, the United States followed a more aggressive path to restructuring. America's policy legacy gave business a few extra degrees of freedom in consolidating their balance sheets. American manufacturing responded to the emergence of efficient international competition, particularly in Europe and Japan, by shifting its costs onto labour. Attempting to restore the profit share, businesses used their dominant position in labour law and in the workplace to downsize and cut wage costs. In an attempt to restore profits, American business tried to curtail wages growth, and rationalise their workforces and technical resources, and marginalising unions were a part of this strategy.[24]

To be feasible, a strategy that passes the burdens of economic adjustment immediately across to labour requires an expedient institutional framework. Employee protections – redundancy laws, hiring and firing rules, legal recourse for unfair treatment, dispute resolution mechanisms – all alter the ease and efficiency of directly transferring costs onto labour. If we take the OECD comparisons of national employee protection systems, the United States affords the least legal protection for workers.[25] With few legal opportunities for institutional forms of recourse, the strength of organised labour on the shopfloor becomes even more critical. But moribund and conservative union leaders have proved no match for well-organised and well-financed de-unionisation efforts by companies. Efforts at a national remedy through legal channels also failed: the Labor Law Reform Bill was defeated in the Senate in 1978.[26] And there has been no subsequent major reform that would assist unions and labour organising.

Objective measures tell us something about the shifting industrial climate. In describing developments in American industrial relations, an otherwise placid textbook in the field says 'the unremitting opposition to unions of most employers has become a fact of [American] industrial life'.[27] There was a massive increase in the number of violations against unions in the 1970s, a good aggregate measure of a tougher industrial climate.[28] Aggressive corporate tactics, weak labour laws, and an ineffective umpire in the National Labor Relations Board led conservative unions to 'concession bargain', generally losing jobs and entitlements, and more militant unions to resist determined corporations. Legal avenues to de-unionise workforces, supplemented by illegal activity that is rarely punished, have made union organising and collective bargaining in the United States increasingly difficult. Corporations simply replaced striking workers.[29] While American law prohibits sacking striking workers, it allows workers to be replaced during 'economic' strikes.[30] And President Reagan's dismissal of almost 2,000 union-organised air traffic controllers and the subsequent deregistration of the union in 1981 were a thumping political endorsement of this kind of industrial aggression repeated later in Australia and the United Kingdom. Peter Crampton and Joseph Tracy claim that '[Reagan's] dramatic action signalled to the private sector that hiring replacements is both legal and acceptable'.[31] They argue the acceptability and increasing use of replacement workers have led American unions to 'hold out' against strikes, a much weaker strategy than striking. Concluding their empirical analysis of US strike patterns during the 1980s, Crampton and Tracy estimate that a 'complete ban on the use of replacements in the 1980s would have increased [strike incidence] by one-third'.[32] However, their estimate does not gauge the effect of replacement threats on general union strategy. Without these threats, a greater propensity to strike may have built on its own momentum. Instead, replacement threats and tactics have become more widespread. In 1999, as the International Confederation of Free Trade Unions (ICFTU) report notes:

recent surveys of employers with impending negotiations have found that upwards of 80 per cent are committed to, or contemplating, replacing workers ... Under the law, employers can hire replacement workers during an economic strike. Although the dismissal of strikers is banned, the use of permanent replacements is, in practice, virtually indistinguishable from dismissal.[33]

David Gordon offers us a compelling story about major changes in the employment structure that reflect the changing industrial relations environment in America. His evidence suggests that corporations did not just gain the upper hand by hardline bargaining and union avoidance strategies. According to Gordon, corporations employed more managers and supervisors (on better pay and with better conditions) to manage their workforce and permanently cement their hierarchical approach.[34] Gordon's evidence demonstrates that corporate America has gradually developed what he calls a 'bureaucratic burden' that has now reshaped and distorted the nation's employment structure. He offers us a general explanation for this: economies geared towards conflict give rise to a particular employment structure that dedicates resources – financial and human – to containing labour.[35] Extending the point comparatively, Gordon claims: 'evidence suggest[s] that among sixteen advanced economies, the more conflictual the labor-management system, the higher the percentage of managers and administrators. Cooperative systems don't need so many bosses.'[36] He explains:

> If a labor–management system relies on hierarchical principles for managing and supervising its front-line employees on the shop and office floors, then it needs more than just the front-line supervisors who directly oversee these workers. ... What guarantees that those supervisors won't be in cahoots with their charges? In such a hierarchy, you need supervisors to supervise the supervisors ... and supervisors above them ... and managers to watch the higher-level supervisors ... and higher-level managers to watch the lower-level managers.[37]

More hierarchical and dominated by service-industries, the American workforce emerged from the recession in the early 1990s to face new economic realities. When the American economy re-established a clear pattern of growth in the 1990s, the recovery was characterised by new developments. America's productivity – still a source of controversy – accelerated. Few inflationary pressures emerged, which the Chairman of the Federal Reserve, Alan Greenspan, famously put down to 'worker insecurity' in 1997. Job insecurity, normally greatest during recessions, was not merely a lingering state of mind. With an already weak system of employee protections, and much weaker unions, the 'hire and fire' corporate culture evidently took hold. As the economy started to grow in the 1990s, the rate of job losses through downsizing actually continued to climb. Peter Taylor notes that 'US corporations laid off some 450,000 employees in 1992 and a further 600,000 in 1993'.[38] Mishel and his colleagues note that 'involuntary job loss (layoffs, "downsizing" and other job displacements not for cause) actually *increased* between the recession of 1992 and the recovery through 1995'.[39] They further suggest that 'job insecurity can help explain why wage growth was slow to respond to falling unemployment throughout most of the 1990s recovery'.[40] This trend continued as the economy continued to grow faster with downsizing reaching almost 700,000 in 1998.[41] Although 'downsized' workers are likely to be re-employed, they are much less likely to sustain their pay and conditions.[42] Certainly, the ability to keep wage costs lower helped boost profits and speculation throughout the 1990s.

Welfare and pro-work social policies

While the American economy and workforce expanded throughout the 1980s and 1990s, the forces that had restructured the workplace eventually caught up with welfare. In most welfare states, welfare policies are closely attuned to conditions in labour markets, and particularly low-wage labour markets.[43] If employment conditions in low-wage labour markets improve, it is not surprising that business seeks access to possible alternative labour supply, and that welfare conservatives will be in a stronger position to promote work for welfare recipients. These conditions certainly prevailed by the 1990s: conservatives and anti-welfare reformers were much more active – and successfully active – in the United States than anywhere else. As many students of social policy learn, anti-welfare currents usually thrive under residual welfare systems. Divided between the Federal system and the states, the American system of public assistance and welfare is residual, overlapping, complex, and difficult to coordinate. But one Federal program, instituted during the Roosevelt era, motivated conservative attacks: the Aid to Dependent Families with Children (AFDC) program which benefited single mothers with children. The AFDC is probably the most talked about, overanalysed, and politically controversial programme in the history of the welfare state. Successful conservative attacks on this programme have had major repercussions for reform prospects elsewhere.

The welfare mix in the United States – a hotpotch of poverty alleviation schemes isolated from broader redistributive measures that exist alongside an extensive private system of middle-class welfare – certainly create political opportunities to discredit welfare. As Martin Gilens demonstrates empirically, public perceptions of many welfare programmes are overlaid with racially driven prejudices about minorities, particularly African-Americans. He argues that while support for the American welfare state (in both anti-poverty and universal programmes) is stable,[44] 'the belief that black Americans lack commitment to the *work ethic* is central to whites' opposition to welfare'.[45] The broader demand that 'welfare recipients should work' is a powerful political lightning rod that attracts widespread support, and critically, part of that support comes from working families finding it difficult to make ends meet who respond to welfare populism. Indeed, we should not be surprised that a country that prides itself on self-reliance and hard work judges harshly those outside the workforce. Republican tacticians and politicians have honed their campaigns to exploit resentful feelings and taken new opportunities to play wedge politics over welfare, attacking welfare recipients ('welfare moms') and demanding populist reforms.[46] The Democrats have had to contend with this populism, largely adopting its rhetoric and avoiding publicly supporting programmes and policies that might be subject to right-wing attack. Under these conditions, the welfare debate has shifted well to the right.

The major Federal reform of the public assistance system came with the Personal Responsibility and Work Opportunity Reconciliation Act in 1996. President Clinton signed it, largely conceding welfare reform to the Republicans who had won a historic victory in Congressional elections two years earlier.[47] His initial welfare commitments reflected a slightly different, less punitive, and more social-democratic agenda. His government's expansion of the Earned Income Tax Credit (EITC) scheme in 1992 attempted to increase after-tax income of low-paid working families.[48] A combination of bi-partisan political support and its pro-cyclical, pro-work design helped the EITC expand during the 1990s and survive Republican attacks. (Because this policy shares both ideological and design elements with the broader idea of a basic income scheme, I shall revisit the EITC in the next chapter.) Still Clinton and the Democrats were obliged to contend with the political boilover, which brought about the Republican Congressional victory in 1994. The tough economy, and a climate of mistrust and frustration were solid foundations for mobilising a hardline approach to welfare recipients and allowed Republicans to capture the agenda. Certainly, welfare reform was a response to the new political climate. But Gilens rightly points out that welfare reform met only one, populist element of public opinion about welfare. He states that:

> these reforms [in the Personal Responsibility and Work Opportunity Reconciliation Act 1996] responded primarily to Americans' cynicism towards welfare recipients and their desire to cut welfare to the undeserving. Only token efforts were made in the 1996 legislation to satisfy the positive desires of the American public to increase welfare spending for the deserving poor.[49]

The Clinton–Republican compromise pushed workfare programmes and work obligations to centre place in programme design. The Act underlined three trends in American welfare policy design: a focus on devolution,[50] a focus on employment, and a focus on individual responsibility and conservative social values.[51] Many critics, activists, and scholars pointed to the worrying implications of the new law. Frances Fox Piven and Richard Cloward summed this up as follows:

> the Personal Responsibility and Work Opportunity Reconciliation Act of 1996 caps at least two decades of confusing calls for welfare reform.... Many states have been clamouring for the authority to slash benefits and limit eligibility. Now they have it, and they're rapidly beginning to use it.[52]

The main changes enforced by the 1996 Act were new Federal conditions on the block funding and design of public and family assistance programs run by states. AFDC funding was abolished and channelled into a new programme – Temporary Assistance to Needy Families (TANF) – that imposed a strict five-year limit on public assistance for individuals and families.[53] About US$55 billion was removed from the social security system, which included cuts in the areas of food stamps and child nutrition.[54] Workfare policies have generally concentrated on reducing the numbers of unemployed or welfare beneficiaries by promoting labour market participation. The reforms have particularly affected women with children who benefited from the former AFDC.

Opponents of welfare reform have raised a number of objections. Devolution worries progressives because state support systems vary greatly and are only weakly regulated by the Federal government. Many states implemented reforms without enforcing Department of Labor guidelines on how workfare programmes should be established. The design of many state workfare programmes places participants in the workplace without the rights and entitlements of ordinary workers. In other cases, workfare participants have been denied some of the entitlements formerly available through public assistance such as Medicaid. Some examples help us see the dilemmas posed by state programmes. In New York City, unions tried to organise workfare participants who were 'employed' in community service jobs as part of the City's Work Experience Program.[55] Unions around the country feared the replacement of workers with workfare participants who were denied the same entitlements and income. In other states, workfare programmes have been criticised for being too close to major employers. Investigative journalist, Christopher Cook, reported on Missouri's Direct Job Placement Initiative which works very closely with large, low-wage employers who need a constant supply of unskilled labour.[56] He comments, 'It's the ultimate public–private partnership, supplying business with a steady reserve of cheap labor while enabling social-service agencies to meet intense caseload reduction targets set by federal and state officials.'[57] The strict time limits of support for women and families naturally raised alarm. Conservatives were able to claim that unlimited welfare support was a thing of the past, and the buoyant employment conditions assisted their argument that all welfare claimants could permanently re-establish themselves through paid employment. While welfare caseloads have fallen dramatically, there are few obligations on states to report on the destinations of workfare participants after employment placement.

While most academic attention understandably focuses on conservative political motivations for workfare style reforms, corporate motivations are also extremely important. An increased demand in some low-wage labour markets during the 1980s and 1990s led business to lobby for reforms that would expand the labour supply.[58] In many instances, local social security offices have become *de facto* recruitment offices for businesses seeking labour. Corporate interest in workfare in the United States is evident in the large conferences held to promote workfare schemes like the 'Welfare to Work Partnership' in Chicago attended by President Clinton in 1999, and sponsored by companies like Monsanto, Burger King, United Parcel Service, and United Airlines.[59] Many workfare programmes have incentives schemes (either direct subsidies or tax deductions) to help recruitment. At the height of the employment boom, *US News and World Report* gave a frank assessment of what lay behind corporate interest in workfare: 'because millions of jobs are at stake, a successful movement of large numbers of people from welfare to work could reduce inflationary pressures by containing wage levels'.[60] Corporations including Monsanto, United Parcel Service, and United Airlines have become large employers of workfare recipients because of the flexible conditions offered by governments and, in some jurisdictions, the legal classification of workfare participants as outside the status of normal employees, without the right to join a union. The United Parcel Service in the United States recruits about 15 per cent of its temporary or part-time staff of 150,000 from workfare schemes. The *US News and World Report* notes that:

> UPS is the most experienced in hiring welfare recipients. Because the package-handling business is seasonal, UPS needs to build up temporary employment at its sorting hubs during certain times of the year. It also needs thousands of workers for only a few hours a night. A blunter truth is that UPS wants to drive down the cost of its labor because UPS is more fully unionized than competitors like Federal Express.[61]

Citing research by the Economic Policy Institute, D. Stanley Eitzen and Maxine Baca Zinn remark that with 'the addition of one million new low-wage workers the income of the bottom 30 per cent of earners will be reduced on average by 11.9 per cent. This drop in wages will be even more severe in those states and locales with large numbers of people on welfare.'[62] While job numbers and incomes managed to remain relatively buoyant during the late 1990s, the long-term wages impact of a large increase in labour supply produced by zealous welfare downsizing worried many. Eitzen and Zinn argue that the new policy effectively 'mandates that poor people will work but without providing the jobs'.[63]

How does the US model perform comparatively?

While the economy boomed and jobs helped reduce unemployment and welfare caseloads, the US model seemed a powerful recipe for other countries to follow. Business benefited from the expansionary fiscal policies of the 1980s and the expansionary monetary policies of the 1990s, which, combined with an institutional framework that made it hard for the workforce to redistribute much of the benefit. Conservatives were able to claim significant victories on the welfare front, and gain greater policy credibility than they had managed to achieve in the past. But did the American work and welfare achievements in the 1990s justify the strong political and business support for the US model that we have witnessed over the past decade? It is this question that I shall now examine in more detail.

The US model: the path to higher employment levels?

Table 3.1 provides some basic comparative evidence about the success of the US model. One of the most important single findings is that the US model has increased its already high employment-to-population ratio (EPR). Of the ten countries reported, the United States has the highest employment-to-population ratio. The United States is one of three OECD nations from the ten surveyed here that have increased their EPR significantly over the past three decades; the American EPR rose about 9 per cent between 1973 and 1998. Canada's EPR has risen by about 6 per cent over the same period. Only the Netherlands has had a larger increase in its EPR, rising over 13 per cent between 1973 and 1998. The Dutch result can be largely explained by a massive increase in part-time work while America has managed to increase employment levels without increasing the overall proportion of part-time employees.[64] The American experience can be explained by several factors. Women's participation is comparatively high, concentrated in the expanding private services industries. And older employees (those aged 55–64) remain in the workforce in higher proportions than all but one of the other nine countries surveyed here.[65] While proponents of the US model argue that high employment levels are evidence of the capacity for deregulated markets to 'supply' jobs, we must also acknowledge 'demand' pressures for employment built into American employment and social policy.

High participation rates among women and older persons in the United States can be explained in major part by the financial pressures on them to enter the workforce and their limited options to stay out of it. The American welfare system provides little income support for the working-age population to remain outside the workforce, encouraging a dependence on

Table 3.1 Unemployment rates, employment-to-population ratios and social expenditures for selected OECD nations

	Unemployment 1978 (%)	Unemployment 1998 (%)	Employment-to-population ratio 1998 (%)	Income support to the working population 1998 (% of GDP)	Net government social spending 1998 (% of GDP)
USA	6.1	4.5	73.8	1.6	14.6
Australia	6.3	7.7	67.2	5.4	17.8
Canada	8.1	7.7	69.0	2.7	18.0
UK	6.3	6.3	71.4	4.9	20.8
France	5.4	10.6	59.4	4.9	28.8
Germany	4.1	8.6	64.1	3.6	26.0
Sweden	2.2	8.4	71.5	7.1	33.1
Italy	4.1	11.5	50.8	3.0	25.1
Netherlands	5.1	3.9	69.8	6.8	24.5
Japan	2.3	4.7	70.8	1.3	12.6

Sources: OECD (1999, pp. 224, 225); OECD (2002, Tables EQ 3.1a,b).

work for income. Table 3.1 also includes data from the ten countries that allows us to compare their EPRs with both their net public social expenditures and their expenditures dedicated to income support for the working-age population. When we compare net social expenditures, we can see that the English-speaking countries spend less on social welfare than their European counterparts. And when we compare the English-speaking countries with the large European nations of France, Germany, and Italy, as is commonly done, we see a clear relationship between higher EPRs and lower social spending (see Figure 3.1). Those who argue that welfare states destroy incentives to work frequently invoke just such a comparison. But this story is complicated by the successful combination of higher EPRs with higher social spending in smaller European nations such as the Netherlands and Sweden, which have augmented their workforces with part-time workers and a large public sector respectively.[66] In both cases, income support to the working-age population is substantial.

The United States stands out because it has both a low level of social spending (only Japan is lower among the ten) and the highest EPR among the countries surveyed. When we make a narrower comparison between

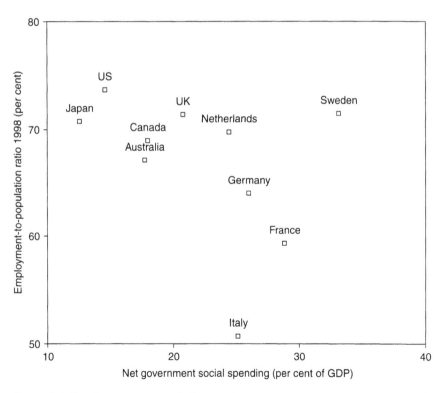

Figure 3.1 Employment-to-population ratios versus net government social spending, 1998

EPRs and public expenditures that provide income support to the working-age population (see Figure 3.2), the United States becomes separated even further from the other countries, spending only 1.6 per cent of GDP (again, only Japan is similar). When it comes to the level of income support for the working-age population, the three other English-speaking countries are not actually dissimilar to their European counterparts. We may infer from this finding that the US model provides fewer exit options – in terms of the generosity and range of benefits available – from paid employment for its working-age population.[67] Higher private spending on health care and pensions in the United States does not appreciably complicate this picture because both apply when the beneficiary is already in the workforce. With fewer resources available to support unemployment or families outside work, there are greater, in-built pressures on working-age people to find and sustain employment.

While it is true that the US model supports a high level of employment, we should be cautious about concluding that this automatically flows from the benefits of deregulated, unequal labour markets. We can qualify such an argument in a number of ways. The first point to make is that fiscal and

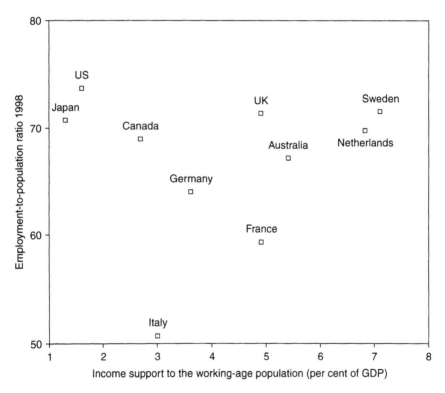

Figure 3.2 Employment-to-population ratios versus income support to the working-age population, 1998

monetary policy stances matter. As James Galbraith points out, America pursued much more expansionary economic policies than Europe did over the same period, which promoted employment growth.[68] The second point to make is that some other countries have managed to sustain high levels of employment without labour market deregulation.[69] While the US model expands dependence on private labour markets, especially the private services sector, to achieve a high level of employment, Scandinavian countries continue to maintain large public sectors to achieve similar goals.[70] Equally, the Netherlands, which has expanded its employment levels, has not entirely relied on the market to achieve this objective.[71] The final point to make is that there are considerable 'demand factors' built into the US model that make it more difficult for working-age people to sustain their livelihoods outside the marketplace. Rather than seeing higher employment levels solely in terms of the 'sound workings of the market' in isolation, we get a fuller picture by considering the structural pressures on the labour market to accommodate the working-age population.

Comparing unemployment experiences: success at the bottom?

When we compare unemployment experiences over the twenty-year period from 1978 to 1998 (see Table 3.1), the United States and the Netherlands are the only countries in our ten-country sample that have experienced an appreciable drop in their headline unemployment rates. The slowdown that coincided with Bush's victory in 2000 has pushed unemployment rates up once again. During the 1980s and the 1990s, the United States achieved substantial employment growth, faster than most European economies but not as fast as Australia or the Netherlands (see also Table 3.3).[72] If we compare current unemployment rates between 1978 and 2003 – a less favourable interval for comparing the United States with other OECD nations – American unemployment remains lower than the peaks recorded in previous recessions despite heavy job losses. Advocates of the US model policy might well claim that the comparatively low unemployment rate during bad times is further proof of the benefits of the American approach.

These certainties appear shakier when we investigate a little further. One problem encountered with the US model is the distribution of unemployment experiences. Mishel and his colleagues show that while the headline unemployment rate may have improved, the United States records *relatively higher* unemployment rates among workers with few formal skills when it is compared with other nations.[73] This finding suggests that the experience of unemployment for workers who miss out on training and education is relatively worse in the United States than it is elsewhere. My own analysis confirms this finding. Using 2001 unemployment rates by education level in the same ten-country sample, I calculated the ratio of the unemployment rate for 25–64-year-olds for all education groups with those with the least formal education, i.e. those who hold less than upper secondary education. This gives us an idea of the distribution of the unemployment burden and, in particular, some idea of how heavily the burden of unemployment in a given country falls on those with the lowest levels of formal education. The results are presented in Table 3.2. I find that for men, the United States has the second highest ratio at 2.0 (equal with Germany), exceeded by the United Kingdom at 2.3. However, among women, the United States is a clear outlier with a ratio of 2.7.

From these findings, we can conclude that unemployment is relatively high for those at the bottom of the education ladder. We learnt earlier on, however, that many economists in the United States and in countries like Australia continue to support deregulated labour markets with lower minimum wages, assuming that they offer the largest benefits to unemployed workers without training and education. At the very least, evidence does not support the relative case: the US model appears to redistribute the burden of unemployment onto those with the fewest opportunities to compete in the labour market. So the case for the US model can only be made in absolute terms, i.e. that it reduces the overall unemployment rate below that which could be achieved by alternative approaches.

Like everywhere else, there is plenty of unemployment and underemployment in the United States that is not properly revealed by official statistics. Economists and industrial sociologists often point to Italy, an example where a relatively large number of informally employed workers are excluded from the official statistics. Critics sometimes point to the disguised unemployment in the United States that is behind bars. The United States has the highest incarceration rate in the world. Is that prison popu-

Table 3.2 Unemployment rates by education level for 25–64-year-olds in selected OECD nations, 2001

	Unemployment rate below upper secondary education		Unemployment rate all levels of education		Ratio of unemployment rates (lowest/all)	
	Male	*Female*	*Male*	*Female*	*Male*	*Female*
USA	7.5	8.9	3.7	3.3	2.0	2.7
Australia	8.1	7.0	5.2	5.1	1.6	1.4
Canada	10.2	10.2	6.2	5.8	1.6	1.8
UK	9.4	4.1	4.1	3.4	2.3	1.7
France	9.7	14.4	6.2	9.8	1.6	1.5
Germany	15.6	11.5	7.7	8.1	2.0	1.4
Sweden	5.6	6.4	4.5	3.8	1.2	1.7
Italy	6.9	14.0	5.8	10.7	1.2	1.3
Netherlands	3.0	2.0	2.0	3.4	1.5	1.5
Japan	6.9	4.3	4.4	4.2	1.6	1.0

Source: OECD (2002a, Table A11.2).

lation large enough to make a difference to the unemployment rate? Bruce Western and Katherine Beckett provide us with clear evidence about just this effect.[74] Western and Beckett see the American prison system as a *de facto* social policy. They point out, as does *The Economist* magazine,[75] that the rate of imprisonment does not reflect rising crime rates but an increasingly tough gaoling policy for those who commit relatively minor offences, and a policy that has a particularly harsh impact on America's minority populations. Western and Beckett claim that the 'US employment performance looks weaker once the size of the prison population is taken into account'.[76] After adjusting unemployment data to account for incarceration rates, Western and Beckett claim their 'modified estimate suggests that unemployment in the economically buoyant period of the mid-1990s is about 8% – higher than any conventional US unemployment rate since the recession of the early 1980s'.[77] They further claim that:

> while European social policy is redistributive, the employment effects of U.S. incarceration exacerbate inequality. Comparative research shows that tax and transfer policies lifted about half the nonelderly poor out of poverty in European countries in the 1980s. Incarceration has the reverse effect. Because incarceration rates are highest among young, unskilled, minority men, the negative employment effects of jail time are focused on those with the least power in the labour market.[78]

Western and Beckett reach a disturbing conclusion: incarceration policies, they claim, 'also implies that sustained low unemployment in the future will depend on continuing expansion of the penal system'.[79] That expansion will be pursued by the profitable US prison industry, which has emerged as an effective policy lobbyist.[80]

Employment growth and the working poor: success of the low minimum wage?

As I suggested earlier, many economists claim that lower minimum wages boost employment and that the apparent success of the US model can be found in its low minimum wages. But is the minimum wage in the United States low when we compare it to other countries in our survey? One useful measure that allows us to make this comparison is the ratio of the minimum wage to the average full-time wage, which is reported in Table 3.3. We find that after Japan the United States has the lowest minimum wage – at less than 40 per cent of median full-time earnings. And the real value of the minimum wage fell by about 18 per cent in the twenty-year period ending in 1999.[81] The problem of trying to live on a very low wage would be minimised if few people actually earned it or there was rapid mobility up the incomes and jobs scale for people at the bottom. But this is

Table 3.3 Incidence of low pay and minimum wages for selected OECD nations, 1999

	Incidence of low pay (%)	Ratio of adult minimum wages to median full-time earnings	Employment growth 1987–97
USA	24.5	0.38	1.4
Australia	14.3	0.59	1.7
Canada	23.7[a]	0.44	1.0
UK	19.6	0.43	0.6
France	NA	0.60	0.3
Germany	12.9[b]	NA	2.9
Sweden	NA	NA	−1.0
Italy	NA	NA	−0.3
Netherlands	14.8	0.47	2.0
Japan	14.6	0.32	1.0

Source: OECD (2002, Tables EQ 9 and EQ11); OECD (2000, p. 14, Table 1.2).

Notes
a 1994.
b 1998.

clearly not the case in the US model. When we look at the incidence of low pay – the proportion of full-time workers earning less than two-thirds of full-time median earnings – we find that one-quarter of the US full-time workforce falls into this category. A breakdown of the working poor by ethnic background gives us an idea of the effects of the falling real minimum wage. While all ethnic groups in the United States have experienced increases in the proportion earning poverty level wages between 1973 and 1997, the sharpest increase occurred among Hispanic Americans, who are a younger new migrant population in the United States.[82] Among African-Americans, proportionately more were earning poverty level wages in 1997 than in the early 1970s.[83] Among the other English-speaking countries, Britain and Canada also share a high incidence of low-paid workers while Australia's traditionally higher minimum 'award wages' continue to limit the numbers of full-time working poor.

Mishel and his colleagues show us that employment growth in the United States has been particularly concentrated in the low-wage sectors of the economy. Their evidence suggests that most jobs have been created in the two lowest paying industries, in retail trade and business, and in personal and health services.[84] This kind of uneven employment growth only further entrenches the high earnings inequality that even advocates of the US model concede.[85] Women are particularly affected. When women entered the American workforce in the 1980s and 1990s in large numbers, finding their way into expanding service industries, they disproportionately filled the ranks of the working poor.[86]

We gain further comparative insight into the American employment structure in Table 3.4 compiled by the OECD, which compares employ-

Table 3.4 The US–EU employment rate gap by wage level and sector, 1999[a]

	Low paid	Medium paid	High paid	All wage levels
Goods-producing sector	0.0	−2.6	1.1	−1.6
Agriculture	−0.8	NA	0.0	−0.9
Mining and utilities	NA	0.2	0.3	0.4
Manufacturing	0.7	−2.4	0.4	−1.3
Construction	0.2	−0.4	0.4	0.2
Service sector	7.5	−0.8	6.9	15.2
Wholesale and retail	2.3	1.5	−0.6	3.2
Hotels and restaurants	1.9	0.4	NA	2.2
Transport and communications	0.1	0.0	0.3	0.3
Financial intermediation	NA	0.5	1.0	1.6
Real estate and business activities	0.4	0.7	2.2	3.3
Public administration	NA	−1.6	−1.4	−3.0
Education	1.0	−0.5	1.4	1.9
Health and social work	1.3	−1.0	2.3	2.6
Community, social, and personal	0.5	1.0	1.6	3.1
Total	7.5	−1.8	7.9	13.7

Source: OECD (2001, p. 108, Table 3.8). OECD estimates based on data from the European Labour Force Survey for Europe and on data from the Current Population Survey (outgoing rotation group file) for the United States.

Note
a For each country, jobs (i.e. employment in 76 industry/occupation cells) are assigned to the same broad wage groups as the equivalent job in the United States. For the United States, jobs are first ranked on the basis of average hourly earnings in 1999 and then placed in one of three wage groups (low, medium, high) of equal size in terms of employment shares.
NA = Not applicable, i.e. no broad occupations in the US for the given industry have average earnings at the given wage level.

ment rates by employment sector and wage levels for the United States and the European Union. Europe has a comparatively larger number of middle-paying manufacturing jobs (2.4 per cent of the total) while the United States has much larger numbers of both low-paying service jobs (7.5 per cent of the total) and high-paying service jobs (6.9 per cent of the total). These OECD findings suggest that the US employment success can be explained by its ability to create low-paid and high-paid service industry jobs. The OECD remarks that the higher US employment rate 'cannot be solely attributed to the fact that it has generated far more low paying service jobs … [it] has also been more successful at generating jobs in relatively high paying occupations in both the goods-producing and service sectors'.[87] But surely these two findings are connected. Recall David Gordon's claim about the 'bureaucratic burden' of US industry. If Gordon's argument is right, America's ability to create high-paid jobs directly stems from its ability to limit the pay and conditions of its low-paid workforce.

Declining real wages were not confined to the lowest paid in the US workforce. According to Mishel and his colleagues, declining wages have been a general labour market development in the United States, only reversed at the height of the Clinton boom in the latter part of the 1990s. From the period 1979 to 1996, only New Zealand rivalled the United States in declines in real compensation growth rates for employees in the private sector.[88] Wages for male workers in the United States have declined in the bottom five deciles between 1973 and 2001 while women's wages have risen.[89] For both men and women at the top, wages have risen sharply.[90] While many factors have contributed to slower wages growth since the 1970s including weak economic growth, deliberate policy-led wage moderation, and a recomposition of the employment structure, several studies implicate the weakness of unions. In their study of OECD wage trends between 1966 and 1992, Western and Healy argue: 'The OECD slowdown seems proximately and partly caused by the economics of the slow-growth era, but fundamentally dependent on the declining power of labour movements.'[91]

The conventional wisdom tells us that the US model produces such upward draughts of earnings and jobs mobility that low-wage employment does not produce a low-wage underclass. Apparently, markets reward hard work. However, Mishel and his colleagues show that low-wage workers in America have the least chance of leaving poverty through income mobility of all the OECD nations they surveyed. They claim that 'the United States had the lowest share of workers moving to the second fifth of earners and the lowest share moving into the top 60%', when compared with European counterparts.[92] They conclude:

> Supporters of the U.S. model generally acknowledge the relative inequality of the United States, but argue that the model provides greater mobility, greater employment opportunities, and greater dynamism than do more interventionist economies. The evidence, however, provides little support for this economic mobility, at least for low-wage workers and poor families, [which] appears to be lower in the United States than in most European countries.[93]

When we look for signs about the future employment structure, we gain a more 'structural' explanation for why income and jobs mobility in America are likely to remain limited. According to the Bureau of Labor Statistics, the fastest areas of employment growth reflect the divided workforce that is emerging in the United States. The fastest-growing employment categories projected for the period 1998–2008 include, at one end, general managers and executives, and system analysts, and, at the other end, health aides, cashiers, retail salespersons, and truck drivers.[94] This profile of faster employment at the top and bottom helps sustain Gordon's general argument about the divided opportunity and power structure that operates across American workplaces and the economy. The divide shows up elsewhere, in basic employment conditions and particularly in health-care. A research report commissioned by the AFL-CIO on the prospects for young workers without university education describes them as the 'forgotten majority'. According to the report, young workers aged between 18 and 34 without college degrees (about 75 per cent) reported lower pay, more trouble meeting basic expenses and more difficulties saving for the future than their college-educated cohorts. Only 39 per cent of this group reported having employer-covered health insurance compared to 67 per cent for young graduates.[95]

Does the low minimum wage in the United States improve its overall employment levels? A few observations can be made on this enormously complex question. First, it is not true that a low minimum wage is an essential ingredient in creating higher employment levels. Countries with higher minimum wages, and less earnings inequality, like Australia, the Netherlands, and Sweden, maintain reasonably high EPRs without low minimum wages. They also achieve relatively high employment levels without creating the very large underclass of full-time 'working poor' that we witness in the United States.

Second, economists hotly dispute the effect of minimum wage floors on the employment level. The economic orthodoxy propounds the idea that raising minimum wages reduces employment. But American economists David Card and Alan Krueger, looking at specific groups of American minimum wage workers in the fast-food industry in two US states, demonstrated the opposite effect.[96] Steve Dowrick and John Quiggan provide an excellent summary of the debates about minimum wages and their employment effects: their comparative evidence suggests there is little correlation between earnings inequality and employment levels.[97] Their findings suggest that higher minimum wages do not necessarily lead to employment losses just as lower minimum wages do not necessarily produce employment gains. In fact, if we take the OECD claim that the US model has produced proportionately more high-paying jobs than anywhere else, we might equally claim that high wages create employment. Few orthodox economists would buy this argument but it is no less clumsy than claiming that lowering wages adds more jobs. Even if wage cuts at the bottom help explain the profile of American employment growth, we are still obliged to deal with the costs of this approach in the high incidence of low-paid workers. And if we commit ourselves to a simple dogma about low wages as a solution to employment, we blind ourselves to alternative policies that create sustainable employment without the poverty.

Working hours: does more sweat pay?

We have established that the United States has managed to increase its employment levels, producing a high number of low-wage jobs. Despite jobs growth and buoyant economic conditions during the 1990s, the

United States did not witness an appreciable decline in either poverty or the number of low-paid workers. However, while we have seen that other countries have managed to produce or restore comparable levels of employment, none of them have managed the overall level of labour utilisation achieved in the US model. This is because the United States has more full-time and longer working hours employees than its high-employment rivals. When we combine three facts about the US model – high employment levels, high numbers of workers employed full-time in the private sector, and long working hours – we start to gain greater insight into America's ability to produce both profits and high income per capita. Working hours are a critical factor in this story. Table 3.5 presents the changes in annual average working hours between 1979 and 1998 for our ten-country sample. Australia, which has undergone economic restructuring, and the United States share the highest working hours among the group. The United States recorded an increase in working hours. The trend elsewhere has been stable or declining. In other English-speaking countries, the decline has been slight but in most of the European countries and in Japan, the decline has been considerable. Sweden is a European exception, recording a large increase in working hours but from a comparatively low base.

Long working hours in the US model have prompted some commentators, notably Juliet Schor, to write about a culture of 'overworking and overspending'.[98] When they combine, long hours and low pay make for a stressful mix, and the deregulated model abets the kind of flexibility that pushes up working hours, particularly in some industries. Financially strained households borrow to maintain living standards when employment income stagnates, and time-pressed families are often forced to make

Table 3.5 Average annual working hours for employees in selected OECD nations, 1979 and 1998

	Working hours 1979	Working hours 1998	Change
USA	1,838	1,850	+12
Australia	1,904	1,856	−48
Canada	1,832	1,779	−53
UK	1,815	1,731	−84
France	1,806	1,603	−203
Germany[a]	1,732	1,507	−225
Sweden	1,517	1,629	+112
Italy	1,820	1,629	−191
Netherlands	NA	1,364	−
Japan	2,126	1,842	−284

Source: OECD (2001, p. 225, Table F).

Note
a Western Germany.

up for the loss of time by entering markets to secure costly goods and services that could be supplied by the household. High levels of household debt in the United States, and in other countries that boomed in the 1990s such as Australia,[99] do not merely implicate those caught up in a consumer culture. Household debt points to the pressures on working families to maintain relative living standards in competitive societies misshapen by the pressures of money and time. Ungenerous entitlements do not relieve these pressures: the United States has the shortest legally sanctioned holidays of any OECD country.[100]

Is the impact of longer working hours in the United States sufficient to challenge the productivity success story frequently attributed to America during the 1990s? The answer is probably yes. OECD data for our ten-country sample for the year 2000 suggests that the United States maintained its comparatively higher GDP per capita by leading the field in its labour utilisation (a composite statistic that measures overall use of labour, combining employment rates and average working hours). While labour productivity in the United States was higher than six of the comparator nations, three – France, Italy, and the Netherlands – had similar or higher productivity rates than the United States. So if the United States has to some extent established its economic superiority through longer working hours and greater numbers of people in full-time employment, the social costs of this achievement must equally be acknowledged. Shorter working hours and job sharing may lower income growth but they allow workers to recover the time required to sustain active lives outside the workplace. This general point is taken by Andrea Boltho who demonstrates that shorter European working hours, and not economic inefficiency, partly explain lower European incomes. Boltho claims that 'European workers do appear a much stronger preference for shorter working hours and longer holidays than do their American or British counterparts.'[101]

Welfare in the US model: is workfare succeeding?

The huge reduction in state welfare caseloads after the Clinton–Republican welfare reform was signed prompted national and international attention. Cases went from 14 million to less than 6 million at the end of 2000.[102] According to its supporters, reform had encouraged mothers to enter the labour market, which was able to take up more workers because of its booming conditions. Critics saw other forces at work, that have raised new problems. The Clinton–Republican legislative programme effectively achieved reforms aimed at expanding work obligations on welfare recipients with few concessions to addressing the practical barriers for many seeking employment: affordable childcare, job creation, and job training.[103] Not surprisingly, those most subject to reforms – women who were previously supported by the AFDC program – encountered new difficulties in managing the work commitments, work and training obligations imposed on them by reforms. In 1999, the Washington-based Urban Institute published findings that suggested the vast majority of women who had gone from welfare to work had found low-paid employment, and were having trouble managing work and childcare. The report's author, Pamela Loprest, reported that, 'More than one quarter work night schedules, and over half are struggling with coordinating work schedules and childcare. At least two thirds do not have [medical] insurance from their employers.'[104] She argued: 'Policies to help former [welfare] recipients move up from initial low-wage jobs could also provide benefits for most of the larger group of low-wage women with children.'[105]

One of the most fundamental weaknesses of workfare, however, is its dependence on the state of the labour market. Rebecca Blank and David Ellwood remark that welfare reforms 'have converted public support from a counter-cyclical program – helping people most when they are unemployed – to a pro-cyclical one'.[106] They further warn: 'Should private-sector jobs for less-skilled workers become much less available in a future recession, it is simply unclear how the newly-unemployed families will cope with this situation or what sort of public assistance will be available to them.'[107] According to the Economic Policy Institute, recessionary conditions have hit single mothers particularly badly. Unemployment among these women has risen sharply but welfare support through the TANF scheme has not risen. The EPI claim that: 'TANF is not functioning effectively in the current recession, as public assistance income has fallen even while jobless rates among the target population have risen sharply.'[108] Other researchers like Kathryn Edin suggest that women are increasingly relying on informal income sources to cope.[109] These findings surely raise questions for the future of workfare reforms and other pro-cyclical policies.

Working life: social integration or social stress?

Conservatives claim that work produces social integration, keeps families intact, and contributes to morals and discipline. They claim work is the solution to a permissive society created by runaway welfare programmes. Liberals, social democrats, and others on the left promote work as a means to autonomy, as a resource for participation, and as an arena in which to 'act out a conflict' as Jocelyn Pixley puts it.[110] Empirical evidence suggests that work *does* have a beneficial impact on autonomy, as liberals, social democrats, and conservatives would variously claim, but we must qualify this finding carefully.[111] In their empirical study, social psychologists Catherine Ross and John Mirowsky found that while working generally improved individual citizen autonomy, citizens who worked in low-wage employment or jobs that were unskilled or tightly supervised did not experience any increase in personal autonomy.[112] These kinds of jobs did not produce either financial independence or opportunities for self-expression. Ross and Mirowsky also found that citizens (mainly women) confronted with both a poor job and household pressures reported even lower autonomy.[113]

These findings help us to make a few general observations about the social consequences of a low-wage employment policy and employment structure. Low-wage, repetitive, and tightly supervised jobs all reduce the autonomy-generating benefits of work. Moreover, women who are forced to balance low-wage employment with their household and child-rearing burdens are particularly vulnerable to this kind of autonomy-sapping stress. What do these findings imply about the US model? First, they indicate that a social policy framework designed to expand low-wage employment either to reduce welfare support or unemployment does not meet our expectations of quality employment or our expectations of public life. We should not be surprised that criminologists studying the links between US crime rates and labour markets have found that low-wage employment areas are as prone to crime problems as areas with high unemployment.[114] Such a finding challenges conservative ambitions for a work-centred social policy that will cure social deviance apparently generated by unemployment and welfare. Increasing work alone looks more and more like a fundamentalist solution to a complex problem.[115] Second, these findings help us appreciate the distinct problems that confront women who must balance work and family when public policy fails to provide intervening support. When our experience of work adds to these kinds of social stress, it produces a sort of social integration we might liken to being 'worn down' by money and time pressures. And this is a far cry from the fantasies of a revitalised civil society we read about in sociology. Such a revitalisation surely requires that full employment is sustained in concert with a generous public policy that supports those at risk of financial and time stresses and those who would benefit from improving the quality of employment.[116]

The end of American exceptionalism? On the export of the US model

Opportunities and obstacles in policy transfer

My assessment of the US model hardly commends it as an international model. But we have identified some features that make the institutions, policies, and ideologies of the US model attractive to international business, national policy-makers, and to reform-minded politicians. Longer working hours boost incomes and profits. Higher levels of labour utilisation are good for governments too providing politicians and policy-makers with a palatable formula for downsizing unpopular income support programmes on the promise of getting people off welfare and into work. National laws and institutions that limit employment protection and union involvement also appeal to business, which benefits from weakening labour's bargaining power. And there are plenty of powerful advocates of the American approach. When we consult major international bodies like the OECD or read analyses in leading economic media, the hallmarks of the US model – low minimum wages and lean employment protections, lean welfare spending, and 'welfare to work' social policy – are widely endorsed prescriptions. In 2003, the OECD published *A Policy Agenda for Growth*, a report comparing the economic performance of the United States and the rest of the OECD. Forecasting that the benefits of the American approach will be long-lasting, the OECD argues that other nations must 'restore healthy incentives to work and employ' to catch up with the United States. The OECD claims that 'tax and benefit reforms, lower non-wage costs, balanced employment protection and more focused active labour-market programmes are often needed'.[117] It sounds bland, and probably written to convince a sceptical European audience, but it demonstrates the OECD's ongoing commitment to US-style reform even as the United States has run into economic difficulties.

Earlier on, I dealt with some competing explanations for American exceptionalism. The 'culture first' argument can only be pushed so far. Alongside a distinctively American cultural history, we observe developments that significantly retarded the social-democratisation of American employment and social institutions – a weak union movement, no social-democratic electoral coalition, and inhibited national employment and social policies. Of course, culture does influence the chances of alternatives taking root and the likelihood of progressive coalitions making changes. But, as I demonstrated earlier, the US model has been a product of social struggles over the twentieth century, and business and conservative forces were able to cede less policy ground than they had to elsewhere. Does their success in limiting the social-democratisation of employment and welfare lead us to expect that the same forces will succeed in changing paths in Europe and elsewhere, so these countries adopt the American approach?

Because the US model is a product of institutional arrangements, and not merely culture, we must surely countenance the prospect of transferring American-inspired policies to other national policy arenas. This prospect is increasingly considered by scholars who refer to international policy learning and implementation as 'policy transfer'.[118] Certainly, the supportive infrastructure for such transfers is in place: international advisers to national governments such as the OECD propose fairly uniform policy reform as though national boundaries must bend to apparent international best practice. And if the idea of modernisation means something in this area, we surely would expect global institutions and communications to further facilitate these experiments. But national employment and social policies remain rooted in path-dependent institutional arrangements, and they are proving resistant to ready reform at a number of levels. Thus, we may anticipate continuing conflict between 'rational economic reformers' (pushed on by international pressures and elite domestic political and business actors) and those social forces anchored in existing national employment and welfare institutions. Some of the factors that would necessarily determine national policy transfer in the direction of the US model would include: business power in the labour market, political and bureaucratic commitment to wholesale reform, limits to change posed by existing institutions and public opinion, and problems created by fundamentalist policy solutions. I will deal with each of these in turn.

1 *Business and union power in the labour market*
For the US approach to employment to find serious policy support, the relative power of business in national labour markets would need to be strong, and business would need to be committed to building political and bureaucratic support for reform. High unemployment, weakening unions, and organised business commitment to change employment policies are prerequisites for building such support. Given these prerequisites, the English-speaking countries in the OECD – Australia, Canada, New Zealand, and the United Kingdom – have long stood out as obvious candidates for reform in the direction of the US model, and they have all experimented with tougher anti-union labour laws and market-driven employment policies. Despite hard times and growing business power, all these countries have substantial labour movements and social-democratic influences in their national polities. For reformers, the European situation is more difficult again. Labour movements are stronger than in the United States, and oppositional influences to market deregulation much more entrenched. Europe has one further disincentive to change that is less apparent in the English-speaking world: successful employment alternatives in Scandinavia and in the Netherlands that compete with the US model.

2 *Political and bureaucratic commitment to reform*
In labour law, and in employment and social policy, a viable political coalition backed up by significant bureaucratic capacity would be necessary to drive US-style reforms. But political commitment to adopt the US model encounters caution, hesitance, and ideological opposition. 'Formal' political opposition from social-democratic parties – either in government or opposition – might count against wholesale reform, and even when these parties are committed to market reforms, as many have been, they may substantially modify the reform agenda just as the Dutch, Swedish, and Australian cases would suggest. Still, competent bureaucracies 'draw lessons' from models and approaches outside their national jurisdictions, and this is a very important source for policy learning and change.[119] Outside organisations also influence bureaucracies. The OECD, for example, maintains steady contact with national governments and is a major source of US-model policy advice. Still, governmental incapacity – conflict between layers of

government, ideological opposition within administrations, and poor policy structures – may hinder or limit reform.

3   *The power of the past: path-dependence and political feedback*
As Paul Pierson tells us, political constituencies are capable of protecting the policies that support them.[120] Political feedback from firmly institutionalised social and employment policies may prevent wholesale restructuring because it raises opposition, and because change generates short-term implementation problems. Pierson has also usefully conceptualised the benefits of maintaining an existing policy regime (he calls it 'path dependence') as a form of 'increasing returns'.[121] Or more precisely, as Pierson rightly claims, 'the costs of exit – of switching to some previously plausible alternative – rise'.[122] These exit costs enter political and bureaucratic calculations about the risks of reform.

4   *The power of the present: public opinion and interests*
Public opinion may be mobilised against wholesale policy reform even when reform is supported by an elite consensus. As Svallfors shows, attitudes towards redistribution and social policy vary according to the type of employment and welfare policies that have become institutionalised in a national context. It is sensible to expect that the policy design contest in those countries will not settle on the simple 'equality versus efficiency' trade-off that we might expect of countries with a lower 'preference' for equality.[123] European constituencies with egalitarian preferences and traditions may mobilise anti-reform blocs when changes are perceived to be inegalitarian, and even if reform is the name of 'jobs' and 'efficiency'.

5   *Policy fundamentalism: simple solutions to complex problems*
Policy transfer scholars claim that policy complexity limits policy transfer.[124] But policy fundamentalism, such as wholesale deregulation of the labour market or the abolition of a policy on ideological grounds, may also limit policy change. This is because under-complex solutions to complicated problems, already subject to existing policies and programmes, generate powerful negative feedback. Simplistic policies tend to unravel as bureaucratic and political activities to repair damage end up undoing the original policy change. And simplistic policies antagonise the community that can readily see their inadequacy. These antagonisms easily stimulate policy challenges, backdowns, and reversals.

The factors I have briefly discussed above lead us to anticipate ongoing conflict between the powerful forces aligned with the US model, particularly international and domestic business, elite policy-makers, and politicians, and the constituencies that have grown out of the institutions of domestic employment and welfare policies. Reformists portray this battle negatively, as a struggle between 'rational policy-makers' and vested interests, backward-looking nationalists, and enemies of modernisation. But, when we look at reformist efforts in the US direction, we do not yet have any convincing examples of wholesale change. Below I consider what has changed in employment and welfare, particularly in the English-speaking countries. To be sure, tough-minded reforms elsewhere are not all inspired by the United States. This would ignore the long-held power of national political and business elites to implement their own national agendas. I do claim, however, that the US model has emerged as the most powerful and developed framework for policy learning and transfer, and is easily the most important indirect source for market-reformist politics today.

Employment policy change: Australia, New Zealand, and the United Kingdom

The most substantial political effort to deregulate national labour markets has taken place among the English-speaking countries in the OECD. The exception is probably Canada, which combines a decentralised system of industrial relations with a relatively resilient labour movement.[125] In the other countries, deregulation took place largely in two areas: (i) to break down the legal regulations over pay and conditions ('flexibility'); and (ii) to dismantle the industrial relations system that institutionalised the role of unions. In each case, governments and employers have sought to introduce increasingly individualised and contractual industrial relations of the type we find in the United States. The British Government gradually restricted the ability of unions to organise through a series of legislative interventions between 1979 and 1997, from the Employment Act 1980 to John Major's Trade Union Reform and Employment Rights 1993.[126] In Australia, successive Labor governments during the 1980s and 1990s gradually dismantled the country's centralised industrial relations system before the conservative Howard Government passed its Workplace Relations Act 1996, an Act that went further in this direction. The Howard Government used the legislation to enshrine individual contracts and enterprise bargaining, limiting the role of the Australian Industrial Relations Commission and restricting the scope of the award (minimum) wages system. New Zealand went furthest of all, as it did in so many areas of economic reform, replacing its industrial legislation with the draconian Employment Contracts Act 1991, which allowed for a sweeping deregulation of the labour market. In all three countries, the union movement lost members, and in Australia and the United Kingdom major unions clashed with conservative governments. We witnessed the miners' strike of 1984–85 over pit closures in the United Kingdom. And the Maritime Union of Australia, the Howard Government and Patrick, the stevedoring company, fought a major industrial battle on Australia's waterfront in 1998. The government emphatically sided with the employers but public opinion was deeply divided.[127]

Conservative governments in the United Kingdom, Australia, and New Zealand have all claimed that lower minimum wages were necessary to re-establish full employment. In the United Kingdom, the Major Government finally abolished wages councils, which provided minimum wages outside bargaining conditions, claiming they priced young people and the unemployed out of jobs.[128] Until the Blair reforms, the United Kingdom did not have a comprehensive minimum wage. In Australia, Prime Minister Howard even claimed the country had sacrificed full employment because it preferred higher minimum wages than the United States.[129] His supportive reference to the US model gave a clear indication of the direction he thought Australia should follow, continuing an already lengthy and broad programme of economic reform.

Reforms have not necessarily become permanent in national industrial systems. In both the United Kingdom and New Zealand, incoming Labour Governments made substantial changes, reversing deregulation and anti-union provisions. The Clark Labour Government repealed the Employment Contracts Act in 2000, restoring a system of collective bargaining in New Zealand. Although the Blair Labour Government made major concessions to the Thatcher-era industrial relations agenda, distancing itself from unions, it created a modest minimum wage and made it easier for unions to organise and collectively bargain.[130] The Blair Government has faced considerable opposition from a resilient union membership that has often challenged the government more effectively than the Conservative opposition. Australia followed a far more gradual path of deregulation but even so, the Labor Opposition remains committed to repealing individual contracts and re-establishing the powers of the Australian Industrial Relations Commission. Although there has been a concerted attempt to shift industrial relations in all three countries towards a US-style labour market, the outcomes have been more muted. One major reason for this is the ongoing influence of previously strong union movements on labour parties. If reforms in the direction of the US model – low minimum wages, contract-based industrial relations, and anti-union provisions – are attempted, they probably will continue to confront domestic political, bureaucratic, and legal obstacles. At the same time, however, there is little sign of a competing model emerging on the left, one that would support job creation through the public sector, limits on the working week, and union-friendly industrial law. But these ideas are off the agenda everywhere.

Welfare and workfare policies: following the United States?

Labour market deregulation has been either limited or reversed in the countries I have mentioned above. Have welfare reforms followed the same pattern? There is little question that the United States has been the leading source for policy transfer especially its welfare-to-work agenda. However, nowhere in the OECD do we encounter retrenchment of programmes that support the working-age population, and that would reduce spending to US levels. Even in the area of welfare-to-work, reform models adopted largely from the United States have had to adapt to local interests, expectations, and resistance. The harsh end of welfare reform has been applied through rule-tightening, greater surveillance, and more work tests. Populist welfare politics have also surfaced, benefiting conservatives. The Howard Government's 'work-for-the-dole' policy introduced primarily for the young unemployed in 1997 met populist demands to make the unemployed work for their benefits.[131] As a serious labour market scheme, however, work-for-the dole makes a very limited contribution.

To consider the scale of retrenchment required to achieve US levels of public spending on supportive programmes for the working-age population, we need only refer back to the comparisons we made earlier. Other than Japan, the United States is an outlier, spending very little public money on working-age income support and programmes. To achieve this low level, other countries would need to retrench sickness and disability benefits, family payments, unemployment benefits, and active labour market programmes. Instead, we encounter steady or rising spending in these areas across our ten-country sample. To 'Americanise' welfare benefits – at least in aggregate spending terms – European and other English-speaking OECD countries would need to supplement programme retrenchment with massive spending cuts. Neither the political will nor the policy rationale for such reforms is evident. However, governments have followed the American lead in enforcing rules and surveillance of welfare benefits that demand much greater obligations on the part of welfare recipients.

One of the more successful areas of policy transfer from the US model has been the Earned Income Tax Credit. This policy is popular among elite policy-makers and politicians for a number of reasons. It is considered to 'reward' work because it benefits only those already in low-paid work. It is also considered to operate in sync with low minimum wages, combining the apparently employment-friendly low-wage regime with anti-poverty measures built into the tax and welfare system. With effect from 1999, the Blair Government introduced a version of the income support scheme – the Working Family Tax Credit – to support the incomes of low-wage working families.[132] Coupled with the adoption of a relatively low minimum wage, Blair's Labour has probably come closest to adopting the American policies of a low-level minimum wage supported by a tax credit for working families. Australia's interest in the same kind of scheme has been more muted. Although the Howard Government has marginalised the award system that protects the minimum wages of Australian workers, it has not been as successful as its allies in promoting deregulation would have hoped. One suspects that the government will move to introduce some kind of negative income tax scheme only after it has dismantled the award wages system.

When we turn away from programmes, and consider welfare politics, we see disturbing signs. Governments win popularity for getting tough on welfare when they are understood as meting out a kind of 'tough justice' to those who don't need support or should be working. Behind this rhetoric lies a different story. As I showed earlier, public opinion in the United States and elsewhere continues to support welfare policies, especially policies that help those considered to be deserving, and policies that appeal to, and benefit, a broad constituency. While public opinion may be swayed by the idea of re-instilling the work ethic among the young unemployed or by the general idea of demanding 'something in return' for public assistance, we do not yet have a clear idea how these current 'welfare to work' programmes will fare with voters in the longer term. Because so many of the policies are pro-cyclical, harsh times necessarily undo their internal logic, throw up problems for welfare recipients, and invite opportunities for challenging policies. An optimistic scenario might involve increasing public discontent with policies that proclaim the end of welfare but do not appear to solve social problems or create sustainable employment.

Convergences and divergences: why social-democratic parties still matter

While they are now dismissed as 'Old Labour', those social-democratic parties that forged an alliance between unions and a larger constituency in support for intervention and redistribution have proved to be electorally formidable. These alliances were never strongly forged in the United States. Recent social-democratic politics has attempted to treat labour very pragmatically, as just another 'interest group' in a complex polity. While 'New Labour' experiments have cropped up everywhere, creating electoral opportunities and pleasing business, these experiments run two risks. First, by moving to the right, these parties risk both weakening and alienating organised labour. In some instances, this may lead to splinter leftist parties emerging within the political system. Second, social-democratic and labour parties would end up destroying a significant part of their electoral capital by weakening organised labour, which has proved to be a resilient voting bloc, source of financial support, and policy credibility. Commenting on New Labour's prospects, Colin Crouch warns that, 'New Labour remains dependent on a party and a wider labour movement which retains many social-democratic concerns; and deregulated global capitalism and the financial markets may not indefinitely remain reliable alternative allies.'[133] Crouch makes a general point about the future relationship between labour movements and social democracy that I shall return to in Chapter 5.

Policy failures: the limits of the US model

Finally, we must entertain the prospect of the US model becoming its own worst publicity. Although I have claimed that it has established itself as the pre-eminent national source for policy learning elsewhere, first among its English-speaking allies, and then among Europeans, problems with the American approach aid critics and unsettle reformers. As James Galbraith points out, the US model faces its greatest challenge in sustaining the public and household debt build-up that allowed for the expansion of the economy throughout the 1990s.[134] Low wages and unemployment will continue to encourage poverty. Workfare programmes that cannot deliver sustainable employment will create new headaches for policy-makers. Slow growth and weak investment will not convince others that a deregulated economy is somehow recession-proof or has 'licked' the economic cycle.

Conclusion: the 'end of work' and the alternative of the US model

Having developed a broad perspective on the US model, we are well positioned to return to the major claims and themes of this book, and to make some further assessments. The American experience of the 1990s tells us two main things about the alternatives facing work in advanced societies. First, the continued growth of employment in the advanced world's largest economy defies the pessimism of many post-industrial thinkers. On the basis of recent American experiences, we could hardly claim the 'end of work'. Ordinary Americans, especially women, have more chance of paid employment than they have probably ever had. And it is women who face the most challenges with paid work – they must contend with lower wages and comparatively undeveloped policies that help manage their entry and commitment to the workforce. Perhaps surprisingly, what we see is more continuity than change. Although jobs, industries, and technology all change, unemployment, inequality, and conflicting interests in the workplace persist. Instead of the inexorable 'end of work', we might still speak of the familiar cycle of boom and bust, one that creates and destroys jobs, and one that still challenges us to redefine the role of governments and markets. The second major observation is that we should continue to think of contemporary America as a work-centred society. We witness this not only in the growth of the workforce but also in the development of workfare reforms to America's public assistance programme. We have no reason to believe that struggles over work in the United States, whether they are battles for union recognition or obligations placed on welfare recipients, will disappear any time soon.

I have claimed here that the US model has established itself as the pre-eminent model for reform. But despite its promises, it falls short of expectations. Even vigorous reformers could not hope to smoothly establish a US-style labour and welfare system elsewhere. Both domestic resistance and long-standing institutional alternatives will continue to block major reform. Meanwhile, an employment-deficient Europe may be inspired by alternatives that also claim to resolve the dilemmas confronting work and welfare without pursuing American-style reforms. The post-industrial alternative is the basic income model that promises to end our over-reliance on work – both economically and culturally. This is the subject of my next chapter.

4   The basic income challenge to work and welfare

America's employment experience throughout the 1990s gives us plenty of reasons to question the 'end of work' scenario we discussed in Chapter 2. While work and welfare developments in the United States point towards a different transformation path to that envisaged by the 'end of work' scenario, we would be hard pressed to say that the US model had resolved the many dilemmas still confronting employment. Even if we believed the US model offered the only possible path to full employment, continuing high levels of inequality and fragmented social policies for the working-age population confront our widely held sense of justice. A generation ago, when Claus Offe wrote about the options facing welfare states, he thought that any effort to re-establish full employment would be disastrous.[1] Many agreed that re-establishing employment growth with tough pro-business economic and welfare policies would fare badly with the public, especially in Europe. In those English-speaking nations that have experienced more determined reform, the public has found policy change more acceptable: it may be that these nations have absorbed these reforms, and are now more tolerant of 'jobs with inequality' than policies that preserve joblessness. But when confronted with the choice between tolerating high unemployment and resolving it through measures that increase inequality, one might be excused for having little confidence in either work-based strategy.

Post-industrial thinkers, social policy scholars, and welfare advocates have turned away from employment strategies to a different policy design, one that they argue severs the already fraught nexus between work and income. The most far-sighted alternative to full employment is the basic income proposal, which extends a universal minimum income to citizens and is not conditional on employment status. Arguments for a basic income, or a guaranteed minimum income as it is often called, vary depending on the ideological commitments of its advocates. Post-industrial thinkers on the left argue that a basic income is the only viable way of maintaining equality in a 'post-employment' era. Others claim a basic income meets our just claim or right to a reasonable income and should be central to a new social contract between citizens and the state. Still others argue that a basic income would combine a higher level of equality with greater efficiency by removing impediments to markets created by welfare legislation. In the first part of this chapter, I will subject each of these claims to scrutiny.

The remaining parts of this chapter extend this analysis in two areas, providing new insights about basic income reform. The second part deals with the problem of building a 'social coalition' in support of basic income. Both advocates and critics of basic income often raise the prospect of citizens rejecting the scheme because it would be too costly, push up taxes, and redistribute income from wage earners to the non-employed. I am therefore interested in finding out what sort of coalition could be mustered in favour of reform. Using data from the British Social Attitudes 2000 Survey and the Middle Australia Project 1996, I look for a basic income constituency among two major groups: (i) those who support the values of a basic income; and (ii) workers who would prefer not to work if they had a reasonable living income without working. While survey data gives us an idea of a basic income constituency, it does not tell us about the electoral viability of far-reaching reforms that basic income would necessarily entail. Still, we get a stronger empirical sense about whether societies are ready to relinquish any of the normative, organisational, and policy weight that work carries.

The third part of this chapter concerns the risks of *partially* implementing a basic income-inspired scheme. Advocates of a basic income concede that a full basic income scheme may be too ambitious and is therefore politically infeasible. As a strategy to overcome these problems, they have turned to the idea of revamping existing modest programmes as the first stage to larger reform. Even in the tough policy environment of the contemporary United States, we find limited acceptance of the basic income philosophy in the Earned Income Tax Credit (EITC) scheme. Basic income supporters like Fred Block and Jeff Manza, and Philippe van Parijs see the EITC as the basis for reforming work and welfare. But would it be possible to build a more generous scheme out of this kind of programme? We might expect problems. The viability of an expanded negative income tax scheme, such as the one envisaged by Block and Manza, would still depend on the economy's ability to produce jobs. And voters and business may resist extending income support beyond the working poor to the non-employed. This problem, some scholars like Robert Goodin and Claus Offe believe, could be overcome by tying a basic income to participating in 'socially useful labour'. But we might wonder whether these solutions – a negative income tax or a participation requirement – sever the nexus between work and income as ambitious supporters of a basic income had originally hoped.

Arguments for a basic income

Advocates for basic income schemes do not all share a 'post-industrial' world-view. But most advocates share ground with new left and new right thinking: a preoccupation with liberty common to the variants of individualism that criss-cross the political landscape. The idea of an unconditional income is not particularly novel either; it has its roots in earlier libertarian and progressive thought.[2] Admittedly there are differences in basic income proposals; these include 'birthright grants', negative income taxes, and, most ambitiously, unconditional basic income schemes financed by progressive taxes. Although the details of the various proposals matter, we can detect three general arguments used to advance the cause of a basic income. The most important and general set of arguments favouring a basic income scheme are citizenship claims: according to this viewpoint, democratic citizenship demands a universal guarantee of the material means required for active participation. Advocates of a basic income claim that no current work and welfare regime can guarantee this right either equally or universally. The second set of arguments emerges from a pragmatic view we encountered previously: that full employment cannot be re-established, and that even full employment in social democracy has never guaranteed an equal minimum income to all citizens anyway. The third set claims that efficiency can be improved by a basic income because it would allow markets to operate efficiently without the impeding presence of welfare and work regulations: such regulations accomplish clumsily what a basic income can accomplish elegantly.

Basic income and citizenship

When we talk about citizenship, we invariably raise questions about the universality of rights, about active participation across all spheres of society, and about mutual respect. One outstanding problem that hangs over the entire citizenship question is how best to ensure citizens have a right to the minimum resources necessary for participation in a democratic society. David Purdy argues that a basic income, in the form of an unconditional grant paid out of taxes secured at or above the level of subsistence is now the best means available to ensure this, and a means that goes beyond the fragile guarantees and unequal opportunities available in contemporary work and welfare regimes. Considering alternative justifications for a basic income, Purdy claims that it can best meet the different but overlapping demands of liberals and socialists.[3] He writes that:

> Recently, ... a certain convergence has occurred. Socialists who are critical of classical liberalism, but care about personal liberty, have begun to overlap with liberals who are critical of classical socialism,

but care about social justice. From this standpoint, it can be argued that universal grants offer the best way to renovate the social rights of citizenship and bring considerations of social justice and questions of economic policy into a common frame of reference.... For the moment, it suffices to say that the aim of liberal-socialism is not to devise a definitive and comprehensive scheme of social justice which, once achieved, is then preserved forever. Rather, the point of the Citizens' Income is to create a conspicuous public framework for handling sectional conflicts.[4]

Purdy's argument is similar to the position developed by John Rawls in *A Theory of Justice*.[5] Rawls grapples with the problem of distribution within a liberal society: he understands that the distribution of primary goods has to be adequate and universal if liberal principles are to be realised.[6] Rawls argues these goods would be provided 'either by family allowances and special payments for sickness and employment, or more systematically by such devices as a graded income supplement (a so-called negative income tax)'.[7] However, Rawls did not fully accept the idea of the state granting a minimum income to people who chose not to work[8] and basic income advocates have sought to go beyond his position.

By guaranteeing universal income resources, a basic income might meet minimum social justice claims for a liberal society. But other scholars have advocated basic income as a remedy for specific inequalities in citizenship. These include the differential recognition given to social groups, inequalities within the opportunity structure, and lop-sided patterns in social and political participation. Feminists rightly point to women's unequal access to the income, recognition, and status currently granted by employment. Carole Pateman, for example, claims that existing welfare states maintain in-built patriarchal arrangements that cannot fully recognise women's real contribution to economic and social reproduction, and therefore advocates a basic income.[9] A basic income recognises equal citizenship claims of men and women to an autonomy-granting income. Other advocates think women would be the main beneficiaries of the plan. Philippe van Parijs claims:

> both in terms of direct impact on the inter-individual distribution of income and the longer-term impact on job options, a UBI [Universal Basic Income] is ... bound to benefit women far more than men. Some of them, no doubt, will use the greater material freedom UBI provides to reduce their paid working time and thereby lighten the 'double shift' at certain periods of their lives.[10]

A different perspective on inequalities in citizenship comes from Loïc Wacquant who implicates the lack of sustainable employment in what he calls the 'advanced marginality' of the kind he encountered in his studies of poor areas in Paris and Chicago. Highlighting the concentration of poverty and exclusion in urban areas, he argues that:

> rethinking the mechanisms that link group membership and advanced marginality will require to [*sic*] examine up close what 'mediating institutions' need to be invented to 're-solidarize' the city and beget the social integration that previously resulted from incorporation into a class or a compact ethnoracial community.[11]

Wacquant sees few hopes in low-wage jobs, rightly claiming they reinforce marginality in deprived communities. Instead, he believes the urban environment is a potential centre for redressing marginality if only the right 'mediating institutions' are in place. He sees the problem in these terms:

> Forsaking the highly dubious assumption that a large majority of the members of advanced society can or will see their basic needs met by formal employment (or by employment of members of their households), public policies designed to counter advanced marginality must work to facilitate and smooth out the severance of subsistence from work, income from paid labor, and social participation from wage-earning that is already happening in a haphazard and uneven manner.[12]

Wacquant's hope for an incomes policy that does more than low-wage jobs do for marginalised people echoes the communitarian ambitions for a basic income we encountered earlier in Chapter 2. Claus Offe, André Gorz, and Ulrich Beck are among those writers who believe a basic income would help revive community interaction, providing not least the time and money to invest community resources such as co-operatives that informally produce goods and services. This would replace some market or government activities with self-regulated ones. Similarly, social policy critics such as Bill Jordan argue for a basic income, claiming it would best satisfy the 'common good' by underwriting a process of community building.[13]

Does a universal basic income meet these ambitions for a more equal and participatory citizenship? Certainly, a universal equal income appears to be an elegant way of reducing the inequality that mars effective citizenship. Outside Scandinavia, where work and welfare regimes expressly aim for universal income support, we find the current work and welfare order in most advanced countries secures only a fragile, unequal framework for recognising citizenship claims. But there are a number of significant problems with presuming a basic income would assist in generating stronger citizenship. Jack Barbalet points out that 'rights are not determinants of action so much as resources which actors might draw upon'.[14]

A right to a basic income may not mean that the resources it provides contribute much to active citizenship. We are still obliged to search for – and protect – 'mediating institutions', as Wacquant calls them, that translate citizenship rights into citizenship activity. A cash grant would only provide preliminary and partial resources for this. Moreover, those who participate most in social institutions today do not merely have access to money and time: we find high levels of participation in civic activity among 'insiders': those who have already accumulated privileged access to social institutions including, notably, good jobs.[15] Without good jobs, outsiders will most probably remain outsiders.

The problem of translating rights into active participation also applies to feminist arguments for a basic income. Carole Pateman and Philippe van Parijs both support a basic income because of its apparent benefits for women, benefits not afforded under most work and welfare regimes. But their arguments miss some of the complexity of the current predicament facing many women. Women's transition to the workforce is transforming their autonomy, recognition, and income-generating opportunities. This reality also poses a complex set of problems for women and for progressive policy-makers. Today, many social policy critics echo women's frustrations at balancing their working, personal, and family lives. Would a basic income address this problem? Certainly, it would increase the financial autonomy of some women. But it does little for – and may even divert policy focus and resources away from – building policy institutions that support many working women who seek to develop skills and careers while raising a family. Women's citizenship is surely enhanced by them obtaining resources to lead full lives: access to rewarding work opportunities, support around the house, assistance in child rearing, and time for self and education. There is a further risk. A basic income might have the same normative and labour supply impact as the arguably conservative proposal to pay women for their child-rearing and household responsibilities.

Problems we encounter with the feminist argument for a basic income underline larger problems in the citizenship arguments for a basic income. By concentrating on the universal right to an income, basic income supporters divert their attention away from those factors that help shape active citizenship. In general, basic income supporters only acknowledge the ways employment *detracts* from citizenship and the ways employment may *enhance* citizenship.[16] Moreover, even under a basic income system, powerful class-structuring forces operating in the labour market would still limit access to good jobs and the benefits they confer on their occupants. So larger inequalities would certainly persist. A full account of citizenship would offer a more balanced assessment of the role 'good jobs' play in building social citizenship, and especially in providing opportunities, recognition and independence for women and marginalised communities.

Basic income and the 'end of work'

If supporters of basic income fail to recognise the value of good jobs in building citizenship, then they frequently do so because they rely on post-industrial 'end of work' arguments we first encountered in Chapter 2. 'End of work' assumptions have inspired progressives to search for social policies that support economic justice without relying on full employment. The basic income model suits the post-industrial left for three interlocking reasons: (i) a basic income would not depend on continuing high employment levels; (ii) a basic income would rely less on economic growth to sustain equality; and (iii) a basic income would challenge the 'work-centredness' of society by supporting citizens – without obligation – outside the labour market.

During the 1980s, many left-leaning European intellectuals decided that full employment was no longer attainable, and threw their support behind a basic income reconstruction of existing work and welfare arrangements.[17] Claus Offe, André Gorz, John Keane, Jürgen Habermas, and Ulrich Beck are among those from this generation of social thinkers who have supported basic income ideals, arguing that full employment was unlikely, and criticising the outmoded, conservative thinking behind full-employment social democracy.[18] As I mentioned earlier, most of these thinkers have come from France or Germany where sour employment trends have understandably inspired fresh alternatives. And most of these writers were influenced by the 1960s social revolution, which produced a new kind of radicalism divorced from traditional socialist objectives and work-centred struggles.[19] Later, and perhaps less plausibly, the same arguments gained prominence in the United States through the writings of Stanley Aronowitz and Jeremy Rifkin. Rifkin's *The End of Work* is the most recent book-length version of this argument.

The post-industrial left has been influenced by green politics and the ecological consciousness that has spread throughout the industrialised world in the past two decades. Like Marxism, green politics despairs at the alienation produced by industrial society but unlike Marxism, it sharply criticises the 'productivist consensus' that commits to environmentally damaging economic growth. For progressive environmentalists, then, the goal of economic policy is somehow to achieve an environmentally sustainable level of growth while pursuing redistributive aims. In the productivist model, both profits and employment suffer when growth slows: this means that dealing with environmental problems forces progressives into an agonising choice between jobs and ecological protection. Van Parijs believes that the basic income scheme offers a path forward:

> The environmentalists' chief foe is productivism, the obsessive pursuit of economic growth. And one of the most powerful justifications for fast growth, in particular among the working class and its

organizations, is the fight against unemployment. The UBI ... is a coherent strategy for tackling unemployment without relying on faster growth. The availability of such a strategy undermines the broad productivist coalition and thereby improves the prospects for realizing environmentalist objectives.[20]

The post-industrial left sees industrial society in a crisis of its own design, becoming less and less able to produce the growth, jobs, and ecological resources upon which it depends. At the same time, culture and society no longer depend on the central place of work – and the work ethic. André Gorz once described displaced workers produced by this society as the 'non-class of non-proletarians'.[21] This became a major theme in European sociology. Ulrich Beck has argued in the past two decades that class-structured industrial societies are becoming individualised, risk societies in which identity, life chances, and employment are more contingent.[22] According to this line of thinking, risk societies generate individual and social risks that cannot be predicted or contained by social policies designed for full-employment societies. As Offe puts it: 'If the particular modes of life, biographical patterns, sexual division of labour, etc., can no longer be privileged or discriminated against, social policy loses its traditional mandate ... to contribute to the cultural anchoring of a hegemonic mode of life.'[23] A basic income, its advocates claim, allows policymakers to avoid making narrow and rigid assumptions about life-circumstances, thereby perpetuating inequalities. Robert Goodin argues a basic income involves minimal presumptions about the inclusion/exclusion categories of the welfare state and the fallible, contestable moral hierarchies that such categories involve.[24] He claims that, 'if people's needs are increasingly non-standardized, so too must be the social response'.[25]

Does the 'end of work' vision of an individualised, less work-centred society provide realistic arguments and evidence to bolster the argument for a basic income? The answer to this rests on the likelihood of a precipitous decline in employment. Some earlier predictions on this score have proved to be over-stated. Gorz, for instance, wrote in the early 1980s:

> It is not an exaggeration to predict unemployment rates of 30 to 50 per cent by the end of the century, as do American economists like Peter F. Drucker or Pat Choate. . . . Considering already existing rates of unemployment, a level of 30 to 50 per cent by the end of the century may seem a moderate prediction.[26]

Rifkin tends towards similar overstatement. Describing the effects of computerisation and new 'machines that can think', Rifkin concludes: 'Norbert Weiner's premonition of a world without workers is fast becoming an issue of public concern in the industrialized nations.'[27]

Even supporters of basic income ideas have criticised the 'end of work' justification for a basic income. Fred Block and Jeff Manza argue that:

> In retrospect, ... analysts misunderstood how automation would reshape the labor force. Rather than a disappearance of all job opportunities, there has been a sharp decline in the full-time, blue-collar manufacturing jobs that had provided an important mobility route for generations of immigrants and minorities. Since the 1960s, there has been considerable job growth, but it has been disproportionately in service sector jobs that are part-time or poorly compensated.... in thinking about 'pensioning off' pre-retirement adults, these analysts failed to consider the long-term negative consequences of living in communities where few adults can find work.[28]

Block and Manza rightly imply that employment trends have not confirmed the drastic 'end of work' scenario in which job losses would take on an almost dialectical force, and produce a natural electorate for a basic income scheme. By conceding that employment trends suggest otherwise, Block and Manza direct us back to the problem of best meeting the needs of low-income workers. But then the basic income proposals must compete with alternatives like raising wages and conditions for the working poor.

When Goodin and Offe speak favourably of basic income as a social policy design that is in Goodin's phrase, 'minimally presumptuous', they too inevitably rely on an exaggerated view about the declining importance of work for citizens. If we take a different view, that work will remain central for most people's economic and social security into the future, it is perfectly sensible for public policy to address the needs of working people as a primary responsibility. Moreover, it is not clear that a universal flat benefit of the basic income type does in fact make minimal presumptions or that making such presumptions is always negative. This is something that Goodin himself recognises.[29] By replacing social policies that discriminate in favour of groups and individuals with special needs like single mothers or people living with disabilities, a basic income scheme would potentially ignore the specific needs claims of these groups or fail to simplify social policy in a way that its advocates envisage. As Elizabeth Anderson points out:

> The main question is whether programs more carefully tailored to meet the needs of the disabled, the disadvantaged, dependents, and their caretakers ... would be more effective in delivering the promised goods, and win greater acceptance, than a [universal basic income].[30]

Basic income and economic efficiency

While much of the appeal of a basic income lies in its ability to address poverty and inequality, the free market right also find a basic income appealing, and largely for its purported impact on economic inefficiency. Some elements of the right have long sought to 'wind back' the regulating, intervening welfare state, claiming that it undermines the market, but they have been forced to deal with the problems of doing so, and in particular the inequality such a reversal would entail. Friedrich von Hayek, who famously rejected the very idea of social justice, advocated a kind of minimum income as a liberal alternative to the welfare state, acknowledging that families and kinship structures were no longer an acceptable insurance against life's contingencies.[31] With similar intent and confronted with the rising welfare ambitions of the 1960s, Milton Friedman restated his case for a negative income tax scheme as a way of achieving a minimum level of justice without regulating the economy.[32] And today, Philippe van Parijs claims that, to be viable, any policy that aims to improve social justice must equally address its impact on economic efficiency.[33] Van Parijs is aware of the potential efficiency costs of extensive basic income reform, namely the economic liability of higher taxes to pay for the reform and the possible effects on labour supply that could lower growth.[34] But, like Friedman, van Parijs sees potential efficiency gains from basic income reform because it would allow for greater deregulation of the labour market.[35] Not only would a basic income subsidise less-than-subsistence wages in the labour market (a boon for business), there would be 'less justification for a number of regulations which currently constrain the labour market, such as restrictions on patterns of working time or even minimum wage legislation'.[36] American writers like Anne Alstott have made similar claims.[37]

Most market-oriented advocates for basic income reform see efficiency gains in (i) reducing the complexity and scale of existing transfer payment and welfare services; and (ii) deregulating the labour market without necessarily lowering the final incomes of workers. Is either of these two options attractive? The prospect of a basic income replacing existing welfare benefits would generate considerable problems. Certainly, not all of the existing welfare state infrastructure could be replaced by a basic income: publicly available services (nurses, carers, social workers) would necessarily continue to demand public planning, staffing, and funding. Moreover, the level of basic income would need to be at least as high as the highest payments for individuals and families with special needs, so that these groups did not lose out from reforms. Even then, the state may lose some of its discretionary spending ability to target needy groups because more of its resources would be channelled into funding basic income.

Further labour market deregulation might be the carrot for business to endorse basic income reform. If deregulation were extensive, and enabled full wage flexibility, two competing pressures would operate: one pressure would exert itself on labour supply as low-wage or disaffected employees left the labour market, and the other pressure would exert itself on wage levels as business exploited deregulation to lower costs and wages. It is hard to predict with any certainty how these effects, and others, would combine dynamically after the reform were introduced. Certainly, the main risk for workers is sometimes referred to as the 'Speenhamland scenario'[38] – wage levels drop for low-income earners when wages are supplemented by a minimum non-wage income. Although advocates of the basic income/deregulation combination might claim that low-wage earners would be better off, the broader impact of labour market deregulation might end up disadvantaging middle-income earners. These workers would be forced to defend their wages and conditions in a deregulated environment. For these workers, 'opting out' of the labour market would be less appealing because they would inevitably incur a large income loss.

The basic income coalition

When we move on to consider how a basic income policy might fare with a distrustful and stressed electorate, we must consider the problem of identifying a 'basic income coalition': the citizen bloc, which would comprise the various constituencies in support of basic income reform. Support might come from citizens who share the values of basic income or from citizens disaffected with their employment situation whether they are employed or otherwise. The British Social Attitudes Survey of 2000[39] asked 1,738 respondents (who were in paid work) the following question: 'If without having to work you had what you would regard as a reasonable living income, would you still prefer to have a job, or wouldn't you bother?' Among the survey questions available in large social attitudes studies, this question comes closest to identifying individual preference for a guaranteed income that is not dependent on employment. As such, the question is one useful measure of the 'work-centredness' of society. By preferring to work when the opportunity to live comfortably without working is available, citizens reveal their intrinsic commitment to work. Responses to this question also give us an idea about the number of working citizens who would prefer to 'opt out' of work altogether if that option was available. This might give us a ready approximation of a potential basic income constituency, and by extension, a basic income electorate. But we can draw only modest inferences from these responses. They would tell us little about whether citizens would support a reasonable living income for everyone (we know only about the respondents' personal preference), and indeed, little about whether citizens would support such a proposal if it were financed through taxes.

Among the British workforce, we find a fairly strong preference to work (see Table 4.1). We find similar results in the Middle Australia Study of 1996[40] (also see Table 4.1). For the British results, most respondents (72 per cent) would prefer to work even if they had an income option that allowed them not to. About 24 per cent would prefer not to work under these circumstances. Depending on one's perspective, these numbers are either discouraging or encouraging. They are discouraging for basic income supporters because British society remains fairly 'work-centred'. This ongoing attachment to work might be evidence of what Offe calls 'a work-centred normative belief system that appears to be largely immune to revision',[41] or evidence of continuing, positive attitudes towards holding a

Table 4.1 Would you work if you didn't have to?

	Still prefer work	*Wouldn't bother*	*Other*
Age 18–24	75	22	3
25–34	72	25	3
35–44	70	26	4
45–54	63	32	5
55–59	60	33	7
60–64	65	32	3
65+	79	11	10
Male (N = 868)	66	30	4
Female (N = 870)	71	25	4
By attitudes to work			
Work is more than that (66%)	74	22	4
Just a means of earning a living (32%)			
Don't have right skills (9%)	61	36	3
No better jobs around here (9%)	62	34	4
Respondent feels same about any job (14%)	50	49	1
By values			
More libertarian (19%)*	61	33	6
More authoritarian (81%)	68	27	5
More pro-welfare (45%)**	67	29	4
More anti-welfare (55%)	68	23	9
Total BSA 2000 (N = 1738)	68	27	5
Total MAP 1996 (N = 200)	72	24	4

Source: National Centre for Social Research, *British Social Attitudes Survey*, 2000, online. Available at <http://www.data-archive.ac.uk>; Pusey, *The Middle Australia Project 1996*, [computer file] Kensington: School of Sociology, University of New South Wales, 2000.

Notes
* Respondents were grouped according to their answers on the libertarian–authoritarian scale. Those who scored less than or equal to 3 (mid-point) were coded as libertarians. The rest (over 3) were coded as authoritarians. There are appreciably more authoritarians than libertarians.
** Respondents were grouped according to their answers on the welfarism scale. Those who scored less than or equal to 3 (mid-point) were coded as pro-welfare. The rest (over 3) were coded as anti-welfare. There are slightly more anti-welfare respondents than pro-welfare respondents.

job. But these numbers are encouraging too because about one-quarter of British workers would opt out of the workforce if they had the opportunity, perhaps giving us some hint of the labour supply impact of a full basic income scheme.

We get a larger appreciation of responses when we break them down according to age, sex, and attitudes towards present job, and as well as according to respondents' value orientations towards social policies and welfare. These breakdowns also help us appreciate which groups might be likely to support – or benefit – from basic income reform. When we consider age and gender, our findings are somewhat unexpected. Young workers (aged between 18 and 24) strongly prefer to work (75 per cent). This number declines with age, only increasing again when we reach workers over 60 and increasing markedly among workers aged over 65, whom we would expect to prefer employment because they have remained in the workforce after they have become eligible for a government pension. The strong preference for work among young people confounds the conventional wisdom on both the post-industrial left – that young people have little interest in work – and on the conservative right – that young people are work-shy. Women are slightly more attached to work than are men, although we may encounter some self-selection bias (i.e. some working women have chosen to work, and therefore we would expect them to hold pro-work attitudes). Still, even if we accept that these results reflect some self-selection bias among young people and women, there is certainly no evidence that either group prefers work less than men and older people. This means that groups usually thought to be natural supporters of a basic income might not be.

When we break down results by respondents' attitudes towards their current jobs, we find 66 per cent of workers believed their jobs were more than 'just a means of earning a living', and 32 per cent thought their jobs were just a means of earning a living. This is further evidence of a widespread attachment to work. Among the majority who think their jobs are more than a means to earning a living, we find a strong majority (74 per cent) who would prefer to work (22 per cent would not bother). When we turn to the remaining 32 per cent those for whom work is just a means of earning a living, the preference for work falls away. But further analysis of this subgroup reveals interesting trends. When we look at the reasons why respondents hold this attitude towards their job, 9 per cent (of the 32 per cent) stated that it was because there were 'no better/good jobs around here', another 9 per cent stated it was because they 'don't have the right skills to get a better/good job', and 14 per cent stated it was because they would feel similarly about any job.

Among those respondents who stated that they couldn't find a better job or didn't have the right skills to get a better job, the preference for work over not working remains fairly high (over 60 per cent in both cases). Only among the truly work-disaffected 14 per cent do we start to encounter a large number of respondents who preferred not working over working (49 per cent). These findings suggest that most people who think that their job is just a means of earning a living do not hold this view because they are disaffected with working *per se*. That a majority of these workers prefer to work suggests that their current job is the problem, and not the idea of working more generally. Would a basic income appeal to these workers? Perhaps. It is more likely, however, that improved employment mobility and opportunities would better meet their expressed needs. Only 14 per cent of workers are what we might call truly disaffected with work. Perhaps a basic income would be a more satisfactory arrangement for these workers but they are relatively small in number.

Two scales in the British Social Attitudes Survey – the libertarian-authoritarian scale and the welfarism scale – help us understand some of the ideological influences on the preference for work. Libertarian and/or pro-welfare values, we posit, may indicate stronger support for basic income ideas. The liberal/authoritarian scale is a composite measure of respondents' attitudes towards various social policies.[42] We find that among those with liberal or libertarian attitudes on this scale – where we might also expect to find more liberal views about work effort – there is a moderate decline in the preference for work. But only a small number of British citizens hold attitudes that are appreciably libertarian on this scale, and even so, their work preferences are not markedly different from the rest of British society. And among citizens with pro-welfare attitudes on a welfarism scale[43] where we would expect to find less discomfort with the idea of not working and being supported by the state, we find that the preference for work is roughly the same as those who hold anti-welfare values (although there is a small rise in the number of those who would prefer not to work).

When we consider these results in a larger perspective, we find that British society remains largely work-centred. Is this work-centredness 'hegemonic', as we have seen Offe suggest, or is it anchored in positive attachment to work experience or the idea of working? Perhaps it is both: no doubt a work-centred society is 'hegemonic' but we would be defying common sense to suggest that the large majority of citizens who hold positive views of their work only do so because they are deprived of alternatives or fail to understand the reality of their working lives. We find that slightly over one-quarter of British workers would prefer to not work if this option were available to them. But among this group, we encounter a decent proportion of workers who also reveal they do not have the right skills for better jobs or that there are no better jobs available. If public policy aims both to provide income and to alleviate unsatisfying life circumstances, it would seem to me that policies designed to improve employment (mobility, quality of jobs, education and training) would be at least as effective for these workers as a basic income would be.

Still, there may well be a substantial minority of citizens whose values or life circumstances would lead them to support an unconditional basic income. But building an electoral majority for such a policy faces understandable obstacles. We should expect opposition to such a policy from taxpayers who would object to providing a higher income to those who do not work. The kind of redistributive politics entailed by a basic income could easily be portrayed as 'redistribution away from wage-earners'. As Purdy writes:

> Disaffected workers may complain that the tax rate required to sustain BI [Basic Income] is excessive; or they may object to Basic Income on principle, as a threat to the work ethic. Depending on their inclinations and opportunities, they may retaliate by working fewer hours, working less hard, putting pressure on their employers to raise pre-tax rates of pay, or resorting to tax evasion, possibly with the connivance of their employer. And as voters, they may lend their support to political parties which promise to lower the 'burden' of taxation or even to restore the old regime.[44]

Perhaps a combination of a much higher level of unemployment, a cultural shift away from work, and rising dissatisfaction with jobs would together produce the kind of political climate in which a basic income would have real prospects. Even then, proponents of a basic income would have to contend with the powerful alignment of forces that would attempt to address the problems of a work-based society by restoring employment and improving job satisfaction. Perhaps for these reasons, supporters of a basic income see more hope in its partial implementation, by building on existing schemes and by lowering expectations for reform.

Partially implementing a basic income: the incremental path to success?

Clearly, the introduction of a universal basic income scheme financed by taxes involves a large-scale exercise in policy redesign, political coalition building, and ongoing administration. Given these complexities, basic income advocates have started to support a partial implementation of a basic income scheme, looking to build on existing programmes. They have addressed two main problems that stem from the lack of a viable political coalition in support of basic income reform, and the lack of any great public understanding about the benefits of reform. The first problem is *feasibility*. A smaller, conditional, and less ambitious scheme like a negative income tax or a revamped Earned Income Tax Credit (EITC) might offer 'institution-building' opportunities for a larger programme even if it did not meet the ambitions of fully-fledged reforms. The second problem is *participation*. If a universal basic income were ever seriously proposed, scholarly criticism of the idea that a basic income gives people 'something for nothing' would surely be magnified among citizens. This has led basic income advocates to support the idea of requiring non-workers to perform socially useful labour. These pragmatic approaches to feasibility and participation might help the basic income cause. But the question is whether adopting such pragmatism would end up achieving larger basic income ideals or fall short of this.

Feasibility

For basic income advocates, building on existing programmes makes a great deal of sense. In Europe, states pay attention to ensuring universal income support. But in most cases, welfare arrangements are quite elaborate, and would not easily yield either politically or administratively to any 'big bang' reform process. Turning to North America, we find some preliminary policy infrastructure for basic income-style reforms. The American EITC scheme is an obvious policy from which to build larger basic income reforms into the US model. The Earned Income Tax Credit is a scheme run by the Federal Government, operates along negative income tax lines, and is available only to low-wage workers and their families.[45] The EITC supplements the incomes of those in low-wage employment – the maximum payment for a family is around US$4,000. Van Parijs agrees that 'in the US context ... the best basis from which to build [a basic income] is probably the EITC'.[46] Fred Block and Jeff Manza advance the same view, proposing to expand the EITC into a more generous negative income tax that is not conditional on work status. They claim that such a tax would protect low-wage workers from poverty, increase labour market flexibility, and reduce the costs of those hardline law and welfare policies designed to contain the problems created by poverty and dislocation.[47]

Without matching Block and Manza's ambitions, John Myles and Paul Pierson offer a pragmatic endorsement of the EITC as a social policy for tough times. They believe the policy is consistent with the current welfare-to-work agenda, a reason for its success. Myles and Pierson claim that:

> a striking aspect of the move toward GI/NIT [Guaranteed Income/Negative Income Tax] programs in both countries [the United States and Canada] has been limited public discussion and conflict over policy change. While 'welfare reform' has generated headlines and protests, major modifications of tax-based income transfers have not.[48]

Myles and Pierson note that the EITC survived Republican congressional budget cutback efforts in 1996: the Clinton administration strongly supported the programme, and it did not suffer from the same political and public opposition that beset other welfare schemes.[49] No doubt the EITC's pro-work design helped in its survival: the policy benefits, and is seen to benefit, those who work. But its success also stemmed from its relatively modest cost. Myles and Pierson argue that the successes of negative income tax schemes in the United States (and in Canada, where the scheme is more generous and effective) derive from their ability to combine 'fiscal restraint with improved social protection for those most in need' – policy virtues consistent with the politics of retrenchment.[50] Moreover, Myles and Pierson observe that:

> these programs [negative income taxes] provide potential common ground for a powerful political coalition. This coalition includes public and private actors interested in controlling public expenditure, those with an interest in increasing labor market flexibility, and those seeking to increase the incomes of poor and near-poor households. Because these programs are much more targeted than universal ones, they offer hard-pressed public officials (and sympathetic private sector actors such as those in the financial community) the promise of expenditure restraint. At the same time, the structure of gradually phased-out benefits is widely considered to be more effective than traditional means-tested programs in sustaining work incentives – a matter of considerable importance to many employers.[51]

They further note that the EITC's 'flexibility, opacity, relatively low cost, and compatibility with the interests of key groups traditionally opposed to generous policies for the poor have allowed the EITC to carve out a successful niche in a very harsh policy environment'.[52]

Does the EITC programme offer the institutional resources for progress towards a partial basic income? To answer this, we must first consider the achievements of the EITC so far, and particularly address the EITC's anti-poverty capacity. Available research suggests that the EITC does make a difference. Citing evidence from the Census Bureau's Current Population Survey, Greenstein and Shapiro state that the EITC lifted about 4.6 million people in low-income working families above the poverty line in 1996.[53] But the authors note that:

> This does not mean that EITC provides more support for poor families with children than any other program. The TANF [Temporary Assistance to Needy Families] cash assistance program provides more aid to poor families with children that the EITC ... But since a much larger proportion of TANF families than of families receiving the EITC have incomes far below the poverty line ... TANF grants are much less likely than the EITC to lift families out of poverty.[54]

This qualification is significant: the EITC's poverty alleviation effects depend primarily on the earned income of the recipient and therefore depend on the employment health of the macro-economy. David Ellwood notes that the success of the EITC cannot be fully separated from the booming economy of the 1990s and the impact of welfare reform on job placement.[55] The EITC is more effective when it is operating in the context of low-wage growth. It is not as effective when employment and economic growth both slow because it does not benefit the jobless or those outside the labour market.

The critics of the EITC see it as an effective 'subsidy' to business for low-wage employment, thereby entrenching the real problem that confronts anti-poverty policies: the deficit in well-paying jobs. Critics think that while the EITC, like similar programmes, does something to help the working poor, it also entrenches low-wage employment. For example, David Howell believes that the EITC is:

> [a] massive wage subsidy which will encourage employers to pay even lower wages than they currently do, and will encourage even fewer government policies that shelter low-skill workers from intense labor market competition. Much of our poverty problem, particularly for working-age adults, lies in the severe wage competition that prevails in low-skill labor markets.[56]

Negative income taxes and tax credits for low-paid workers have proliferated in the 'liberal' welfare states of the United Kingdom, the United States, and Canada, which all have relatively low minimum wages and a large number of working poor. So while the EITC may assist poor workers, it is harder to claim that the policy deals with the root problem of working poverty. Drawing on published and unpublished evidence about the wage and employment effects of the EITC, Ian Watson argues that the policy has

> placed downward pressure on wages at the bottom of the labour market, expanding the size and reach of the low wage sector. Turnover in jobs has been high and the size of the 'working poor' has continued to expand. The EITC has allowed low wage jobs to proliferate because it operates as a public subsidy to low-paying employers.[57]

In Australia, for example, the main support for tax credits has come from a group of pro-market economists, who see it as a vehicle for cutting minimum wages to stimulate jobs without raising too much opposition and increasing poverty.[58]

Would expanding the EITC into a broader, more generous negative income tax scheme along the lines Block and Manza envisage – a universal scheme with a base payment for those who do not work[59] – assist low-income people, remain feasible, and meet the ambitions of the basic income movement? First, it would effectively guarantee a minimum income by extending a flat sum to alleviate poverty among non-workers, and more generously assist the working poor than the present EITC. Of course, as Block and Manza acknowledge, this would raise opposition from a sceptical public, conservative politicians and business, and especially so in the United States.[60] The main strength of the EITC – and probably the main reason for its survival – is its deliberate focus on the *working* poor: so extending income support to non-workers is no trivial revision of the policy's original intent. As Myles and Pierson point out: 'Any strategy that proposed to extend the NIT model beyond the working poor would ignite the traditional flash point of American social politics, namely, race.'[61] It would face employer opposition, and politicians, and the public may resist higher taxes to pay for it.

Second, it is not clear whether a more generous negative income would automatically transform the plight of low- or middle-income wage earners. Block and Manza argue that their proposal would increase the bargaining power of low-wage workers and improve flexibility in the labour market. They argue:

> if the grant level were closer to 80 per cent to 100 per cent of the federal poverty line, many individuals and families would be able to manage without earned income for some months at a time by cutting out all but the most essential purchases. This would make the Speenhamland scenario unlikely because employees could afford to walk away if employers were reducing wage levels or degrading working conditions.[62]

While the 'opt-out' option for low-wage workers may be strengthened by such a policy regime, higher wage earners may not fare so well. As I mentioned previously, they would face pressures from employers in a deregulated labour market, and opting out would be less feasible.

Third, it is difficult to see how the policy would reduce dependence on the labour market, one of the main ambitions of basic income advocates. The policy would still depend on employment growth to keep its overall cost under control. If too many workers opted out of the labour market, the programme's costs would rise, and business would object to the scarcity of labour. If there were too much unemployment, the costs of the programme would also rise rapidly. My point is plain: such a plan would still depend primarily on the health of the labour market, and its capacity to generate jobs, and especially well-paid jobs that supply tax revenue and help cut poverty. For basic income advocates, an expanded negative income tax might disappoint their hopes of ending reliance on the labour market.

Participation

Clearly, one of the feasibility problems confronting a full basic income scheme is building the political will and fiscal resources to support people outside the labour market. As we saw above, this has led basic income advocates to propose modest reforms. But others prefer to tackle the problem of supporting non-wage earners differently. Dealing with what Goodin, van Parijs and others call the 'something for nothing' problem – that basic income subsidises the undeserving idle – is more than a philosophical question. These writers understand that the public, especially in the English-speaking world, remain largely hostile to extending welfare benefits to people who are deemed to be active and able to work. A number of basic income advocates have proposed that the design of the basic income programme oblige non-working beneficiaries to perform some kind of socially useful scheme, thereby turning the scheme into a 'participation income'.[63] A participation model for basic income would deal with the political problems that are anticipated for a universal basic income, and it would offer additional resources for the development of a viable third sector. Goodin, for example, claims that:

> the most politically saleable form of a basic income, for now and the foreseeable future, may be a participation income. Under that scheme, everyone could draw a basic income on condition that they perform some socially useful labour ... they can satisfy it by caring for young, old, or disabled members of the community, by participating in community service or environmental projects or through some other activity.[64]

A similar view is expressed by Offe and Heinze who make an ambitious case for expanding the voluntary sector as well, to help rebuild communities, and to limit the domination of markets on one side and bureaucracy on the other.[65] Rifkin sees the development of a third sector (financed by a participation income) as inevitable. He claims that 'the globalization of the market sector and the diminishing role of the governmental sector will mean that people will be forced to organize into communities of self-interest to secure their own futures'.[66]

Would a participation income meet the aspirations of basic income advocates? Certainly, by conceding the need to promote participation in socially useful labour, earlier hopes that a basic income would underwrite a post-work society are diminished. Essentially, the participation income proposal forces us again back to the problems of how we organise work. While the participation income may be more competitive politically once the 'something for nothing' problem is conceded, the plan would face a different kind of challenge. Would expanding third sector employment, underwritten by basic income, be a viable alternative to an enlightened jobs creation plan of similar scope and magnitude? While there has been enormous enthusiasm for reviving the third sector, and a basic income could help its development, there are necessarily problems. Although volunteers perform important, often unrecognised work, we should not romanticise the voluntary sector. Boris Frankel is right when he says that 'many proponents of various forms of barter and self-help networks in the "informal sector" ... often fail to realise they are merely advocating informal labour markets'.[67] Rifkin bases his argument for an expanded third sector on the unqualified view that 'the nurturing commitment of volunteers often leads to better results in the providing of care services than the more detached care of salaried professionals'.[68] Although Rifkin is dismissive of public employment alternatives (they are too costly and politically unpopular), the public would surely expect that the rising demands for individual and community care made necessary by longevity and technology will be met with a professional workforce accessible to those in need. The public may well prefer to deal with unemployment by expanding professional, public employment in caring, and welfare services.

Conclusion

The strengths of the basic income plan lie in its simplicity, its universality, and its treatment of joblessness, ecology, and human diversity. But a basic income scheme is unlikely to resolve the ongoing problems of work in at least two ways. Basic income supporters do not fully grasp the persisting relationship between *work and citizenship*. And viable proposals for basic income still rely on work: a negative income tax depends on the economy's ability to generate jobs, and a participation income ends up inventing new forms of work to secure public support.

Most supporters of basic income hold pessimistic views about the future of work. Many see wage-labour as an inherently limited source of social identity. Other supporters credit the importance of work to citizenship but doubt the viability of pro-employment strategies. But public attitudes and expectations also matter here. Survey evidence presented in this chapter gives us a somewhat abstract, and therefore qualified, picture of social attitudes towards working and not working. This evidence is not definitive but it is a guide to the public mind, and to the ongoing emphasis many seem to place on work in their lives. We cannot rationalise away these results by declaring that work is hegemonic only in a negative sense. For many, it would seem, work remains a preference as much as a necessity. This does not mean that work induces an equal sense of commitment across society. But it is an open question whether we deal with the problems of working life through strategies that reduce reliance on employment or whether we re-engage with an agenda focused clearly on creating and maintaining decent jobs. This is a question that particularly confronts most women and those individuals stuck in dead-end jobs. But we should be careful not to assume that the problems that work can generate including unemployment and alienation mean we should dispense with pro-employment strategies. The picture is more complex. Criticising van Parijs's reference to the difficulties facing working women, Edmund Phelps reminds us that:

> [women] have the self-knowledge to know something that van Parijs appears not to know about them: the sociability, the challenges, and the sense of contribution and belonging that those jobs provide are an important part of their lives, as they are of the lives of others.[69]

Phelps's point leads to a more general conclusion: we cannot necessarily deal with the problems of employment today by assuming work will further diminish or by designing public policy to avoid these problems.

When we focus on pragmatic approaches to implementing a basic income, namely, a negative income tax scheme and a participation income, there still remain two vital clashes with the problems of work. A negative income tax scheme critically depends on employment growth to maintain its viability. Too few jobs mean too little tax revenue and too many families on the minimum income line. We may also doubt whether supporting further labour market deregulation, as many basic income advocates do, is a reasonable return for a negative income tax scheme that gets the thumbs-up from business. Supporters assume that further deregulation will have, at worst, neutral effects on the wages and conditions of employees. If this does not transpire, the reforms might exacerbate what critics claim the EITC already does: entrench a low-wage labour market. If instead we designed a participation income that helped expand the third sector, we would then be obliged to consider if this is reinvented 'job creation' in another guise. Given the pressing needs for social services and professional employment, the community might prefer to see new needs taken up in a revitalised employment strategy. If these proposals reflect back to us the larger problems of work, we must turn to viable alternatives that address them. Given the weakness of the forces most closely identified with work, unions and social-democratic parties, we must ask ourselves if these forces are now capable of finding new, energetic solutions to joblessness, working poverty, and unequal access to good jobs – all subjects we have raised over the last two chapters. This is the question for my next chapter.

5   Labour movements and work
Exhausted alliances or new challenges?

In the previous two chapters, I have presented two alternative visions of the future of work: the US model characterised by a sprawling, uneven dependence on the labour market, and a basic income reconstruction of work and welfare. Whatever claims are made for the US model, lowering inequality is not among them. And even if a realistic basic income scheme came to fruition, say, in the form of a generous negative income tax, policy-makers would still have to deal with the problem of creating jobs, and well-paid ones at that, to make it viable. My view is that neither model decisively resolves the problems of work that confront advanced societies. But advocates of both approaches are on solid ground when they claim that 'old' solutions no longer apply. On the face of it, they have a case for saying that old ways of dealing with the employment question – through union recognition in the workplace and full employment in the polity – are now exhausted. However outmoded these ways may seem, there is compelling evidence that strong labour movements helped produce both greater equality and greater political commitment to full employment. Yet, almost everywhere in the countries we have surveyed, those movements face real challenges. Unions are losing members, losing strikes, losing their presence in the workplace, and losing influence in politics. In recent times, only the French labour movement has demonstrated a capacity to head off major reforms when it challenged the government in November 1995.

If prospects for a fairer, fully employed society depend on reversing the decline of the labour movement, then we must confront the question of union revival. With the current balance of power tipping further towards 'market solutions' or anti-union intervention, it is unrealistic to talk about how a strongly social-democratic agenda for work could emerge without also talking about revitalising labour. To consider the likelihood of a progressive pro-work agenda, we must first of all concern ourselves in some detail with the prospects for unions in the countries we've discussed. Are the forces producing union weakness primarily beyond the control of labour movements, confirming the pessimism of the post-industrial left, or do unions themselves contribute to their present situation, and therefore hold some of the keys to their own destiny? Answering these questions enables us to then consider a two-fold problem: whether unions might regain lost industrial and political authority, and whether they might increase their influence in labour and social-democratic parties, which in some countries have now taken a right-wing direction. In seeking new policies and alliances, has the 'New Labour' model we find in Britain, Australia and elsewhere been a rational response to the labour movement's weakness? We must ask whether labour movements can influence these parties so that they commit themselves to the goals of 'jobs with equality' and justice in the workplace.

Labour movements and the democratisation of work and welfare

Before we begin the substantial analysis of this final chapter, we must visit a larger stage by considering the impact of organised labour on democratisation. We do this to get some sense of the real contribution of unions to advancing society. Labour movements have been forceful campaigners in the struggle to enlarge and deepen the democratic sphere. But not all accounts of labour movements have fully appreciated this. Leninist versions of Marxism tended to adopt, in both theory and practice, an elitist stance towards organised labour. They held out no great prospect for radical reform without the leadership of a revolutionary intelligentsia, and were not fussed about assisting the development of 'bourgeois democracy' anyway. The Fabian socialism of the Webbs and others was committed to democratic reform but shied away from any idea of radical democracy; that is, the active democratic participation of workers in workplaces and unions. And, as we first discussed in Chapter 1, Max Weber and Roberto Michels inspired the dominant negative view in sociology. They were pessimistic about – and even hostile to – labour's commitment to deepening democracy.[1] The verdict reached by subsequent mainstream sociology was clear: labour's democratising impact would not withstand the 'oligarchical tendencies' that would eventually strangle unions and labour parties. Kim Moody summarises this pessimistic perspective when he writes that:

> This 'common sense' view of unions is widely held on the left as well as in the academic mainstream. It is rooted in a quintessentially twentieth-century view resting heavily on the theoretical works of anti-socialist sociologists such as Robert Michels and Max Weber, elitists like Sidney and Beatrice Webb, and others who saw rising bureaucracy as the central and inevitable feature of 'modern' society. In one form or another, Michels' theory of 'Iron Law of Oligarchy' has informed most twentieth-century analysis of trade unionism. The Webbs, who observed the phenomenon of bureaucratization even earlier, took this

type of thinking further by endorsing the growth of trade-union bureaucracy as desirable.[2]

Later sociological investigations into the potential for union democracy seemed to confirm these pessimistic legacies. Seymour Martin Lipset, Martin Trow, and James Coleman's study of union democracy in the International Typographical Union in the 1950s concluded that the bureaucratisation of unions was inevitable, a by-product of history and modernisation.[3] Others, like Mancur Olson who influenced the current generation of rational choice and public choice theorists, saw the very idea of union organisation as a form of 'unfreedom'. In his treatise, *The Logic of Collective Action*, Olson sees collective bargaining as restricting individual freedom, assuming that union democracy could be exercised only on the smallest, 'group-like' scale.[4]

Despite these pessimistic forecasts, labour's practical contributions – both direct and indirect – have been substantial. When we speak of 'direct' effects, we mean labour's tangible impact in the workplace and in the political economy. 'Indirect' effects include labour's larger benefits for democratic societies. Understandably, the direct presence of unions is now taken for granted. Their activities are now 'routine'. But they have been and remain a powerful institutional presence, both industrially and politically. Industrially, unions have contributed to the shape and scope, continuity, and institutional life of all industrial relations regimes. Politically, unions have been the organisational base for labour and social-democratic parties, have turned out to vote for these parties, and have kept social-democratic policies focused on work and full employment.

While labour's direct impact on social-democratic politics has been substantial, its indirect impact on the democratic complexion of societies has been just as important. But this impact remains under-recognised in both sociology and our historical memory. Labour movements have rarely limited themselves to the 'bread and butter issues' of the workplace, as various 'business union' traditions would have it. At the beginning of *Citizen Worker*, David Montgomery reminds us that, 'in autocracies, where any popular mobilization could be regarded as subversive, even strikes over economic issues frequently activated demands by workers for freedom of speech and association and access to the decision-making power of government'.[5] And Samuel Cohn's study of French coal strikes during the Third Republic suggests that labour's broader campaign for democracy and social reforms had a distinct impact. As Cohn discovers:

> A critical finding from the analysis is that the increase in wages from nonpay strikes was greater than from strikes that contained a salary demand. Demanding control over the labor process or demanding major political reforms is a credible way of demonstrating ideological commitment to a radical program. This ideological posture convinced

authorities of the seriousness of the union's commitment to social conflict, and to strikes as a means of pursuing larger social goals.[6]

So labour movements ultimately find themselves challenging the distribution in society of money and power. In pursuing their direct objectives, unions cannot help but to thematise larger problems of inequality in democratic societies. Their impact on twentieth-century politics defies the standard pluralistic account of democracy over that period, one that sees the state stilling a pool of diverse interests of which labour is only one. An account of democratic change must not limit itself to understanding how the state *balances* social interests; rather, it must also acknowledge the impact of social movements on the development of the state itself. David Kettler and Volker Meja help us develop such an understanding. They write that:

> we are not arguing merely, with S.M. Lipset, that unions have contributed to a pluralistic political field that limits the powers of all. Twentieth-century democracy, in our view, is about economic distribution and power sharing, not about effective system maintenance and limitations of governmental power. Unions in union-oriented labor regimes have not been simply one of a multiplicity of interest groups. By virtue of their projects, they have been structurally linked to the generation of distinctively democratic issues. The rise of nineteenth- and twentieth-century democracy is inseparable from the emergence of the 'social question', and unions have given organizational expression to that question, forcing it onto all political agendas, whether or not their own strategy has addressed it in an effective or defensible way.[7]

Kettler and Meja understand labour's indirect contribution to the entire structure, conduct, and scope of democratic politics. By opening up the 'social question', labour movements forced democratic politics to address a greater range of rights and social problems and gave impetus to the structures and policies that would recognise other, later, movements. Of course, acknowledging this fact does not mean we must adopt an uncritical, romantic view of labour movements. As Kettler and Meja further stress:

> unions have served to activate and reproduce democratic politics because their activities institutionalize the political agenda items of power sharing and economic redistribution. This does not mean they have been necessarily or even commonly dedicated to egalitarian objectives in these regards. The point we are making need not be harmed by the recognition that unions have often pursued quite particularistic policies under these regimes, seeking access to privileges rather than the abolition of privileges. As principal players in a labor regime, their activities and conditions of existence have nevertheless

implied generalizable politics forming issues that ramify beyond unions' manifest purposes or those of their competitors or antagonists, rendering all settlements provisional, while reproducing contests and choices.[8]

Although this book is only concerned with a few advanced countries in a much larger world, we find continuing evidence of labour's transformative influence elsewhere, in South Korea, South Africa, and Brazil, for example. Gay Seidman's study shows how township struggles in South Africa and struggles in the workplaces of Brazilian manufacturing were critical for wider democratisation.[9]

Labour's role in politics and society would mean less if we were unable to substantiate its beneficial impact on the character and performance of work and welfare regimes. According to an International Labour Organisation (ILO) *World Labour Report* published in 1997, the effects have been real and substantial. In countries with strong labour movements (measured by union membership levels), we can identify the clear imprint of social democracy: higher public sector employment,[10] higher levels of social expenditure,[11] and lower inequality.[12] Contradicting perceptions of labour's 'protectionist' bias, the ILO also argues that labour movements are part of a constellation of factors that lead to greater 'global openness' in the trading environments of the countries studied in the report.[13]

Have labour movements improved the political commitment to and achievement of social democracy's main goal – full employment? Certainly, this was one of the main claims that Göran Therborn made in his survey of European employment outcomes until the 1980s.[14] The ILO report also endorses labour's role: 'Trade unions and their political allies have often been fervent advocates of expansionist macroeconomic policies to encourage full employment.'[15] But the report goes on to claim that the recent period of fiscal austerity, putatively the product of global economic realities, has left the labour movement bereft of alternative policies.[16] Still, evidence suggests that strong labour movements continue to make a difference to employment outcomes, and not in the direction of higher unemployment that their critics claim. Scandinavian countries, with the strongest presence of organised labour in their societies and politics, continue to defy critics on the left and right, performing well by combining high employment levels with low inequality.

Is high union membership a major 'cause' of these beneficial outcomes or is it an 'effect' of a political system already committed to social democracy? This is a challenging question. Perhaps it is more difficult to separate out the role of unions in the complex patterns of cause and effect that shape mature policy configurations. Many commentators might think that high union membership is now more an effect than a cause of social-democratic regimes. Even if strong labour movements seem like a mere effect in these regimes, they still have the power to block anti-labour reforms or to force compromises. This influence of course cannot withstand the falling membership and declining workplace presence that confront many labour movements. Their organisational and industrial decline has compromised their political power. What are the causes for this decline: is it a simple matter of declining 'class consciousness' in post-industrial societies, as the post-industrial left would have it? Or of structural change in the economy? Or are national institutions mediating factors in union decline?

Explaining labour's decline

When we say or hear that 'unions are in decline' or that the 'labour movement is finished', what evidence is there to support these claims? Several measures help us to answer this question. These are: union density (membership) figures, strike rates, and collective bargaining rates.[17] Table 5.1 provides us the first and most commonly cited measure – union density figures (union members as a percentage of the labour force) in 1985 and 1998 for the ten countries we've surveyed in this book. With the exception of Sweden, union density has fallen considerably everywhere. The largest decline, almost 20 per cent, occurred in Australia whose economic and labour reforms have involved a partial deregulation of the labour market and dismantling of the centralised system of industrial relations that once protected unions. The second largest decline, almost 13 per cent, occurred in the United Kingdom during the Thatcher–Major years, again a period of labour market deregulation.[18] (Incidentally, an even larger decline occurred in New Zealand, which introduced 'big bang' economic reforms after the mid-1980s, reforms now partially reversed.) As I mentioned in Chapter 3,

Table 5.1 Union density[a] changes in selected OECD nations between 1985 and 1998

	1985	1998	Change
Australia	45.6	26.0	−19.6
Canada	37.1	30.1	−7.0
France	13.9	10.0	−3.9
Germany	35.9	26.2	−9.7
Japan	28.4	22.5	−5.9
Italy	42.3	38.0	−4.3
Netherlands	28.0	23.1	−4.9
Sweden	81.5	88.0	+6.5
United Kingdom	45.4	32.8[b]	−12.6
United States	18.0	13.9	−4.1

Source: Visser (2000, pp. 12–14).

Notes
a Union members as a percentage of the labour force.
b 1995.

union density in the United States started falling a few decades before declines occurred elsewhere. And it has continued to decline slowly through the 1990s, ending up at 14 per cent of the workforce. While decline is to be expected in America, it is not true that Europe has remained a 'fortress' of unionised workforces. French unions have low private sector membership, offset by militant organisation in the public sector. And the traditionally powerful unions of Germany's industrial economy have failed to slow union membership decline. Only in Scandinavia, where unions have achieved the greatest institutional power, do we see little or no decline in union membership.

We turn now to a second measure – the level of strike activity. Of course, strike activity whether measured by the number of strikes or the total workdays lost due to strikes and lockouts varies from year to year, and in a quite unpredictable fashion. These figures give us a different impression of labour's activity than union density levels do. They tell us about the actual level of contention between unions and employers. Trends since 1980 generally point in a steep downward direction. We get some idea of this in Table 5.2, which includes data for our ten countries on the number of days lost to strikes and lockouts in the years 1980 and 1995. Other evidence confirms that strike rates are at historic lows in many countries.[19] Even recent upturns in strike activity in some countries have come nowhere near reversing the general downward trend.

The third measure is the collective bargaining coverage of the workforce (see Table 5.3). Collective bargaining matters when it comes to achieving equality in the labour market. The ILO states that 'countries where the proportion of workers covered by collective agreements is greatest generally have the highest degree of earnings equality, and in these countries inequality has increased less'.[20] Australia was the only country outside

Table 5.2 Workdays not worked (from strikes and lockouts) in selected OECD nations, 1980 and 1995 (000s)

	1980	*1995*
Australia	3,320	548
Canada	8,975	1,569
France	1,523	521[a]
Germany	128	247
Japan	1,001	85[a]
Italy	16,457	909
Netherlands	57	691
Sweden	4,479	627
United Kingdom	11,694	415
United States	20,844	5,771

Source: International Labour Organisation (1997, pp. 253–254).

Note
a 1994.

Table 5.3 Collective bargaining coverage rates in selected OECD nations, mid-1990s

	Mid-1990s	*Trend**
Australia	72	–
Canada	37	–
France	75	+/–
Germany	80	–
Japan	21	–
Italy	70	NA
Netherlands	79	+
Sweden	72	+/–
United Kingdom	35	–
United States	11	–

Source: Visser, (2000, pp. 17–18).

Notes
* + = increasing, – = decreasing, +/– = steady.

Europe among the ten with coverage above 70 per cent. With the exception of the United Kingdom, all the European countries among the ten we've surveyed have collective bargaining coverage rates at 70 per cent or above. So, it is not surprising we find labour market inequalities in the United States where collective bargaining coverage is very low, and rising inequality in countries like Australia and the United Kingdom, both of which have moved away from collective bargaining.[21]

Having established significant union decline, how do we explain this? Although we might naturally look to two decades of slow growth and 'recessionary economics' that have produced unemployment across the OECD, we need to consider other endemic factors to build a comprehensive explanation.[22] Here, I shall consider four main factors, obviously interrelated.[23] These are: structural change, regime change, societal change, and internal change. *Structural change* refers to 'secular' changes in the economic structure, for example, the decline of manufacturing, increase in services, and macro-industrial shifts linked to greater international integration. Depending on how we define it, structural change may also incorporate changing demographics and labour market structures. *Regime change* refers to changing political and employer tolerance of organised labour, sometimes culminating in reconfigured labour market institutions. *Societal change* refers to shifting attitudes and behaviour towards unions, particularly the propensity to join a union and support for the activities of unions. And finally, *internal change* refers to those inner-organisational dynamics that influence union density, such as the capacity to learn from and cope with adversity by developing new forms of militancy, recruitment strategy, and political influence.

Structural change: industry restructuring and global integration

The most frequently identified source of union decline is structural change. The automotive, capital goods, and textiles industries in advanced economies have become more efficient and more capital-intensive or have relocated to lower-cost countries. And new service industries – health care, retail, and professional services – have expanded rapidly. In some countries, like Australia and New Zealand, the decline in traditional manufacturing has been dramatic, fitting the profile of 'de-industrialisation'. Alongside industry change we encounter demographic shifts and labour market restructuring that affect the type of workers and jobs in the economy. Structural change affects union density in two ways: traditional unionised workforces shrink as downsizing and efficiency drives take hold, while new workforces, dominated by women, remain under-unionised. The combined effect of these two forces is even more powerful: just to maintain the status quo, unions must offset the loss of existing members in declining industries with recruits from new ones. Bernhard Ebbinghaus and Jelle Visser estimate that structural change explains about 40 per cent of membership decline in Europe between 1970 and 1992.[24] David Peetz's study of declining union membership in Australia suggests that structural change accounts for about half of the membership losses 'over the decade to 1992', playing a smaller role thereafter.[25] Henry Farber and Alan Krueger find that 25 per cent of union decline in the United States between 1977 and 1991 (a time when membership fell about 10 per cent) could be explained by the combined effect of industry change and changes in demography.[26]

There is, of course, a larger aspect of structural change: greater global economic integration. Does the 'globalisation factor' driving some national industry restructuring make a difference to union density? Or, in other words, does the pessimistic view that global competition will erode union density, stand up? According to a sixteen-country study that explores the impact on union density of direct investment, trade flows, and capital openness, the answer is no. The study concludes, 'these results thus provide little support for the thesis that globalization produces general convergence in union density (or hurts all union movements severely)'.[27] In addition to these findings, the ILO *World Labour Report* suggests union movements thrive in some of the economies with high levels of trade and capital openness.[28]

At first glance, the declining union membership we find in 'post-industrial' service economies seems to confirm the pessimistic forecasts of post-industrial social theorists who thought that unions would fade along with traditional industries and class-structured societies. But this perspective assumes that employees in post-industrial service industries – teachers, nurses aides, call centre workers – are incapable of being organised. This is not necessarily the case. All the authors of the studies referred to here qualify the place of structural change in union decline. They see it as a 'background' feature, always present and powerful, but not as central to the union decline story as we might expect.[29] Peetz observes that 'structural changes can be quite small when compared with the influence of union, employer and state strategy'.[30] While structural change affects the fortunes of labour movements, it should not be read as a unidirectional explanation for union decline as is sometimes done in theories of social change.

Regime change: states and labour market institutions

While structural change partly explains trends in union density, a more immediate explanatory factor is the character of labour market institutions, which is determined over time by states and employers as well as unions. Governments are central players in establishing and reforming the labour market institutions that define union rights and access to workplaces, and that maintain dispute resolution mechanisms and collective bargaining systems. Bruce Western finds that pro-union labour institutions are conditional on the Left maintaining office at a national level.[31] Employers are typically the most important outside influence on the shape of industrial relations and labour market institutions, although labour movements are occasionally able to force compromises in labour law and industrial relations as well as obtain reforms in their interest. Employers exercise a similarly dominant influence over the 'informal' balance of power within the workplace, only challenged by the strongest and most visionary unions.

Ebbinghaus and Visser's study of European unionism underlines the important role of labour market institutions in producing and sustaining union density. Their analysis concentrates on union access to the workplace, the presence of 'closed shops', union control of unemployment schemes and union involvement in corporatist politics.[32] When one or more of these arrangements was in place, union density was higher, and less vulnerable to decline. They find that 'if unions do not run an unemployment insurance system [the "Ghent" system found in Belgium and Scandinavia], or do not combine workplace unionism with macro-level corporatism, they are unable to maintain the level of unionization achieved in the mid-1970s'.[33] In their sixteen-nation study, Peter Lange and Lyle Scruggs find that union density levels were closely predicted by the combined presence of what they call 'union-compatible institutions'.[34]

Labour market institutions are critical. The empirical findings presented here help explain why union membership is lower in the United States where labour market institutions have been hostile to unions for decades, and why membership is higher in countries where institutions are conducive to union participation and coordination. So government policies that limit union access to the workplace or abolish collective bargaining not only remove formal rights, they also have a real impact on union density. The dramatic declines in union membership in Australia and New Zealand since the mid-1980s demonstrate the effects of labour market reform in these countries. As I mentioned in Chapter 3, labour govern- ments in both countries started to deregulate the labour market, moving away from a centralised wage-fixing system and collective bargaining. Later conservative governments built on these reforms with the Workplace Relations Act 1996 in Australia and the Employment Contracts Act 1991 in New Zealand. The ILO makes it clear that 'the weakening of the protec- tive legislation and institutional recognition accorded to workers' organi- zations in the United Kingdom, or more recently in New Zealand, has had a definite impact on union membership'.[35] In Australia and New Zealand, unions have struggled in the new environment. The old system afforded unions some level of institutional protection, especially for closed shops, that did not necessarily involve much workplace activism, the very resource unions need in the new system.[36]

Employers have a direct interest in pursuing labour market deregula- tion. These reforms make de-unionisation or union avoidance strategies more viable. Unions have fewer legal protections and must contend with the organisational superiority of employers. In Australia, the reformed labour market environment spurred employers like Rio Tinto and BHP into confrontations with both mining and manufacturing unions, and the stevedoring company, Patrick, into a protracted conflict with the Maritime Union of Australia.[37] Regime changes give new opportunities to militant employers, and make it harder for unions to fend them off either industri- ally or legally. Of course, beyond national institutions lie international ones. Trade arrangements like 'free trade deals' offer employers new avenues to resist unions. For example, Kate Bronfenbrenner shows that since the United States signed the North American Free Trade Agreement (NAFTA), employers there have threatened to close in over half of all union-organising campaigns and, 'where union organizing drives are suc- cessful, employers do in fact close their plant, in whole or in part, 15 percent of the time – triple the pre-NAFTA rate'.[38]

Societal change: joining and supporting unions

One of the strongest claims of the post-industrial left, particularly of writers like Alain Touraine and André Gorz, is that class consciousness is no longer the main social and political 'organising principle'. According to this perspective, which we explored in Chapter 2, unions depend on class consciousness to motivate collective contention in the workplace, which in turn keeps class politics active. Without this, unions lack the vital element that enables them to act like social movements, and to enter into social and political contests.[39] Rather, they are only capable of maintaining a scaled-down organisational and political presence. And the gradual emergence of welfare states and industrial relations systems further weakens class politics: changes in labour laws, workplace rights, and rising living standards all contribute to a reduction of the class tensions that once motivated unionism. At the same time, individual and social expectations of work change: work environments offer incentives to 'get ahead', and encourage instrumental behaviour. For many people, according to this view, unions have become obstacles to individual achievement at work, and the public views strikes, militancy, and collective action as pointless.

So the story goes. But is it correct? Certainly, neither the decline in class awareness nor the decline in class politics and voting are inconvertible facts.[40] And even if class awareness had fallen by some objective standard, we would not expect this to necessarily translate into a reduced propensity to join unions or to approve of their political purpose. By imagining that class awareness is about strikes on the docks or blue-collar men marching, we confine ourselves to *one* image of class activity that misrecognises new types of class awareness in modern corporations, among cleaning staff and hotel workers, and among women and minority workers in emerging sectors of the economy. Moreover, workers join unions for many reasons other than giving expression to what we might call class consciousness. They do so to express immediate grievances with a boss or an employment situation, to affect collective bargaining outcomes, and gain other types of benefits that might be more personal or instrumental. American evidence indicates that far from losing support among workers, unions are becoming more attractive to workers in that country. Higher numbers of workers tell opinions pollsters they would prefer to belong to a union. One survey conducted on behalf of the AFL-CIO shows that the public is becoming more sympathetic to unions, and that more workers wish to belong to one. Young people (aged between 18 and 34) were both the most sympathetic in their attitudes towards unions and the most likely to want to join a union – 54 per cent in 1999.[41] Another Australian survey has shown support for unions is strongest among young people.[42] These findings are promising for unions, telling us that union membership still interests the people who are most likely to work in the post-industrial service economy. Of course, expressing interest in joining a union is not the same as actually joining. For this to happen, as we shall see, other factors must be in place.

Support for the political, industrial, and social roles of unions is also improving.[43] Walter Galenson reported in the mid-1990s that public support for unions in many countries was increasing, not falling.[44] And support for unions is increasing in countries where they have been politically attacked like Australia and the United Kingdom. Table 5.4 reports the results from the Australian Election Studies of 1993 and 2001, and the British General Election Studies of 1987 and 1997.[45] These results provide some idea of the evolution in public opinion about unions at a time when conservative governments in both countries were attacking organised labour. In 1993, 64 per cent of Australians thought unions had too much power.[46] By 2001, and after five years of conservative government, this number had dropped to just 48 per cent – a decline of 16 per cent in eight years. Over the same time period, the numbers of Australians who thought big business had 'too much power' had increased from 62 per cent to 72 per cent.[47] As union membership has declined, so have perceptions of union power. In fact, by 2003, one-quarter of Australians who responded to the Australian Survey of Social Attitudes thought unions should actually have more power.[48]

The British results are even more compelling (again, see Table 5.4). In 1987, at the height of the Thatcher years, 44 per cent of British voters (a plurality) thought that it would be better for Britain if unions had little power. In 1997, at the time of Labour's victory, a large majority of Britons – 68 per cent – disagreed with the statement that unions had too much power. Differences in the two questions mean that these results are not directly comparable. Nonetheless, we may see that the long-dominant perception of union power that has helped conservatives win elections is waning, at least in the United Kingdom.

Major disputes in recent years have revealed popular support for unions, even when politicians and the media have portrayed them negatively. In France, the public sector strike-wave of November 1995 was widely supported by the public, and no doubt the union campaign against the reforms contributed to the defeat of the conservatives in parliamentary elections less than two years later. In Australia, the unpopular Maritime Union of Australia managed to win a surprising level of public support in its battle over waterfront de-unionisation with the conservative Howard Government and Patrick, a stevedoring company. And in the United States, the public expressed support for the huge Teamsters strike against the United Parcel Service in 1997, which involved 180,000 workers.

Table 5.4 Attitudes towards unions in Australia and the United Kingdom: selected years

	Agree	*Disagree*	*Undecided/Other*
Australia			
The trade unions in this country have too much power 1993	64	18	19
2001	48	23	29
United Kingdom			
It is better for Britain when trade unions have little power 1987	44	33	23
Do you think that trade unions have too much power or not 1997	22	68	10

Source: *Australian Election Studies*, 1993, 2001; *British General Election Studies*, 1987, 1997.

Countless other campaigns in Europe, America, and Australia have found public support as well.

While workers may be starting to express stronger preferences about belonging to a union, this is not the same as actually joining one. For this to happen, workers must be organised, and labour market institutions must support union organising. Progress seems unlikely in the United States and in other countries that have weakened labour market institutions that once supported unions. But these considerable obstacles are further compounded by a fourth and final factor – the incapacity or unwillingness of unions to change, by organising new workers, and particularly those in new industries.

Internal change: incorporation, top-down leadership, and union inertia

While external factors – changes in industry, industrial relations regimes, and the propensity to join or support unions – all make a difference to union density and capacity, the internal dynamics of union organisations are also important. We may generally summarise the internal problems facing unions as follows: while unions gained their industrial and political power through the grunt work of strikes and campaigns, they have now developed a more bureaucratic character, one that is conditioned by access to legal and political power and which is less effective when unions are challenged by hostile forces. As complex organisations with their own internal dynamics, unions do not necessarily encourage either workplace activism or mobilise their membership in ways that fit the profile of a 'social movement'. Unions must somehow maintain tremendous organisational discipline – to represent their memberships in the courts, in the workplace, in corporatist negotiations, and in politics – and *still* motivate their members in a broader sense, to a vision of a more equal and just workplace, and a more equal and just society. While unions benefit from their 'incorporated' status within political and industrial relations systems, this advantage can contribute to organisational pathologies that weaken labour's capacity to organise and mobilise workers. I shall discuss some of these organisational problems, commenting on why they matter in explaining union decline.

Incorporation

Invariably, unions become 'incorporated' into industrial relations regimes whose scope and practices they themselves partly influence. Of course, the activities and preferences of the state and powerful employers usually prove more decisive influences on the legal and political environment within which unions must operate. As J. Samuel Valenzuela explains, interaction between labour movements and states varies widely, from the corporatist social-democratic regimes of Europe, to the 'minimal inclusion' model of the United States, and the co-opting labour relations of authoritarian states.[49] But, with the exception of states which exclude labour altogether, most union movements develop organisational characteristics that offer them internal stability and protection within an industrial relations and political system.

While labour movements benefit from their partial or complete acceptance, incorporation poses organisational dilemmas that become painfully apparent during times of change. Claus Offe and Helmut Wiesenthal offer us a general framework for understanding these dilemmas.[50] They argue that unions must balance the organisational demands required to operate formally within a legal and industrial system with their capacity to mobilise workers. These two imperatives – exercising formal power and social power – require potentially competing organisational 'logics'. Formal power depends on exercising bureaucratic capacities, which requires a disciplined, legally oriented leadership and organisational structure. Social power, exercised by striking or engaging in larger social struggles, requires the energetic determination of the membership. But 'incorporation' leads labour movements to operate in legally confined and political conditioned environments, which reinforce 'formal' mechanisms of dispute resolution and management over 'social' ones, which involve direct forms of contention and activity.

As Offe and Wiesenthal point out, learning to participate in formal power structures greatly enhances the labour movement's ability to influence political and industrial outcomes. But incorporation sets in train a number of internal changes that expose movements to new vulnerabilities. Because labour relies on its social power for ongoing access to formal decision-making, developing an organisational and political orientation conditioned to the use of formal resources risks depleting the capacity to mobilise. Sometimes active participation is discouraged, and unions pacify their members by managing labour problems 'above the heads' of the rank and file. While this makes union 'business' more orderly and even more effective, labour movements are left vulnerable when they are confronted with adverse external change or reforms that can quickly hit membership levels and marginalise union influence.

Top-down leaderships, domesticated memberships

Studies show there is a strong relationship between industrial relations systems and politics and the organisational culture of unions.[51] Those unions incorporated into a larger industrial relations system ordinarily place strong emphasis on top-down bureaucratic organisation. They do so for at least three reasons. The first, as we've just seen, is the impact of the external environment on union organisation. The insights of social movement theorists help here. As Doug McAdam, John McCarthy, and Mayer

Zald make clear, macro-structural conditions help shape patterns of 'micro-mobilisation' or, as the case may be, the lack of any such mobilisation.[52] A legal and industrial framework conditions, even disciplines, unions to act *within* its structures; for example, to employ industrial officers or lawyers to settle disputes, deal with legal problems, negotiate with political parties or officials, or represent workers on management committees. This means that a bureaucratic, leadership-driven approach to labour problems quickly becomes an entrenched *modus operandi*, providing a formulaic basis for union micro-management disconnected from active member involvement. While this organisational approach has benefits when confined to its proper place, it becomes ineffective when it operates as the sole means of union conduct.

The second reason for emphasising top-down organisation is that, over time, union leaders reinforce their own political and industrial power. This happens with or without competitive elections for leadership positions. Leadership has a far-reaching impact in organisations, and unions are no exception. C. Wright Mills understood the dangers of 'bureaucratic' labour leadership well when he wrote, 'the labor leader who tries to integrate his union with the corporate bureaucracy is also including himself in the bureaucracy'.[53] Social movement theory leads us to similar conclusions. As Mayer Zald and Roberta Ash write, 'the organizational leaderships' commitment to a set of goals may also influence the structure [of organizations]'.[54] Top-down organisation suits incumbents because it is disciplining, creating a climate of political and organisational predictability. Top-down industrial relations structures, among which we could include European corporatist arrangements, Australian industrial commission representation, and Japanese and American business unionism, all invest real power in union officeholders and negotiators. Although union leaders do not always recognise it, these structures are potentially demobilising. Moreover, they may encourage the leadership to 'domesticate' members in pursuit of organisational objectives.[55]

The third reason why unions produce top-down structures is ideology. Since their arrival on the industrial scene, unions have developed their own ideologies or adopted others to guide their organisational conduct. Some examples illustrate my point. Business unionism ideologically accepts the right of business to manage, limiting the scope of its activities accordingly. Business unionism found in America or Japan usually discourages militant involvement by the membership or the leadership will only allow it subject to strict limits. Unions influenced by varieties of socialist thinking have also adopted organisational models consistent with their broader ideologies. These have ranged from very decentralised and democratic organisation through to the democratic centralism Soviet-style we find in, say, the communist Confédération Générale du Travail (CGT). A democratic socialist leadership orchestrated some of the most innovative union activity such as the pro-environment 'Green bans' undertaken by the Builders'

Labourers Federation in Sydney during the 1970s.[56] But it would be wrong to assume that all socialist-inspired unions attempted this radicalism or decentralisation. Most developed bureaucratic characteristics. As we see in other organisations, ideologies often legitimise a leadership cadre or reflect the 'hegemonic constraints' of the broader environment.

I am not suggesting that 'incorporated' unions are ineffective merely because they exercise and become accustomed to exercising bureaucratic power. On the contrary, within the predictable world of a stable industrial relations system, unions can use the resources of that system with extraordinary efficiency. Nor do all incorporated unions pacify their memberships. Writing about social movements in general terms, Zald and Ash remind us that 'while there is often an association between growing institutionalization and bureaucratization *and* conservatism, there is no evidence that this is a *necessary* condition'.[57] This is further supported by empirical studies of even large unions. Stepan-Norris's study of union democracy in the United Automobile Workers demonstrates that democracy flourished when there were factions and political competition within the local union chapter, and there was a commitment to democratic process.[58] This evidence suggests that union organisations need not deteriorate into unrepresentative bureaucracies, and, as we shall see, there are signs that bureaucratic organisation is now being challenged in several national contexts.

Union inertia in the face of change

Given the tough realities facing labour movements, especially in Australia, New Zealand, the United Kingdom, and the United States, are unions prepared to meet the challenges of falling membership and political presence? Kim Moody is among many who do not think so. And he points the finger at the incumbent leaders of major unions, in English-speaking countries and elsewhere. Moody describes the kind of 'leadership inertia' that characterises many unions. He claims that:

> This new generation of top labor leaders took office in a moment of transition across much of the developed industrial world. Most of them built their upward-bound careers during the long period of paralysis and restructuring during the 1980s. They tended to embrace the cooperation agenda of those years as something appropriate to the new global era.... They did so without strong opposition from a membership still in shock from the enormous changes. The activists in the workplace might be more suspicious of the new ambience of cooperation that inevitably pushed for more work and longer hours, on the one hand, and destroyed good jobs, on the other.[59]

We can identify three signs of leadership inertia. Union leaders prefer routine methods for dealing with problems and conflicts, even when their expediency diminishes. Leaders replicate themselves, anointing protégés with similar political and organisational preferences. And leaders resist opening up union structures to the membership by adopting an 'organising culture'. Quite often, union leaderships have preferred to maintain a minimal connection to their members, something that has been called a 'servicing' approach or model. In this approach, union officials understand themselves as service providers, handling the employment problems of their 'clients' at arm's length. Officials and members alike see the union as a 'third party' in the industrial relations systems. Providing services is a necessary part of any union organisation. But, as an overarching organisational method, service provision tends to coincide with low levels of workplace activism and little direct input into union structure and goals. When the servicing culture multiplies across union organisations, the labour movement begins to lose its vitality. The failures of this model keep multiplying. Many of the 'incentives' that are supposed to passively motivate joining unions, for example, frequent flyer schemes and cheap consumer services, have been abject failures. But there is a larger problem. Service-driven unions end up with uncommitted members, and are forced to rely on external protections or deal making with employers to survive. Because leaders often have different preferences to their memberships, adversarial or crisis situations often expose real weaknesses. Union leaders may willingly 'concession bargain' at the national, industry or firm level, leading to job losses and wage cuts. Poor outcomes for workers, in turn, produce a demoralised climate for future activism.

Centralised union bureaucracies favour insiders, reproducing institutionalised cultures and power networks, which are typically dominated by men and frequently by leaders whose educational and class status is higher than that of their membership. Entrenched leaderships often have little affinity with or even relationship to the changing industries they represent. Leadership selection usually reflects the skills and training required for success and promotion within institutionalised cultures, and these skills include legal or economic knowledge together with an 'insider' connection to party politics. Not only does this kind of selection produce a distinct leadership cadre, it also perpetuates the distance between union officials and members that we already find entrenched in top-down unions. As such, all kinds of biases in selecting union leaderships come into play. Barbara Pocock reports an ongoing male bias in leadership selection in Australian unions that operate outside the public sector.[60] And these biases matter. Public sector unions in Sweden, for example, have undergone a distinct 'feminisation', choosing women leaders and successfully unionising women.[61] We might contrast Swedish union success in recruiting women with the situation in Germany, which has not undertaken such a feminisation. And gender biases may end up making a difference to union density: low female membership is a significant factor in explaining why Germany's union density is lower than that of Sweden.[62]

During the long phase of union decline, we might have expected active adaptation to new times. But with entrenched leaders and a reliable *modus operandi*, union organisations are prone to resist change, or make only superficial efforts at change. The Australian, British, and New Zealand labour movements are good examples of movements that went into decline when a favourable institutional environment collapsed. Perhaps we naturally expect adverse change to induce rebuilding efforts. But this is by no means guaranteed. Sclerotic unions have usually run down their activist base – the group most likely to make a difference in tough times. And an additional complication is middle-level resistance to change when 'enlightened reformers' start to act from above. Referring to the Australian situation, Peetz claims that:

> A centrally coordinated union movement can effect change with the top of [the movement] and can in limited ways facilitate the development of activism at the bottom of the [movement], but the central layer, armed with the rhetoric of solidarity, the advantages of incumbency, and the culture of defensive attack, can be impervious to all but the most radical environmental changes.[63]

As we shall see, this kind of problem is among many we encounter when we examine efforts to rebuild unions after several decades of stagnation or decline.

Changing labour movements: the challenge of organising

By the 1990s, declines in membership, workplace presence, and political clout had started to catch up with labour movements and, in several countries, discontent began to rumble. I'll briefly look at some recent changes in France, the United States, the United Kingdom, and Australia. Consistent with historical and institutional differences, we see diverse responses to pervasive problems. However diverse union realities are, there are common threads. In each case, we find conflicts between unions and governments, efforts at reforming unions, and attempts to organise new members. There is a dawning sense that labour movements must fundamentally change if they are to rebuild, and that this places pressure on unions to undertake internal reforms. These internal reforms invariably involve reviving an 'organising culture' that emphasises workplace activism, closer links between leaders and members, and a desire to make a difference in the workplace and in politics.

The 1995 strike-wave in France stood out as a symbol of hope for labour's renewal. Over a million public sector workers went on strike for several weeks against the conservative government's plans to reform the French pension system and parts of the public sector including the rail system. The strike-wave signalled a major shift in national mood. While

French unions have very low membership in the private sector, their presence in the public sector is much greater. In a centralised state like France, militant industrial action in the public sector can shut the country down. And it did.

The strike-wave was significant in at least two respects. It reminded politicians and public alike of the awesome political and symbolic authority of a major strike. The public sided with the strikers. Pension reforms angered many workers. And, as Georges Ribeill points out, the government's unpopular plan to reform French railways helped fuse disparate union groups into a defence of the railway system, the SNCF, as a 'public service'.[64] The Juppé government was forced to withdraw the reforms, and met electoral defeat two years later. The unexpected victory of the left alliance – *la gauche plurielle* – obliged the incoming administration of Lionel Jospin to adopt one of organised labour's most sought-after policies: new regulations on working hours that would help combat long working hours and reduce unemployment. The public warmed to the new policy, and economists estimate the 35-hour week mandated by *la loi Aubry* has created 250,000 extra jobs – no mean feat in a country with a chronic unemployment problem.[65] But the strikes were significant in another respect: they revealed the energies of the rank-and-file who overrode the caution – and even conciliatory gestures – of union leaders. Leader of the social-democratic Confédération Française Démocratique du Travail, Nicole Notat, was denounced for her support for 'dialogue' with the government over the reforms. Her accommodating response misjudged the mood of French workers.[66] As Moody reports, discontent started to challenge France's post-war labour boundaries and schisms:

> The strikes increased the strength of the new union SUD (Solidarité Unitaire Démocratie), which had originated at France Telecom and the post office, helping to postpone the plunge of the telecom workers into the marketplace. SUD stood at the head of a loose alliance of eighteen independent unions called the 'Group of 10'. In the wake of the strike, about 300 rail workers who had been in the CFDT formed SUD-Rail. The independent teachers' union, the FSU (Fédération Syndicale Unitaire), also played a big part in the strike and in pushing a more aggressive style of unionism than the National Education Federation (FEN, Fédération de l'Education Nationale) from which it had split a couple of years earlier.[67]

The intellectual reaction to the strikes was also telling. Some intellectuals demonstrated strong support for the labour movement. In his speech to striking workers at the Gare de Lyon, Pierre Bourdieu described the strike as a revolt against the destruction of a civilisation built on public service.[68] Claude Lefort affirmed that the labour movement was the force most capable of altering the course of politics in the interests of broader solidarity.[69] Alain Touraine, however, did not see the strikes with the same optimism. In his edited collection on the strikes, *Le Grand Refus*, Touraine remained tentative about the 'social movement' quality of the strike movement, preferring to call it a 'shadow of a movement'. Touraine insisted that the strikes had a defensive element that limited its social purpose.[70] Writing in the same collection, Michel Wieviorka saw the strikes as a defence of the existing privileges of state-sector workers. He also considered the rhetoric of the strike movement as a left-wing variant on National Front politics, therefore playing to its agenda.[71]

Was Touraine right to claim that the defensive nature of the strike-wave signalled its limitations, qualifying its significance? Moody points out that *defensive* struggles are often the *first stage* of new movement activity, forging new networks and producing experiments.[72] It is true that the strikes lacked a central social conflict of the kind that would define the strike movement *as a social movement* on Touraine's terms. But others see the diverse claims of the strike-wave as a distinct advantage. Arnaud Gallois summarises the counter-position offered by Farhad Khosrokhavar who also contributed to *Le Grand Refus*. Gallois states:

> For Khosrokhavar ... those qualities [of not having a single claim or purpose] are not the signs of a regression or a negation, but rather of a novel and positive reinvention of political action: by not having central actors or an alternative programme or utopia it enabled maximum participation, by not having a clear direction or strategy and being fragile and ambiguous it was able to be flexible, responsive, inclusive and non-hierarchical. Khosrokhavar interprets the protests and strikes of December 1995 as the renewal of citizenship rites, a celebration of fraternity and collective adventure. In a society riddled with injustice, the strikes and rallies are ways of making public, deprivatizing, and hence regaining some dignity: they are a 'self-affirmation of civil society'.[73]

The strikes signalled a restive mood in French society and politics. While ambivalence (especially on the left) towards the policies of Lionel Jospin led to the government's defeat in 2002, the incoming conservatives have been cautious and pragmatic, committed, at least in rhetoric, to maintaining the 35-hour week. However, despite the limited reforms of the French socialists, the tide is still running against European labour movements. Living within the strictures of EU fiscal austerity, neither the Socialists nor the victorious Chirac–Raffarin team have committed themselves to any serious job creation scheme. And German unions had only a small influence in limiting Chancellor Schroeder's reforms to the welfare state and labour practices as part of his 'Agenda 2010', which passed through the Bundestag in late 2003. While labour's institutional status in most European countries has not been seriously challenged (as it has been in the

English-speaking countries), the environment is not without daunting challenges.

The US labour movement could only dream of causing the kind of political disruption that the French strike of 1995 caused. By the mid-1990s, the union movement was in a moribund state. Membership fell from 18 per cent in 1983 to 14 per cent in 1998, and with the exception of France, America had the lowest level of union density in the industrialised world. As we saw previously, structural change and unfavourable economic conditions could only account for part of this collapse. Unions had failed to expand their membership into large, growing employment areas like retail trade and health care. And if leadership mattered, then these results are hardly surprising. According to Nelson Lichtenstein, the AFL-CIO's long-time leader George Meany had once boasted that he had 'never walked a picket line or led a strike'.[74] Losses accumulated in the food and automotive industries where concession bargaining led labour into depressing compromises.[75] And, as we saw in Chapter 3, labour's legislative influence was equally ineffective. As Richard Rothstein observes, the 'labour movement has won some battles over social legislation . . ., but has lost every major recent national legislative attempt to defend its institutional interests, and thus its ability to have continued social and economic power'.[76] Labour has not been able to secure reforms that would punish illegally acting employers, eliminate strike replacements, and legalise pickets.

The US labour movement finally faced up to its serious decline when John Sweeney led the 'New Voice' team to victory in an election for the top positions at the AFL-CIO in 1995. Sweeney's team included Richard Trumpka from UMWA and Linda Chavez-Thompson, a Hispanic-American woman from AFSCME.[77] Sweeney's leadership bid was bolstered by his previous successes at the SEIU, which is the fastest-growing major union in the United States. From 1984 onwards, Sweeney had devoted more resources to organising, encouraging combative tactics in labour disputes, such as those deployed in various 'Justice for Janitors' campaigns in Washington, DC, and Los Angeles.[78] These campaigns mobilised immigrant workers, many of Hispanic background, in militant actions unprecedented in the cleaning industry.

At the AFL-CIO, Sweeney set out to rebuild the labour movement 'from above' by breaking with the worst practices of its business union past, emphasising the need to organise millions of low-paid workers, encouraging international labour solidarity in a post-Cold War world, and increasing its political and policy influence.[79] The new leadership committed to an organising strategy: unions would devote far more resources to *internal organising* by extending rank-and-file participation in unionised workplaces and to *external organising*, by recruiting and winning union elections in new workplaces. If there was any proof of bureaucratic inertia, it is in the paltry resources devoted to organising: the typical US union devotes only about 5 per cent of its budget to external organising. By placing additional resources at the disposal of the Organizing Institute, which trains activists in the skills of workplace organising, the leadership has tried to shift the focus of the union movement onto growth and renewal.

In national politics, the New Voice team moved the AFL-CIO to the liberal-left on social issues. By involving itself in other social struggles such as campaigns for the rights of Hispanic and African Americans, gays and lesbians, and illegal immigrants, the new leadership of the AFL-CIO has attempted to assert American labour's social conscience. In international politics, AFL-CIO has started to wind back its focus on Cold War anti-communism, committing more resources to union organising in other countries. In the economic world of NAFTA, cross-national activity is paramount, and the Solidarity Centre in Mexico City is a good example of this. Although Sweeney has occasionally added a more militant tone to the leadership of the AFL-CIO, the New Voice leadership has promoted a modest kind of 'social contract' unionism abroad and at home.[80] Sweeney's strategy has operated within the boundaries of labour's post-Second World War role, perpetuating the alliance with the Democrats. Far from breaking with labour's conventional political alliance with the Democrats, the AFL-CIO has tried to prove its electoral and campaigning capacity to a wayward Democratic Party.

The two offensives of the New Voice leadership – to bolster organising and political influence – have produced mixed results. On the organising front, overall union density has started to stabilise in the low teens but there is no sign that the labour movement is on the verge of a substantial recovery in union density. However, campaigns in some industries have been promising. In 1999, unions organised the largest textile plant in the United States. And the SEIU won representation of 74,000 Californian home-care workers.[81] And, as I remarked earlier, victories in some large-scale strikes in the automotive, telecommunications, and transport industries in the late 1990s and early 2000s were promising signs. Perhaps the most significant of these strikes was in 1997, when Ron Carey led the Teamsters into a battle with the United Parcel Service. Moody claims the Teamsters' victory was a product of a change of national leadership in 1991, and a commitment to vigorous campaigning thereafter. He explains:

> Big steps toward greater democracy and militancy were taken during Carey's first five year term. In addition, the union adopted a progressive stance toward political and social issues. The Teamsters also joined with other, more progressive, unions in cross-border relations with Mexican workers. His 1996 52–48% victory over old-guard stand-in Jimmy Hoffa, Jr, whose only qualification was his name, guaranteed the reform process would continue.[82]

146 Three alternatives for work and society

The Teamsters strike represented a new level of coordinated campaigning. Rothstein observes that:

> not only did the Teamsters spend months preparing for the UPS strike, polling members to determine the most salient issues and developing a sophisticated public relations campaign; but the AFL-CIO also demonstrated its commitment to the 'new' Teamsters by subsidizing strike benefits with contributions from other unions.[83]

The well-planned strike won public support, and the company eventually agreed to many of the union's demands. Carey's departure (after allegations of election funding impropriety) and James Hoffa's election in 1998 represented a setback for reformist Teamsters.

Some major unions have embraced organising together with greater militancy and more open union structures. But their limited success in making inroads into labour's problems has prompted new debates and actions. An alliance, the New Unity Partnership, made up of five large unions including the SEIU, has established what Aaron Bernstein calls their 'own mini labor federation'.[84] They want the AFL-CIO to reform faster, and they plan to devote more resources to organising. To increase membership, they propose more targeting of large national companies, and more organising around geographic areas, building on existing union strength in industries and in cities. Other activists argue that plans continue to concentrate on top-down institution building, and do not encourage deep grassroots activism that will build a committed membership. This ongoing debate has one benefit: both the leadership and activists of America's main unions increasingly recognise union decline will only be reversed by organisational change. What this will entail is yet to be fully comprehended.

By contrast with the organising foundations of America's unions, which are shaky and still leadership-driven, AFL-CIO political strategy has made inroads. Rather than distancing itself from the Democrats, the New Voice leadership has set out to re-establish labour's electoral importance to the Democratic Party. Unions have put more resources into voter registration and motivating union households to vote. This strategy is supposed to force the Democrats to take labour's industrial and social agenda more seriously, if only to appeal to the Party's electoral expediency. After 1996, unions made a difference to Democrat electoral fortunes, especially in the mid-term elections in 1998 when the Republicans fared unexpectedly badly. Union votes were critical to Gore's primary vote success against George W. Bush in the November 2000 presidential elections. According to the AFL-CIO, voters from union households accounted for 26 per cent of the electorate in 2000, an increase from the 19 per cent they managed in 1992, when Bill Clinton was first elected.[85] Has their strategy paid off? Labour's improved electoral bloc has led to some minor policy shifts and greater attention by leading Democrats to winning the union vote. But there is little sign that labour's voting power is sufficient to create a pro-labour political majority to reform America's anti-union labour laws.

In the somewhat different political and industrial context of Tony Blair's Britain, there is also renewed contention. After years of decline in union density during the Thatcher–Major Governments, the labour movement managed to halt this trend by the late 1990s.[86] Labour's victory in 1997 brought improved collective bargaining provisions for unions, and these improvements have no doubt aided organising efforts. Despite Labour's modest reforms, the unions and the Labour Government are more politically estranged from one another than in the past. Earlier on, British Labour had deliberately distanced itself from the labour movement, to make itself more attractive to 'Middle England' in the lead-up to the successful 1997 campaign. 'New Labour' was as much an effort to distance itself from its union-dominated 'Old Labour' image as it was a superficial political makeover.

Like the AFL-CIO, Britain's Trade Union Congress (TUC) promotes a moderate, reformist, and cooperative outlook though it too has increased its focus on organising. The TUC's tame approach, however, is not reflected in all developments among British unions. Membership has voted out moderate, pro-Labour leaderships of some of the largest unions, replacing them with leaders more critical of the government. Take Derek Simpson's victory in the manufacturing-based union, Amicus, in 2002. New union leaders from both within the Labour Party and outside have become Tony Blair's main political opponents. The Labour Government's plan to privatise parts of the public sector and its support for the American-led invasion of Iraq in early 2003 were defining moments. These developments are indicative of greater member activism and a willingness to vote for union leaders who will challenge employers and the government alike. How this changing climate will affect union density and union political campaigns remains to be seen.

Of the ten countries we have surveyed, Australia has experienced the largest decline in union density. Structural change in the Australian economy has been important, but labour market decentralisation and deregulation have also made a big difference. Unions were historically protected by centralised wage fixation and by their formal recognition within the industrial relations system. As this system has been dismantled, unions have struggled to maintain their membership levels. Since 1993, the Australian Council of Trade Unions (ACTU) has attempted to deal with rapid union decline. Like other national union federated bodies, the ACTU has prodded unions in the direction of organising. It has been inspired mainly by North American experiences such as the successful organising campaigns of America's SEIU and Canada's CUPE and CAW.[87] The ACTU has followed the AFL-CIO lead in calling on its member unions to devote resources to organising, especially in the service sector. Some successes are evident in growing membership in community services, hospitality, and transport. To assist this, the ACTU developed an initiative called Organising Works, which has recruited and trained mainly younger union organisers from diverse backgrounds to undertake union organising campaigns and recruitment. This initiative has had some success. Take the strike led by new union organisers like Rebecca Reilly against Star City Casino in Sydney during 2000. The union involved had managed to mobilise mainly young workers with no prior union experience in a difficult-to-organise part of the economy. But, as we see in the United States, efforts like these would need to occur on a much wider scale for unions to recover.

The tensions between the Australian labour movement and the Australian Labor Party (ALP) are not as public or as pronounced as they are between the two groups in Britain. The ACTU and the ALP were in a close partnership during the Hawke and Keating Labor Governments that undertook extensive 'pro-market' reforms of the Australian economy and industrial relations system between 1983 and 1996. Discontented unionists believe that this process undermined unions and paved the way for the conservative Howard Government's industrial relations reforms after 1996. The evidence presented in this chapter seems to confirm that belief. One sticking point will remain: how far an incoming ALP government will follow the lead of New Zealand Labour, and 'roll back' or replace anti-union provisions in Federal labour law, including provisions for individual contracts.

Common to these country-specific experiences is an awareness of the need for unions to open up, embark on vigorous organising campaigns, and adopt a stronger role to increase the voice of workers in politics. As Margaret Levi says, 'Long dormant, the debate about union democracy is surfacing again.'[88] The organising model demands both internal democratisation and a major effort in organising new workforces and advancing their political and social interests. It also offers a practical critique of existing union bureaucracies, and the limits of top-down union organisation. And at its core, the organising approach explicitly recognises something I've stressed throughout this book: that the workplace remains a vibrant centre of social life and social identity. Rank and file organisers make this very point. Take, for example, American waterfront organiser, Stan Weir's comments on the 'informal relations' of work. He sees employees working alongside each other as a team:

> which works together daily in face-to-face communication with one another, placed by technology and pushed into socialization by the needs of production. It is literally a family at work torn by hate and love, conflict and common interest. It disciplines its members most commonly by social isolation and ridicule, it has a naturally selected leadership, makes decisions in the immediate work area and can affect the flow of production.[89]

Weir's understanding of the workplace matches up with the more formal language of social movement scholars when they write about the background environment for 'micro-mobilisation'. As McAdam *et al.* explain:

> micro-mobilisation contexts ... are the primary source of resources facilitating movement emergence. These groups constitute the organizational context in which insurgency is expected to develop. As such their presence is as crucial to the process of movement emergence as a conducive political environment.[90]

Informal social relationships in the workplace continue to provide the sustaining resources for collective action. Organising depends on these social relationships developing a character that produces solidarity and collective coordination. Without developing these, and building them into the heart of union organisation, it is hard for unions to sustain an active committed membership capable of translating their work experiences into a larger capacity to act, in concert with others, to influence work and politics. And without these resources, macro-reforms that threaten unions like changes in legislation or tougher employer tactics cannot be effectively combated. As McAdam *et al.* point out, 'if one lacks the capacity to act, it hardly matters that one is afforded the chance to do so'.[91]

Recent studies of union successes demonstrate the impact of the organising model. Peetz's study of Australian unions shows that the presence of workplace delegates militated against membership decline.[92] Kate Bronfenbrenner and Tom Juravich have produced a profile of the kinds of activities that proved successful in union victories in National Labor Relations Board elections between 1987 and 1994.[93] Although they note that employers had become more aggressive, using more anti-union tactics, and most unions still clung to conventional, narrow campaigns, some factors and tactics lifted the success rate. Encouragingly, service industry results were stronger than they were even in manufacturing, and workplaces with higher representation of women and people of colour reported higher success rates as well. Tactics were decisive: unions were more successful where they employed proactive and creative tactics to gain representation by conducting workplace meetings and surveys, door-knocking, and encouraging rank-and-file participation. Building on their empirical arguments, Bronfenbrenner and Juravich argue that:

> there is much more at stake in a grassroots union-building campaign than just getting new members ... Organizing should also not be viewed as independent of other unions ... Particularly in an anti-union climate, organizing is just one step in creating a strong and viable bargaining unit and local unions. It not only needs to achieve real dignity, justice, and fairness for its members but it must be ready to stave off many challenges it will face over time. ... [N]ot only does

the union-building approach allow for victory, it also creates an opportunity for the union to become strong and viable as workers early in the organizing process gain leadership skills and understand the real power associated with their involvement.[94]

While it seems clear that organising strategies provide the *micro context* for rebuilding unions, raising the challenge of creating 'democracies within bureaucracies', labour movements cannot ignore the *macro context* of laws, institutions, employers, and states. Of course, unions do not control their larger environments, and so we must turn to the capacity of labour movements to secure supportive labour market institutions and laws from the world of politics.

Changing labour movements: the challenge of politics

Margaret Levi summarises the conditions for union prosperity when she writes, 'a comparative perspective on labour unions reveals that the best of all worlds for the workers is coordinated bargaining at the national level and significant rank-and-file engagement at the local level'.[95] Our survey of union debates, leadership challenges, and organising successes demonstrates the critical importance of workplace organising. But to rebuild a larger movement based on workplace activism requires a strong and supportive institutional cradle. Union recognition in the workplace, extensive collective bargaining provisions, and the right to strike are types of preconditions for sustained union power. Yet, for weak labour movements, reforming national institutions in this way seems beyond reach.

If unions must take organisational risks to revive their grassroots power, then must they also take political risks to revive their institutional power? To answer this question, we must briefly consider the political relationship between labour movements and political systems. It is true to say that, with the exception of union links to Christian Democrat parties in Europe, labour movements have traditionally found allies on the left. But these alliances varies considerably. In the United States and Canada, labour is only indirectly represented in politics.[96] Neither the American Democrats nor the Canadian Liberals are 'labour parties'. In the United States, despite labour's independence from major political parties, unions generally support the Democrats and especially in presidential elections. In Canada, labour has a good deal of influence over the New Democrats, a party with some political power at the provincial level but which is nationally weak.[97] In Australia and the United Kingdom, unions founded labour parties, maintaining formal links and voting rights within each party. This relationship has changed over the last decade, with both Australian and British Labour reducing union voting and representation. In Europe, Scandinavian, Dutch, and German social democrats have varying levels of union affiliation and influence.[98] The strongest link in French politics rests between the CGT and Communists but the CFDT is closely linked to the Socialists.

In 1997, Bruce Western claimed that his 'evidence ... suggests that unions can and do elicit support from labor parties. Parties and unions share close organizational links, and labor and social democratic parties have strengthened the rights and powers of unions.'[99] The relationship, of course, also goes the other way: unions have provided an enormously important political constituency for labour and social democratic parties. Quite apart from their common mission, unions and their political allies have developed a 'symbiotic' relationship: unions have 'supplied' votes, members, and a leadership cadre for political parties in exchange for legal protections, institutional support, and progressive reform. So we would expect the current crisis in unions to unravel this relationship, weakening the political capacity of unions on one side, and damaging the electoral base of their political allies on the other. The electoral equation for social-democratic and labour parties now looks different: declining union membership equals a declining union 'voting bloc'. Without members and voters, union leaders begin to lose their political clout with parties and governments. In the brazenly instrumental world of politics now, the business lobby, with its ready access to power and money, is a more attractive partner than a shrinking, often maligned, union movement. Even for social-democratic parties.

How much of its 'voting power' has organised labour lost in some of the countries we've surveyed? The scale of the decline is reported in Table 5.5.

Table 5.5 The 'union voting bloc' for main left-of-centre parties: trends in Australia, the United Kingdom, and the United States

	Late 1980s	Early 2000s
Australia	(1987)	(2003)
Union members (% of voters)	42	19
Union members who identify as Labor (%)	63	46
Union bloc for the ALP	27	9
United Kingdom	(1987)	(2001)
Union members (% of voters)	27	20
Union members who identify as Labour (%)	40	47
Union bloc for Labour	11	11
United States	(1988)	(2002)
Union members (% of voters*)	15	14
Union members who identify as Democrat (%)	42	41
Union bloc for Democrats	6	6

Sources: *Australian Election Study*, 1987; *Australian Survey of Social Attitudes*, 2003; *British General Election Studies*, 1987, 2001; *National Election Studies*, 1988, 2002.

Note
* Voters in House of Representatives elections.

First to Australia, which has experienced dramatic union density decline. Using results from the Australian Election Study of 1987 and the Australian Survey of Social Attitudes of 2003, we find that union members declined from 42 per cent of the electorate in 1987 to 19 per cent in 2003. Moreover, many fewer union members identified with the ALP. In 1987, some 63 per cent of union members identified with Labor. In 2003, that number had fallen to 46 per cent. This means that the union 'voting bloc' for Labor – the percentage of union members in the electorate who identify with the ALP – has fallen from 27 per cent of the electorate in 1987 to just 9 per cent in 2003.

In Britain and the United States, the union-voting bloc for Labour and the Democrats respectively has not declined as sharply as it has done in Australia. But the bigger picture is no better. According to the British General Election Studies of 1987 and 2001, increasing partisan support among unionists offset declining union membership. This kept the union voting bloc for Labour at about 11 per cent. In the United States, we see a stable but even more depressing picture. According to the National Election Studies of 1988 and 2002, union membership decreased slightly but Democrat identification among unionists remained about the same. This means unions offer the Democrats a voting bloc of only 6 per cent.

Certainly, the votes that unions deliver to their political allies are not confined to a sturdy bloc of partisan members. Union campaigns stimulate non-union workers and others in the community, and many unionists vote for the main left-of-centre party even though they express no deep allegiance with it. But the size of the union bloc tells us something important: it is the regular, year-in, year-out voting constituency that will deliver a baseline support for the preferred party of the union movement. As this support shrinks, we would expect labour and social-democratic parties to be less responsive to union demands and to organised workers as a whole, responding instead to other demands, some of which conflict with the traditional political objectives of unions. These electoral realities place in stark relief the political misfortune confronting unions in these countries, and help explain, at least in electoral terms, why their political allies have both distanced themselves from unions and tried to broaden their electoral base. They also explain why the post-Thatcher Labour Party has kept itself at a greater distance from the union movement by both reducing the formal influence of unions over the party and ignoring union political demands. Equally, we can grasp why unions in the United States offer the Democrats only a limited amount of political capital. Labour would need to literally transform itself into a larger, more powerful constituency if its quest for major changes to America's labour laws were to come to fruition. This current political weakness helps explain why, in spite of renewed union vigour, the relationship between the AFL-CIO and the Democrats remains largely unchanged.[100]

With declining membership, unions cannot expect left-of-centre parties to maintain a disciplined commitment to the rights and living standards of working people when there are better funded and more powerful organisations to appeal to, organisations with different ideas about the workplace. How might unions respond politically to their reduced bargaining power? Table 5.6 sets out two broad approaches that union movements may follow. In the first, unions seek to harness their 'exchange-like' relationships with their main political allies by maintaining their loyalty while rebuilding their political force. This certainly has been an objective of the AFL-CIO: to increase the size of the union voting bloc for the Democrats by recruiting members through organising, and encouraging partisanship through campaigning. By gaining in strength while remaining loyal, labour movements have the political resources to increase their bargaining power with, or even control over, their political allies. The success of AFL-CIO voter mobilisation in recent years is a starting point. But the movement would need an enormous increase in its voting and campaigning capacity to obtain the kind of national leadership by the Democrats that would strengthen collective bargaining and union recognition. In other national jurisdictions, where unions still have more members and greater institutional sway over their political allies, more remains possible. But if bargaining resources diminish further, remaining loyal would leave unions facing a cold political reality.

The second broad approach is that labour movements become more 'independent' of their political allies. This may allow labour to 'punish' ineffective or unresponsive politicians, party officials, and governments, or to take up a more 'social movement'-style role within the political system. Acting with an independent streak may well be the political equivalent of workplace organising. This might include greater political disruption, tactical political campaigning and bargaining, supporting unpopular causes, and setting up alternative parties. In some countries, union leaders and activists have been helping form smaller, breakaway parties with varying success.

The ultimate object of more social movement-style politics would be to bring a major social democratic party 'back to its roots', so to speak. If the

Table 5.6 Transforming labour movement–labour party relationships: four scenarios

	Failure	*Success*
Movement–party relationship remains close	Union loyalty weakens bargaining power (lower membership and votes for ally)	Union loyalty strengthens bargaining power (higher membership and votes for ally)
Movement–party relationship draws apart	Union independence weakens political power and bargaining power	Union independence strengthens political power and bargaining power

evidence we've presented here is any guide, this strategy would seem foolish. The success of mainstream political allies does make a difference to union prospects, and injuring allies can only backfire. And many already say, 'a bad labour government is better than the alternative'. But this is not a universal truth. As we know from the Australian and British examples, strong union–party links do not necessarily produce clear advantages for labour. And relatively independent union movements that can stir up the political establishment, as we find in Canada or France, are able to represent their interests just as effectively. Narrow strategic or instrumental action will produce dependable results but it is always bounded by systemic constraints. Political risk-taking by unions can, on occasion, exceed those constraints. As Levi points out, sometimes political disruption 'may actually aid their purposes rather than hurt them, as [unions] seem to have been relearning in recent years'.[101]

The choices may not be as stark as 'all in or all out'. Labour movements may begin to experiment with a repertoire of conventional allegiances and methods while also harnessing stronger and more credible threats to 'make a difference'. Of course, this sober assessment of union prospects should not lead us to think that all problems are on the side of organised labour. Do labour and social democratic parties have anything to lose from weak labour movements? The answer is clearly yes. They risk long-term electoral fragility while unions decline as their historically most powerful support base. Unless labour and social-democratic parties can galvanise a more broadly constituted electorate or can continue to win the votes of large numbers of disaffected non-union workers, then union decline will eventually hobble left-of-centre parties. We have every reason to expect that the large number of non-union workers and their families would start to drift away from a 'New Labour' politics that appears hollow and indifferent to labour concerns. Other political forces can and do fill the political void, taking up popular grievances. Far right parties preach anti-immigrant solutions to unemployment, and rightist parties blame high taxes on the 'welfare burden'. For these reasons, labour and social-democratic parties have a clear stake in the ongoing strength of unions even though their actions seem to deny this. It would be in their interest to maintain pro-union labour institutions but the 'Realpolitik' of business-dominated societies complicates this interest remarkably.

Labour movements and the work and welfare agenda

To rebuild, labour movements must extend their organising capacity, mount successful campaigns, and challenge sclerotic political allegiances. And to do this, they must exert political pressure to build or maintain favourable organising conditions. Looking to the future, where do the policy priorities of labour movements lie? Obviously, these priorities would be mediated by national contexts, which vary considerably. Swedish labour faces different problems than, say, the American or Australian labour movements. So most of my short contribution to this section is directed at labour movements that are confronted with the tasks of building and rebuilding. But I will also try to sketch out some, hardly exhaustive, objectives that I believe union movements everywhere might have in common. I'll confine my comments to four areas: full employment, policies for the working poor and working women, collective bargaining, and labour's democratic purpose.

Full employment: working hours, the public sector, and 'transitional labour markets'

In the past, labour movements had a strong interest in full employment. This interest is surely ongoing. Narrow forms of unionism are interested in protecting the jobs of their immediate members. But high unemployment eventually impacts on even the most insulated union. Certainly, labour movements cannot 'produce' full employment. That ability lies jointly with states and business. But labour's political power is a crucial component in building a 'full employment' political coalition, which might combine the electoral forces of a resurgent labour movement, working women and the working poor, welfare groups committed to alleviating poverty, and people seeking partial access to work while also occupied in other social activities. This coalition could be guided by a labour movement capable of keeping its political allies focused on the needs of the whole working population.

For labour movements, full employment has never been a technical term, confined to some macro-economic state in which complete resource utilisation is achieved. Rather, it has been a normative and strategic goal: normative because organised labour recognises the human costs and lost potential caused by unemployment; and strategic because unemployment weakens labour's industrial and political capacity to act. Part of this book has been devoted to criticising exaggerated claims of the 'end of work' but the question remains: is full employment a desirable and achievable goal? Certainly, we must accommodate the intelligent critics of full employment we've mentioned throughout this book who see it variously as defending male access to jobs or economically infeasible. To meet their criticisms, we must discard any idea of full employment that either explicitly or implicitly is committed to a 'male breadwinner' social model. While we should reject the idea that we are facing an imminent 'end of work', we must not be deluded about the economic and social coordination problems governments face in achieving full employment.[102]

Three planks of a revived full employment strategy are critical: counter-cyclical policies, structural policies, and policies designed to cope with transition in and out of work. We'll deal with each in turn. Labour's political imperative is to push for political and economic solutions to unemployment that do not redistribute the burden of adjustment onto low-paid workers or onto those who are left out of work for reasons of political expediency. Undoubtedly, this imperative commits labour to policies of economic expansion and counter-cyclical economics. These policies would challenge the employment-draining monetary and fiscal austerity that prevails today, and which is more of a problem for Europe than elsewhere.[103] Post-industrial critics argue that a 'high growth' policy is now untenable, akin to environmental myopia.[104] But 'low growth' policies damage environments as well by forcing government and populations to exploit natural resources or lower environmental standards to service debt and create jobs. Low growth also encourages informal economies, which sometimes again involves environmental risk. Surely the better goal is to invest in sustainable industry, a source of growth, employment, and environmental benefit.

The second major plank is structural policy. Of course, business cycles matter: low growth increases unemployment. But structural measures can ensure higher levels of employment over the economic cycle. One important way of combating unemployment is to keep working hours under control. In countries like Australia and the United States, where working hours are either high or rising, there is a clear need for legislative intervention. Other governments have recently acted in this area. As I mentioned earlier, the French Socialists legislated a 35-hour limit to working hours after they won the elections of 1997. Critics of shorter working hours, mainly business representatives and market economists, claim that the shorter working week lowers productivity by forcing businesses to employ a larger workforce to achieve the same output. Because of this, the policy actually impedes real employment growth. Are their claims correct? Certainly, these policies impose additional costs on business but these costs are small compared with the social costs of unemployment. Do shorter working hour regulations create jobs? Evidence suggests they do but perhaps not so many as its proponents hope. Jennifer Hunt's analysis of work-sharing in Germany during the 1980s finds that it has small, positive employment effects, but they are not as great as creating a 'low wage' employment sector.[105] The French experience appears to have produced a similar result: reducing working hours has a significant but small effect on overall employment.

Reformists seeking to lower unemployment by regulating working hours must deal with critics, supportive of the US approach, who claim that creating a larger low-wage sector is simply more effective. They need to marry working hour reductions with other structural policies. Though quite out of fashion, public-sector job creation remains an important structural component of full employment. Sometimes local, state, and national governments have used government as an employer of 'last resort', primarily to alleviate long-term unemployment. But should we hold greater ambitions for the public sector? The wide range of personal and social needs arising in two major areas – education and health care – suggest we should. Carers for elderly people and the disabled, adult-learning teachers, childcare workers, health professionals and researchers are among those who will increasingly work in the public sector. And governments would be well advised to invest in them for two reasons. To ensure equality of access to these services, something that's unlikely to result from private or voluntary provision. And to ensure that well-trained professionals carry out these services. A professionally trained public-sector workforce offers a distinct advantage over an under-trained, under-paid voluntary or private-sector workforce.

Critics complain that, however innovative, public-sector job creation is too expensive, and will lead to higher taxes. But communities end up being 'taxed' by cheaper, socially defective solutions too. Take the example of America's health insurance system which chews up huge resources as it fails to cover one in five Americans. Aren't the profit margins of this industry a form of 'taxation' that the community bears? By expanding public sector jobs, taxes may go up. But the public and the economy stand to benefit from a transformed 'social infrastructure' that contributes to a sophisticated, healthy, and adequately employed workforce into the future.

The third plank is a policy designed to deal with transition in and out of employment. Günter Schmid presents us with a compelling redefinition of full employment that breaks with the 'male breadwinner' norm. This is a model for overcoming some of the structural and normative problems of full employment we raised earlier.[106] He argues that today we must see the goal of full employment at two levels: creating an economic environment to sustain employment growth in full-time labour markets; and creating a series of well-integrated, publicly subsidised 'transitional labour markets'.[107] A social-democratic policy would redefine full employment in the following terms. Everyone would have the right to a good job. But for various reasons, individuals inevitably undergo 'transitions' between work and other life situations – between work and education, between work and unemployment, between work and family, and between work and retirement. At these critical junctures, transitional labour markets that supply employment with public subsidies will go far in meeting the employment and income needs of a diverse public, recognising the claims of women and men of different ages, life situations, and abilities.

A full employment strategy founded on working time regulations, public-sector job creation, and an institutionally nourished set of transitional labour markets goes well beyond the old male, breadwinner model. It would offer a distinct advantage over the US model, which stimulates private sector employment but at the cost of high inequality. In the US model we noted the distinct lack of government support for working-age people outside the labour market, and for managing the boundaries of work, family, and social life. The transitional labour market approach to full employment would devote particular resources to people in these situations by recognising their needs for employment and income and their particular life-stage needs. This approach would also offer a richer policy framework than a basic income policy, meeting the needs of a large number of people who are not in a position to work full-time. Rather than assuming that people outside conventional employment (the under-employed, those involved in education, those caring for others or those newly-retired) want nothing more to do with paid work, this approach also assumes that many people wish to maintain a connection to working life while pursuing other goals. Taking the proposal a step further, we might envisage developing transitional labour markets so that 'dead-end' jobs are taken up temporarily by people who seek only marginal contact with employment while they are occupied with other goals. Combined with opportunities and training, people who would otherwise work in menial jobs for long periods would have greater mobility.

Policies for the working poor and working women

We saw in Chapter 4 that proponents of a generous, universal negative income tax see topping up wages through the tax system as a sensible way of dealing with low wages without destroying jobs. This approach, as we saw, is best thought of as a compromise between the US model of deregu-lated, private sector job creation, and the basic income goal of guarantee-ing a minimum income. However, others continue to stress the fundamental importance of living wages in reducing the number of poorly paid workers. One reason why Australia's deregulation experiment has not led to a large increase in the number of low-paid full-time workers (those earning under two-thirds of average weekly earnings) is the continued intervention of the Australian Industrial Relations Commission to set a minimum level of award wages. The ACTU has managed to achieve increases in the minimum wage at a time of considerable employment growth in Australia. The situation in the United States is more difficult. While labour lacks the political power to get legislation through Congress to keep the Federal minimum wage level with the cost-of-living, it has suc-cessfully pressured state governments to increase the state minimum wage, and pushed for 'living wages' for 'service contractors using public money' at the city or county level.[108] The idea of a 'living wage', a foundation prin-ciple of the Australian model, is compelling. While there is mixed public support for poor people who subsist outside the labour market, the public is sympathetic to low-wage workers. Labour movements in more unequal advanced countries will find both their greatest opportunities and greatest difficulties in organising poor workers. Poor workers are likely to respond to campaigns for living wage increases but are often in sectors of the economy that are hard to organise.

Institutionalising living wages in a country like America would also produce flow-on benefits to that country's 'discontented middle'. By reducing downward pressure on middle-income paying jobs, living wages would help alleviate economic frustrations that are one indirect element in the rising discontent with politics, an ingredient for right-wing populism and 'wedge politics' in some countries. The power of wedge politics among white working-class voters is an important factor in Republican gains among these voters after 1964.[109] Stronger unions, and a Democratic Party committed to greater wage protection for low- and middle-income earners, would go some way to limiting conservative gains among these voters.

The number of women entering the workforce in all the countries we've surveyed is growing. As we saw in Chapter 3, working women in countries like Canada, the United Kingdom, and the United States are over-represented among the working poor. Women will prove an increasingly important group in organising efforts and in political campaigns. The difficulties of managing family, education, and employment needs with limited resources are starting to receive due political recognition. But action sometimes lags behind; such as Australia's failure to devise a comprehensive maternity leave plan. Labour movements must continue to address these problems by forcing public policies to reflect both the full employment needs of many women and the particular 'transition circumstances' women face between work and family life.[110]

From collective bargaining and union rights to democratic workplaces

The evidence we have presented in this chapter points to the importance of widespread collective bargaining for more equal labour market outcomes. In countries with higher levels of collective bargaining, we find greater wage compression and less variation in the rights and conditions of employment. Collective recognition of unions in the workplace, and the ability to set collective agreements at firm, industry or national level are the best ways to ensure that crude market outcomes are smoothed out, and that working life can be satisfactorily organised for many more workers. So defending and extending collective bargaining rights must be a common union priority. One country that stands out in this respect is the United States. Extending collective bargaining will require a Herculean organising effort, and that seems impossible in the current legal and institutional framework. One benefit that varies with access to collective bargaining in the United States is health care: as health care costs spiral in that country's largely privatised system, we can expect health care will become an important organising resource for unions. Of course, collective bargaining is just one step, important though it is, in the struggle for 'democratic workplaces' where workers have a greater voice in decision-making about company or organisation direction, and more say over their own work. While we find some limited participation of this kind in European work councils, to pursue this path further would require a change in the ownership structure of advanced economies, something that leads us into pure speculation at this point.

Labour movements and democratisation

As I suggested earlier, labour movements cannot help but thematise the problems of inequality in democratic societies. The collective experiences and capacities of people at work provide a significant opportunity for 'social learning' that has implications beyond the workplace. Unions have always provided a voice for workers in politics. This role will continue and, with some luck, will be governed by wider ideals of inclusion and participation. Encouraging voting, campaigning with other social movements, and challenging the top-down power of corporations and elite money-driven politics are among the many activities that will push labour's efforts beyond the workplace and into the spheres of society and politics.

Labour movements have been among the first social movements to give substance to the idea of internationalism. Far from being a dreamy ideal, the practical significance of cross-border cooperation is now very clear. Most commentators focus on the gloomy side of global restructuring. But there is a more positive aspect as well. By engaging and cooperating across borders, unions will start to face up to the challenge of union avoidance strategies by national governments and multinational employers.[111] And a growing awareness of the realities of Third World labour will make a difference to the way labour movements operate in the future, and the kind of solutions they will accept. This kind of solidarity may seem feeble. But the 'global campaign' launched by mining and other unions over Rio Tinto's labour and environmental practices gives us a glimpse of the direction future cross-border campaigns could take.

Conclusion

This chapter has led us to several conclusions. A strong commitment to policies that will promote good jobs and build workplaces where workers have a voice will depend on the ongoing capacity of the labour movement to act industrially and politically. There are good reasons to think that, without a redistribution of power, labour market solutions will continue to follow their present path, only minimally addressing the interests of a growing number of disaffected workers. In some national jurisdictions changing this reality is no mean feat. If full employment policies that will benefit the public and unions alike are to be conceived and implemented, they will require a powerful new political coalition at the centre of which we would find unions.

To successfully reclaim a policy alternative that would rival either the US model or basic income approach, two clear problems must first be addressed. On the industrial front, unions need to experiment with tactics and strategies. They must attempt to create 'democracies within bureaucracies' that combine grassroots strength with organisational might so unions can operate within and beyond the constraints of industrial relations systems. On the political front, unions must re-establish their political voice by developing a more comprehensive repertoire of political strategies to increase labour's voting clout and its ability to use social movement style politics to reshape the political agenda.

6 Conclusion

What have I done in this book? By criticising the premises and arguments of the 'end of work' scenario envisaged by the post-industrial left, I have set out a three-way comparison of models for regulating work, which first considered the dominant US model of employment creation through deregulated labour markets, and then considered two alternatives, a basic income model guaranteeing a minimum income that is independent of employment status, and a full employment model of job creation that depends on a renewed political coalition built around stronger labour movements. I claim that these alternatives are a set of choices regulated by institutional factors and economic and political power as much as they are 'determined' by brute technological and economic constraints. These choices attach different priorities to employment in overall institutional design and to equality in the labour market. The result can be summarised as a choice between a 'jobs with inequality' approach (the US model), an 'equality without jobs' approach (the basic income model), and a 'jobs with equality' approach (a full employment model). I shall return to these three options to clarify my overall argument. But first some comments about the 'end of work' scenario, particularly about how it understands social change and, more broadly, about its place in the social sciences.

The 'end of work' and social change

I have shown that the 'end of work' argument has attracted a long line of distinguished thinkers since Karl Marx first articulated it. It is true Marx held varied, even divergent, views about work and social change. In highlighting the 'end of work' scenario we can trace in his writing, I am not claiming to offer a definitive account of Marx's ideas about the transformation of work. Rather, my approach is exegetical. My claim is that Marx's formulas and speculations resonate in the work of later thinkers. The 'end of work' position continues to directly and indirectly inform the social theories of a group of contemporary thinkers I have identified with the post-industrial left: Alain Touraine, Claus Offe, Ulrich Beck, André Gorz, and Jürgen Habermas. In the arguments of these thinkers, we find two interlocking claims: that work is likely to further diminish as an economic activity, with labour-saving technologies becoming increasingly available, and that work is likely to diminish as a social activity, with fewer people participating in work and more developing identities in other social contexts.

Understanding macro changes

My main objection to the 'end of work' scenario is that it exaggerates the decline of work. Empirical evidence, something post-industrial thinkers tend to overlook, helps a great deal here. I have relied on historical employment-to-population ratios to show that, in the ten countries we studied, we do not encounter anything like a universal decline in employment levels. In criticising 'end of work' arguments, Manuel Castells reminds us of how, during the 1990s, employment in the world economy expanded rapidly.[1] There are European exceptions. And, as I have stated in this book, it is not just a coincidence that post-industrial, 'end of work' thinking has taken strongest hold in France and Germany where employment levels have declined substantially. It is thus understandable that intellectuals cannot see the point of extending employment, or have lost faith that any political and social changes might still emanate from the workplace.

If we discount the 'end of work' scenario, how are we to account for changes in employment levels, and in the relevance of work for society and politics? Any account would depend on how we understand macro-social changes. Summarising various theoretical positions, Anthony Giddens says in an introductory textbook that 'social change is difficult to define'.[2] It is easy to understand why. Whether inspired by evolutionary concepts, the idea of differentiation or the momentum of rationalisation, theories of social change have enough difficulty attempting to account for the past and the present. They run into even greater difficulties when they forecast the future of work, social relations, or technology.

I shall make one distinction that I believe assists us in accounting for the changing relationships between work and society that we've looked at here: a distinction between the 'first order' and 'second order' characteristics of social change. By first-order characteristics, I am referring to the broadest structures of modern societies. Alongside a rational legal and bureaucratic system and a differentiated society, we would include a socially and technologically complex division of labour. My view is that the 'end of work' scenario presents the transformation path of employment as a *first-order* change for modern societies. In this scenario, technological change and rationalisation are an all-conquering force. Other sociological inquiries are prone to similar exaggerations about what has changed with little attention to what stays the same. In this vein, we often hear claims about the 'end of tradition', the 'end of ideology' or the 'end of the family'. Even the 'end of history'. Yet traditions, ideologies, families – and history – have continued strong.

When it comes in describing changes in work, I think that they are 'second order' in character and magnitude. By second order, I mean that they are changes *within* the larger, slower moving structures that belong to the modern division of labour. Viewing changes in this way is more balanced and cautious. Changes in industry composition, the role of women in the workforce, unemployment levels, the level of technology, and in social attitudes towards work may all be large and disruptive for society, prompting fears and speculation, but they do not necessarily challenge society's continuing dependence on paid employment. In their rich empirical study, Chris and Charles Tilly offer what I believe is a more sensible forecast:

> Work is unlikely to change character massively during the next few decades because low-wage workers in poorer countries compete their capitalist cousins out of business, because capitalist workers' preferences shift from wages to leisure, or because someone invents the ultimate labor-saving device. It is likely to change because international circuits of capital are gaining power, because governments are losing their capacity or propensity to enforce workers' established rights, and because long-distance migration is bringing new groups of workers into previously closed labor markets. Changing power relations will have larger impacts than new technologies or alterations in market efficiency.[3]

Sociologists and political economists like anyone else are entitled to their view that work is over-emphasised in our culture and society. But this remains a normative view, shared by some but not by all.

Micro realities

Marx and Weber bequeathed to us the idea that technological change and rationalisation are powerful enough to dissolve the social relationships of work. 'Alienation' and the 'iron cage' tell us something of the pathos of these large-scale forces. But do technology and rational organisation extinguish the 'micro-social contexts' of work that make employment a meaningful experience for our social identities and conflicts over social organisation? It seems unlikely. Technology and rational organisation are still embedded in social institutions. In surveying recent studies of technical change and the workplace, Joanne Miller puts it as follows:

> Technological changes in modes of production were assumed to follow a specific logic affecting the social organization of production ... The effects of technology on jobs and the work force are no longer

viewed as inevitable outcomes but the product of multiple and recipro-
cal constraints of a technical and nontechnical nature.[4]

As Miller suggests, we have increasingly moved away from understanding
technology as an independent force. And the 'nontechnical' elements in
work to which Miller refers are hardly trivial. They include power and
social relationships, which make work a rich experience; indeed, an
experience that provides millions of people with opportunities to practise
technical and social skills as well as exposure to the 'abstract' forces, of
markets and of power, that help shape their lives.

Perhaps in many respects the most convincing of the grand theories of
social change is offered by Jürgen Habermas. He challenges the idea that
'work' or 'production' can remain the central analytical category for social
theory. But, in developing his alternative position, he does not leave us
with a convincing account of the importance of work to social change.
Without achieving this, Habermas leaves us with the view that work is
increasingly rationalised in a technical sense, and that the social institutions of work today matter less. We probably need stronger 'micro
foundations' that avoid understanding work in the grandiose terms we find
in Marxism, and that identify experience at work as a powerful source of
social action. Others recognise this. Habermas's protégé, Axel Honneth,
has persuasively argued that work is still important for social recognition.[5]
And, sorting through new ways of understanding the workplace as an
intersection of technical and social organisation, Andrew Feenberg offers
us a conceptual path to understanding the ongoing social potential of the
workplace when he speaks of 'democratising rationality'.[6] Something akin
to this democratic rationality is meant when today's union organisers
speak of 'organising' workers so that they may redefine the power-laden
social relationships of the workplace.

Understanding macro and micro perspectives

How can we link together 'macro' and 'micro' claims? If we understand
most changes in employment to be 'second-order' social changes, by which
I mean they are contingent, open to challenge, and highly variable in their
effects, we avoid understanding technology and organisation as immutable
forces, understanding them instead as factors that must inevitably find
their context in the micro-social foundations of the workplace. That is
why the sociology of work increasingly understands technology as 'socially
embedded', industrial relations systems as 'politically driven', and gender
segregation on the job as 'socially determined'. We see the powerful influence of our social and political environments in workplace management,
rules about the use of technology, and employment policies. I began this
Conclusion by referring to the 'choices' societies end up making about
employment alternatives. They too are a product of social processes, made

within the 'hard constraints' of economics, organisations, and power. It is to these alternatives I now turn.

Jobs with inequality: the limits of the US model

Characteristics defined

The clearly dominant alternative in the debates about how to solve the problems of unemployment is the US model. I have called the US model the 'jobs with inequality' approach. The model's greatest claim is to maximise employment in the private labour market. Although the United States has gained a certain notoriety for perpetuating low minimum wages, a large pool of working poor, and weak unions in an otherwise affluent society, it has managed to generate more full-time private sector employment than the other societies we've surveyed here. By re-establishing strong employment growth, the US model has been somewhat of a challenge to the 'end of work' scenario, and provided a new impetus for policy-makers elsewhere to consider the American alternative. Creating jobs without raising public expenditure or rewriting the rules of the labour market appeals to government so policy-makers and politicians thus have an obvious interest in America's recent successes, even as these successes now fade.

Was the employment success during the 1990s a product of free market forces and 'market clearing' minimum wages, as its defenders claim? The answer is probably not. More likely, success followed from other factors: expansionary monetary and fiscal policy over the past two decades combined with a fragmented welfare system that leaves the working population with few alternatives to paid employment. We often hear the claim made for the US model that its success lies in a cruel fact, 'low minimum wages produce jobs'. Is this an iron law of economics at work? Evidence we included in Chapter 3 suggests not: raising wages can also have positive employment effects, and certainly other countries with higher minimum wages still manage comparable levels of job creation.

What of the 'inequality problem' that is identified with the US model? Its defenders are largely unapologetic. Their world is a 'second-best' world, with a story that goes like this: to create jobs, we have to accept the market, and thus individual life chances must also depend on market forces. If markets work well, we keep hearing, they will create 'laws of justice', generating incentives for mobility that will motivate achievers. But the evidence, such as that presented by the authors of *The State of Working America*, denies the US model's 'mobility' achievements.[7] Regulated labour markets in other countries do better. Just as regulations and government support can promote economic efficiency, regulations and government can encourage mobility. When we look at the share of GDP that goes to the working-age population in the form of transfer payments and welfare services, only Japan competes with the United States for bottom place among the ten countries we surveyed. By spending comparatively little on maintaining income and social support for the working-age population, governments commit themselves to a weak 'social infrastructure' of inadequate arrangements for childcare, health services, training and education opportunities, and public sector employment. A weak social infrastructure ends up weakening mobility and, more fundamentally, weakens equality of opportunity.

What's 'American' about the US model?

Sceptics might say it is wrong to speak of a 'US model', that this is just 'capitalism at work'. But all economic systems are mediated by powerful political and social influences. The various forms of capitalism depend not only on different regional, technological, and industrial foundations but also on the social and political institutions that regulate work, and regulate the boundaries between work and welfare.[8] As a powerful nation, with an ongoing experiment in deregulated labour markets and lean welfare, the United States is an important source of inspiration for policy transfer, especially when business and technocratic elites dominate politics, and therefore social choices about institutional design. Although I do not suggest that even the English-speaking countries, ones most likely to follow the US model, will converge with the policies of the United States, I do think the US model will remain the benchmark for 'top-down' reforms elsewhere. In this respect, the US model will remain a fundamental point of reference in future conflicts over reforming national work and welfare regimes.

Equality without jobs: the disappointments of a basic income

A European vision

The strongest proponents of basic income reform are from France and Germany, where employment-to-population ratios are low and falling. It seems quite plausible to imagine a post-work social system in which the links between work and income distribution are modified in the direction of a universal income guarantee. Certainly, the idea is highly appealing in the abstract, especially for those who believe in justice but see faults in the existing welfare states and have little confidence that the 'old' forces for full employment can any longer make a difference. And a basic income may well be feasible in some national contexts. Where states already come close to guaranteeing a minimum standard through a hotchpotch of welfare and employment programmes, a basic income scheme would represent a mere simplification rather than a splurge of social spending, and, as Robert Goodin suggests, would 'presume less' about welfare clients. So we must wonder why such a good idea has struggled to find a political foundation and a public audience beyond reformist academics and social policy critics.

The search for an economic and political foundation

A basic income would seem to offer a clear improvement over the US model in at least one respect. If creating jobs in the future depends on forsaking the goal of equality, it is more rational and humane to forsake the goal of full employment instead. But what signs are there that national economies and societies are willing or ready to make this choice to maintain equality? Two conditions would need to apply: joblessness would need to become even more substantial and intractable, and the public would need to lose its normative and structural attachment to paid employment. In the 1980s, rising unemployment, new social movements, and tired unions appeared to contribute the necessary momentum for basic income reform. But even in Europe, high unemployment has not persisted everywhere, and we have little evidence that the so-called 'postmaterialist generation', distant from labour struggles and attracted to new identity politics and environmental causes, have actually turned their backs on getting good jobs. With the help of data from the British Social Attitudes survey conducted in 2000, I have argued that most workers value their jobs, and do not just see employment as a source of income. I expect that this will continue to be the case, which means that, for better or worse, employment questions will remain at the centre of political and social life.

Negative income taxes as halfway reforms

In Chapter 4, I argued that there is now a clear opportunity for a convergence between supporters of the US model, who believe that markets are best for creating jobs but acknowledge their model's inequalities, and supporters of a basic income who acknowledge the unfeasibility of a full basic income but seek a streamlined way of delivering justice to citizens that also protects them from the hazards of the labour market. A middle way between the US model and a basic income model could be found by implementing a partial basic income in the form of a negative income tax. Proposals like this, such as the well-argued negative income tax proposal offered by Fred Block and Jeff Manza, build on the experience of America's Earned Income Tax Credit. The EITC provides additional income to low-wage workers through the tax system, alleviating poverty without mandating the higher wage rates that would have negative effects on employment. Some advocates see this kind of policy compromise as a viable way of combining a deregulated labour market that creates jobs with tax-based measures to reduce poverty. Critics see it differently. For them, it is a policy that avoids, even entrenches, the real problem: the proliferation of low-wage jobs. Certainly, supporters of a full basic income scheme, who hope to completely sever the nexus between work and income, would see this as a mixed blessing. To keep costs under control, a negative income tax policy regime would still depend on a steady supply of good, well-paying jobs. But without a viable political coalition and a powerful economic rationale, it is hard to envisage a basic income scheme that goes beyond this point of compromise.

Jobs with equality: labour movements and full employment

The need for a full employment coalition

Can we still commit, as a serious social and political choice, to a model of 'jobs with equality'? In my view we can, but subject to other developments. As I argued in Chapter 5, the main condition would be a strengthened political coalition supporting full employment. Given present configurations of money and power, it is unrealistic to expect governments will commit to greater equality without political pressure. A glance at the past gives us a clear idea about the social forces most capable of pressuring government: labour movements have made a real difference to the shape of work and welfare regimes. Their continuing viability is a necessary but not sufficient condition if a 'jobs with justice' policy is to develop in countries that have let employment equality slip.

The role of unions

Prospects for the 'jobs with equality' approach look dim while union movements are losing industrial and political influence. But when we look closely at the factors that make a big difference to comparative union strength – a commitment to organising workplaces as well as supportive labour market and industrial relations institutions – it becomes clear that these factors remain contingent, open to contention and redefinition. We do not confirm the pessimistic view of unions we find among the post-industrial left that tends to think new industries and new social identities will weaken labour's presence in the political and social structures of post-industrial societies. While we cannot confidently predict a major union revival, we should not dismiss the prospect of unions strengthening in the workplace and in politics.

Labour movements and political parties

In many countries we've surveyed, the historical relationships between labour movements and parties of the mainstream left have been challenged or scaled back. In Australia and the United Kingdom, for example, labour's role in the parties they originally established has been formally reduced. And the declining voting bloc that unions can deliver to their political allies has weakened informal 'exchange' relationships between movements and parties. Unions have delivered votes, political candidates, and money, and social-democratic parties have protected workers. Times are now more challenging. Well-organised business, bureaucratic, and political interests are in a stronger position to influence the economic and social policy of governments including labour and social-democratic governments. This has left unions in many countries with a daunting challenge: to somehow re-establish their influence over political allies by strengthening their workplace presence and increasing the power of their voting bloc. There are some promising signs from AFL-CIO efforts that have recently made a difference to election outcomes in the United States. But unions in America and elsewhere will still need to experiment in riskier social movement activity that pressures the *entire* political system to take notice of injustices in work.

The struggle over work

This book has challenged the post-industrial 'end of work' argument. I have shown that much rests on how we account for the relationship between employment and social change. By varying our baseline assumptions about the number of jobs that will be created, and the balance of political and social interests and power, we arrive at starkly contrasting scenarios. In the political world, with power tilted to business and business-friendly governments, we find the US model dominant. It is a work-centred vision without an emphasis on justice. In the academic world, where the 'end of work' scenario remains a powerful argument, we find the basic income model dominant. It is an equality-centred vision without a clear recognition of the ongoing importance of work. I believe we can still combine employment and equality. But, as always, achieving a 'jobs with equality' approach will depend on a change in industrial and political power.

Notes

Introduction

1 J. Rifkin, *The End of Work: The Decline of the Global Labor Force and the Dawn of the Post-Market Era*, New York: Jeremy P. Tarcher/Putnam, 1995.
2 *US News and World Report*, 'World-Class Workaholics: Are Crazy Hours and Takeout the Elixir of America's Success?', 20 December, 1999.
3 J. Habermas, 'The New Obscurity: The Crisis of the Welfare State and the Exhaustion of Utopian Energies', in S. Weber Nicholsen (ed. and trans.), *The New Conservatism: Cultural Criticism and the Historians' Debate*, Cambridge, MA: MIT Press, 1994, pp. 48–70.
4 Bureau of Labor Statistics, *Comparative Civilian Labour Force Statistics: Ten Countries: 1959–2002*, 2002, online. Available at www.bls.gov (accessed 23 October 2003).
5 A. Touraine, M. Wieviorka, and F. Dubet, *The Workers' Movement*, trans. I. Patterson, Cambridge: Cambridge University Press, 1987, p. 290.
6 See L. Mishel and J. Schmitt, *Beware the US Model: Jobs and Wages in a Deregulated Economy*, Washington, DC: Economic Policy Institute, 1995.
7 J. Myles and P. Pierson, 'Friedman's Revenge: The Reform of "Liberal" Welfare States in Canada and the United States', *Politics & Society*, vol. 25, no. 4, December 1997, pp. 443–472.
8 A. Honneth, *The Fragmented World of the Social: Essays in Social and Political Philosophy*, ed. C. Wright, Albany, NY: State University of New York Press, 1995, p. xvii.
9 For a very useful perspective on the 'joining processes' in micro/macro sociology, see R. Munch and N. Smelser, 'Relating the Micro and Macro', in J. Alexander, N. Smelser, and R. Munch (eds), *The Micro-Macro Link*, Berkeley, CA: University of California Press, 1987, pp. 356–373.
10 E.C. Hughes, *On Work, Race and the Sociological Imagination*, ed. and intro. L. Coser, Chicago: University of Chicago Press, 1994, p. 33.

1 Pessimistic origins: work in classical sociology

1 C. Offe, *Disorganized Capitalism: Contemporary Transformations of Work and Politics*, ed. J. Keane, Cambridge: Polity Press, 1985, pp. 129–150.
2 G. Friedmann, *The Anatomy of Work: The Implications of Specialization*, trans. W. Rawson, London: Heinemann, 1962, p. 94.
3 When Marx refers to the 'abolition of labour', he is referring not to the 'end of work' in a philosophical sense but to the end of the 'naturally given' division of labour and the relations of production that govern it. On this point, I am indebted to Márkus's insights. See G. Márkus, *Marxism and Anthropology:*

The Concept of 'Human Essence' in the Philosophy of Marx, trans. E. de Laczay and G. Márkus, Assen: Van Gorcum, 1978, p. 75, n.10. Markus makes it clear that the exact transformation path of work in post-capitalist society stands as an unresolved feature of Marx's writings (see ibid., pp. 81–82). I accept that Marx describes different scenarios in various places. In the *Grundrisse*, for example, he mentions that 'machinery presupposes a mass of workers', but this work is stripped of its social meaning; see K. Marx, *Grundrisse: Foundations of the Critique of Political Economy (Rough Draft)*, trans. M. Nicolaus, Harmondsworth: Penguin, 1973, p. 690.

4 H. Joas, *The Creativity of Action*, trans. J. Gaines and P. Keast, Cambridge: Polity Press, 1996, p. 92.

5 Adam Smith replaced the existing theories of value (such as the physiocratic economics of land) with a labour theory of value, reflecting the changing reality of wealth creation and economic and political power in Europe. On Hegel's concept of labour, see H. Marcuse, *Reason and Revolution: Hegel and the Rise of Social Theory*, London: Routledge & Kegan Paul, 1968, pp. 76–79. Hegel's social theory (his *Jensener Realphilosophie*, for instance) draws on a connection between needs and labour. Marcuse notes, 'Labour, for Hegel, connects individuals to the social whole, and "abstract and universal labor" is connected with concrete individual need through the "exchange relationships" of the market' (p. 78). He further comments on Hegel's description of the early-modern labour process:

> The tone and pathos of the descriptions point strikingly similar to Marx's *Capital*. It is not surprising to note that Hegel's manuscript breaks off with this picture, as if he was terrified by what his analysis of the commodity-producing society disclosed'.
>
> (ibid., p. 79)

Marcuse notes that Hegel resolves this problem through the 'strong state' (ibid., p. 79).

6 Márkus, *Marxism and Anthropology*, pp. 5–15.

7 K. Marx, 'The German Ideology: Part I,' in R. Tucker (ed.), *The Marx–Engels Reader*, New York: W. W. Norton, 1972, p. 120.

8 A. Heller, *The Theory of Need in Marx*, New York: St. Martin's Press, 1976, pp. 31–32.

9 Ibid., p. 33.

10 Joas, *The Creativity of Action*, p. 98.

11 Ibid.

12 For Marx's discussion of surplus value, productive and unproductive labour, and the nature of capitalist competition and change, see K. Marx, *Capital: A Critique of Political Economy: Volume I, Capitalist Production*, trans. S. Moore and E. Aveling, ed. F. Engels, London: Lawrence & Wishart, 1970. For Marx's discussion of capitalist 'breakdown' (falling rate of profit, etc.), see K. Marx, *Capital: A Critique of Political Economy, Volume III, Book III: The Process of Capitalist Production as a Whole*, ed. F. Engels, Moscow: Progress Publishers, 1966. For an excellent summary of Marx's political economy, see P. Sweezy, *The Theory of Capitalist Development: Principles of Marxian Political Economy*, New York: Monthly Review Press, 1970.

13 Marx, *Grundrisse*, p. 705.

14 Marcuse, *Reason and Revolution*, pp. 295–312.

15 K. Marx, 'Capital: Selections', in Tucker, *Marx–Engels Reader*, pp. 319–320.

16 Heller, *Theory of Need*, pp. 101–102.

17 Ibid., p. 117. Heller further states that, 'without doubt Marx imagines the society of associated producers as one in which the measurement of wealth is

not the proportion of necessary labour to surplus labour, but the proportion of necessary time to disposable time' (p. 116). She notes that when Marx refers to labour time as a basis of measuring activities, he is effectively conceiving society 'as one single individual' (ibid.)

18 Ibid., p. 119.
19 Ibid., p. 123. See also F. Feher, 'The Socialism of Scarcity', *Thesis Eleven*, no. 37, 1994, 105. He states that,

> Marx's position, ... implies the inadmissible naturalization of use values. In reality, use values 'stand in history', so do the ways of producing for them and satisfying them. Producing for the complex use values of modernity is an extremely costly process, drastically different from the simplifying presentation of the 'naturalist' Marx.

20 M. Postone, *Time, Labor, and Social Domination: A Reinterpretation of Marx's Critical Theory*, Cambridge: Cambridge University Press, 1993. Postone takes up this discussion, distinguishing between labour defined according to the 'historical necessity' of capitalism (which takes on the familiar characteristics of exploitation and alienation) and labour defined by 'transhistorical necessity', that is, 'goal-directed social activity that mediates between humans and nature, creating specific products in order to satisfy determinate human needs' (ibid., p. 5). I have no disagreement with this distinction. However, Postone could give more attention to the possibility that transhistorical necessity might develop in ways that do not conform to the minimisation of labour time and the rationalisation of production.

21 H. Braverman, *Labor and Monopoly Capital: The Degradation of Work in the Twentieth Century*, New York: Monthly Review Press, 1974.
22 C. Tilly and C. Tilly, *Work under Capitalism*, Boulder, CO: Westview Press, 1998, pp. 158–159. In their survey of the empirical literature of deskilling and reskilling, Chris Tilly and Charles Tilly note:

> Following Marx himself, Harry Braverman held that capitalists narrowed jobs in order to *deskill* them.... Employers can fill narrowed, deskilled jobs with less expensive grades of labor, cutting costs.... Marglin ... posited that – as in the case of centralization – capitalists established a fine division of labor in order to wrest control of the labor process away from workers.... All of these theories call for a progressively finer and finer division of labor. But case studies demonstrate a far more complex pattern. Narrowing and deskilling alternates or coincides with reskilling. Repetitive jobs are automated out of existence, while new, broad jobs are born. David Howell and Edward Wolff's careful study of changes in the skill composition of the U.S. workforce between 1960 and 1985 finds that overall, the mix of jobs shifted in the direction of *increasing* cognitive and interactive skills.
>
> (ibid., pp. 158–159, authors' emphases)

(The study by Howell and Wolff is D.S. Howell and E.N. Wolff, 'Trends in the Growth and Distribution of Skills in the U.S. Workplace: 1960–1985', *Industrial and Labor Relations Review*, vol. 44, 1991, pp. 486–502.)

23 Friedmann, *The Anatomy of Work*, p. 115.
24 M. Radin, *Contested Commodities*, Cambridge, MA: Harvard University Press, 1996, p. 105. Radin notes:

> Many teachers and scholars identify this way with their work. So, of course, do many performers, artists, and writers; and editors and publishers. So do many doctors, and nurses, and people who care for children, the

> elderly, the retarded, the handicapped, and people who counsel students, or married couples, or those who have trouble with drugs and alcohol. Firefighters, paramedics, and law enforcement officers can do their work as givers to others while being paid.
>
> (ibid., p. 105)

25 Ibid., p. 106.
26 Ibid., p. 107.
27 H. Arendt, *The Human Condition*, Chicago: University of Chicago Press, 1989, p. 5.
28 H. Marcuse, 'On the Philosophical Foundations of the Concept of Labor in Economics', *Telos*, no. 16, 1973, pp. 9–37. See also D. Kellner, 'Introduction to "On the Philosophical Foundation of the Concept of Labor"', *Telos*, no. 16, 1973, pp. 2–8.
29 H. Marcuse, *Eros and Civilization: A Philosophical Inquiry into Freud*, London: Abacus, 1972, p. 42.
30 Ibid., pp. 47–48.
31 Ibid., p. 116.
32 Ibid., p. 117.
33 See A. Gorz, *Farewell to the Working Class: An Essay on Postindustrial Socialism*, trans. M. Sonenscher, London: Pluto Press, 1982. See also A. Gorz, *Critique of Economic Reason*, trans. G. Handyside and C. Turner, London: Verso, 1989.
34 Marcuse cited in Kellner, 'Introduction to "On the Philosophical Foundation of the Concept of Labor"', p. 7. Kellner observes that, in Marx,

> the realm of material production is devaluated as a realm of mere bondage, as submission to natural necessity. The philosophical root of the claim that labor in the realm of necessity is bondage is a desire, central to Heidegger, German Idealism, and existentialism, for an unconditioned freedom of the self. Marcuse counterposed to the idealist-Heideggerian notion of the primal, absolute freedom of the self, the claim that the labor system was a fetter on the individual's free self-activity
>
> (ibid., p. 6)

35 A. Feenberg, *Questioning Technology*, London: Routledge, 1999, p. 79.
36 M. Weber, *The Protestant Ethic and the Spirit of Capitalism*, trans. T. Parsons, London: Allen & Unwin, 1930. See also K. Löwith, *Max Weber and Karl Marx*, ed. T. Bottomore and W. Outhwaite, trans. H. Fantel, London: George Allen & Unwin, 1982, pp. 42–43.
37 G. Ingham, 'Some Recent Changes in the Relationship between Economics and Sociology', *Cambridge Journal of Economics*, vol. 20, no. 2, March 1996, pp. 256–257. Ingham notes:

> the necessary additional component of a sociological explanation, Weber argued, was the interpretative understanding (Verstehen) of the motivational link between the observation of conduct and its meaning to both actor and observer. In this case, it was the attempt to establish an affinity between the unique capitalistic *spirit* and the *ethical* (i.e. normative) force of Protestantism.
>
> (ibid., pp. 256–257)

38 M. Weber, 'The Origins of Industrial Capitalism in Europe', in W.G. Runciman (ed.), *Max Weber: Selections in Translation*, trans. E. Matthews, Cambridge: Cambridge University Press, 1985, p. 340.
39 W.G. Runciman, 'Ideology: Introduction', in Runciman, *Max Weber*, pp.

135–136; Runciman notes that 'the question whether the influence of Protestantism was decisive in this way is virtually impossible to settle conclusively' (p. 135). See also G. Poggi, *Calvinism and the Capitalist Spirit: Max Weber's Protestant Ethic*, London: Macmillan, 1983.
40 A. Giddens, *Capitalism and Modern Social Theory: An Analysis of the Writings of Marx, Durkheim, and Weber*, Cambridge: Cambridge University Press, 1985, p. 179.
41 R. Brubaker, *The Limits of Rationality: An Essay on the Social and Moral Thought of Max Weber*, London: George Allen & Unwin, 1984, pp. 85–86.
42 M. Weber, *The Theory of Social and Economic Organization*, trans. A. Henderson and T. Parsons, ed. T. Parsons, New York: The Free Press, 1968, p. 248.
43 Ibid., p. 275.
44 R.J. Holton and B.S. Turner, *Max Weber on Economy and Society*, London: Routledge, 1989, p. 53.
45 D. Rueschemeyer, *Power and the Division of Labour*, Cambridge: Polity Press, 1986, p. 70. See also W. Mommsen, *Max Weber and German Politics, 1890–1920*, trans. M.S. Steinberg, Chicago: University of Chicago Press, 1984, pp. 433–440.
46 G. Therborn, *Science, Class and Society: On the Formation of Sociology and Historical Materialism*, London: New Left Books, 1976, p. 301.
47 Ibid.
48 K. Polanyi, *The Great Transformation*, New York: Farrar & Rinehart, 1944, p. 150.
49 D. Montgomery, *Citizen Worker: The Experience of Workers in the United States with Democracy and the Free Market during the Nineteenth Century*, Cambridge: Cambridge University Press, 1993, ch. 2. Montgomery remarks:

> over the course of a century a new machinery of 'law enforcement' had been created for America's cities. Magistrates paid by fees had either been replaced by or incorporated into a system of criminal justice that was based on the initiatives of salaried police, prosecutors, and judges. The capacity of the state to govern had been greatly increased where it mattered most: in the suppression of popular behavior that disrupted the mastery of society by capitalist markets.
>
> (ibid., p. 71)

50 Ibid., p. 114.
51 Ibid.
52 Weber, *The Theory of Social and Economic Organization*, p. 261. Poggi, G., 'Max Weber's Politics as a Vocation', lecture at the University of New South Wales, School of Sociology, 11 August 1999. In this lecture, Professor Poggi remarked that Weber was one of the few European intellectuals to take trends in the United States seriously, visiting there.
53 D. Montgomery, *Workers' Control in America: Studies in the History of Work, Technology, and Labor Struggles*, Cambridge: Cambridge University Press, 1979, p. 25.
54 Ibid., p. 27.
55 Ibid., p. 108.
56 R. Boyer and H. Morais, *Labor's Untold Story*, New York: United Electrical, Radio and Machine Workers of America, 1972, pp. 216–217. See also Braverman, *Labor and Monopoly Capital*. Braverman notes:

> the birth of the 'human relations' idea coincided with the Depression of the 1930s and the massive wave of working-class revolt that culminated in the unionization of the basic industries of the United States. In the illumination cast by these events, the workplace suddenly appeared not as a

system of informal group relations as in the interpretation of Mayo and his followers, but rather as a system of power, of class antagonisms. Industrial psychology and sociology never recovered from this blow.

(ibid., p. 145)

57 A. Johansson, 'Taylorism and the Rise of Organised Labour; United States and Sweden', in B. Gustafsson (ed.), *Power and Economic Institutions: Reinterpretations in Economic History*, Aldershot: Edward Elgar, 1991, pp. 302–336.
58 Feenberg, *Questioning Technology*, p. 80.
59 Ibid., p. 79.
60 D. Kettler and V. Meja, 'The End of Western Trade Unionism?: Social Progress after the Age of Progressivism', in J. Alexander and P. Sztompka (eds), *Rethinking Progress: Movements, Forces, and Ideas at the End of the Twentieth Century*, Boston: Unwin Hyman, 1990, p. 130.
61 M. Weber, 'Class, Status, Party', in H.H. Gerth and C. Wright Mills (eds), *From Max Weber: Essays in Sociology*, London: Routledge & Kegan Paul, 1974, p. 181. See also J. Barbalet, 'Marx and Weber as Class Theorists and the Relevance of Class Theory Today', in C. Jennett and R. Stewart (eds), *Three Worlds of Inequality: Race, Class and Gender*, South Melbourne: Macmillan, 1987, p. 140.
62 However, Durkheim's contribution to historical and methodological issues is evident in the range of studies he published in *L'Année Sociologique*. See E. Durkheim, *Emile Durkheim: Contributions to L'Année Sociologique*, Y. Nandan (ed.), trans. J. French *et al.*, New York: The Free Press, 1980.
63 S. Lukes, *Emile Durkheim: His Life and Work; A Historical and Critical Study*, London: Penguin, 1973, pp. 146–147.
64 K. Thompson, *Emile Durkheim*, New York: Tavistock, 1982, p. 82. However, Thompson argues that, 'by the end of *The Division of Labour*, it is clear that Durkheim had doubts about the possibility of organic solidarity emerging automatically from the increasing division of labour' (ibid.).
65 E. Durkheim, *The Division of Labour in Society*, trans. G. Simpson, Glencoe, IL: The Free Press, 1980, p. 79.
66 J. Alexander, *Theoretical Logic in Sociology: Volume Two: The Antinomies of Classical Thought: Marx and Durkheim*, Los Angeles: University of California Press, 1982, p. 155.
67 Durkheim, *The Division of Labour in Society*, p. 335.
68 Ibid., p. 109.
69 Ibid., p. 128.
70 Ibid., pp. 338–339.
71 Ibid., p. 368.
72 Ibid., p. 377.
73 Alexander, *Theoretical Logic in Sociology*, p. 155.
74 R. Perrin, 'Emile Durkheim's *Division of Labour* and the Shadow of Herbert Spencer', *The Sociological Quarterly*, vol. 36, no. 4, 1995, pp. 791–808.
75 Friedmann, *The Anatomy of Work*, p. 80.
76 Ibid., pp. 78–79.
77 A. Gouldner, *The Coming Crisis of Western Sociology*, London: Heinemann Educational Books, 1973, p. 250.
78 E. Mayo, *The Human Problems of an Industrial Civilization*, New York: Macmillan, 1933, p. 183. In his own discussion of anomie, Mayo realises that the source of resistance lies within the informal association and solidarity networks in the workplace. Writing during the Great Depression, Mayo notes that the Taylorist revolution did not create effective forms of group interaction, a point made obvious by the Hawthorne studies, which clearly revealed that

informal groups were the basis of workplace decision-making. Mayo urges that there is an 'immediate need to restore effective human collaboration' (p. 183).

79 Thompson, *Emile Durkheim*, p. 86.
80 Ibid., p. 88.
81 See E. Durkheim, *Socialism and Saint-Simon*, ed. A. Gouldner, trans. C. Sattler, London: Routledge & Kegan Paul, 1959.
82 A. Oberschall, *Social Conflict and Social Movements*, Englewood Cliffs, NJ: Prentice-Hall, 1973, pp. 135–136.
83 G. Rocher, *Talcott Parsons and American Sociology*, trans. B. Mennell and S. Mennell, London: Nelson, 1974, p. 7.
84 T. Parsons and N. Smelser, *Economy and Society: A Study in the Integration of Economic and Social Theory*, London: Routledge & Kegan Paul, 1964, p. 49.
85 Ibid., p. 148.
86 N. Mouzelis, *Sociological Theory: What Went Wrong?: Diagnosis and Remedies*, London: Routledge, 1995, p. 95.

2 Work and the post-industrial pessimists

1 J. Habermas, *Toward a Rational Society: Student Protest, Science and Politics*, trans. J.J. Shapiro, Boston: Beacon Press, 1970, pp. 81–122.
2 J. Habermas, *Knowledge and Human Interests*, trans. J.J. Shapiro, London: Heinemann Educational Books, 1972, pp. 43–63.
3 Ibid., p. 62.
4 G. Márkus, *Language and Production: A Critique of the Paradigms*, Dortrecht: D. Riedel, 1986, pp. 76–77.
5 Ibid., pp. 91–92.
6 J. Habermas, *The Philosophical Discourse of Modernity: Twelve Lectures*, trans. F. Lawrence, Cambridge: Polity Press, 1990, pp. 79–82.
7 A. Feenberg, *Questioning Technology*, London: Routledge, 1999, pp. 189–190. See also A. Honneth, *The Critique of Power: Reflective Stages in a Critical Social Theory*, Cambridge, MA: MIT Press, 1991, p. 254.
8 Habermas, *Toward a Rational Society*, p. 93.
9 J. Habermas, *The Theory of Communicative Action: Volume 1: Reason and the Rationalization of Society*, trans. T. McCarthy, Boston: Beacon Press, 1984, p. 273.
10 See J. Habermas, *The Theory of Communicative Action: Volume 2: System and Lifeworld: A Critique of Functionalist Reason*, trans. T. McCarthy, Cambridge: Polity Press, 1987, pp. 140–148. Habermas's uncoupling thesis relies on a reconstruction of Durkheim and Mead. Building on Weber's disenchantment thesis, Habermas argues that modernisation leaves social rationalisation processes less dependent on the *conscience collective* (ritualistic social solidarity) and more dependent on *normative agreement* that embodies communicative action. A legal process attempts to harmonise the processes of differentiation, steadily replacing the repressive function of law. At the same time, the growing complexity and formality of systems 'demoralise' organisations, also undermining traditions and opening up social identities to communication. Relying on Kohlberg's insights, Habermas further argues that the uncoupling of system and lifeworld is driven by successive shifts in moral consciousness that increasingly tie morality to our communicative attainments.
11 See, for example, J. Berger, 'The Linguistification of the Sacred and the Delinguistification of the Economy', in A. Honneth and H. Joas (eds), *Communicative Action: Essays on Jürgen Habermas's* The Theory of Communicative Action, Cambridge: Polity Press, 1991, pp. 165–180. See also T. McCarthy, 'Complexity and Democracy: or the Seducements of Systems Theory', in

Honneth and Joas, *Communicative Action*, pp. 119–139 and H. Joas, 'The Unhappy Marriage of Hermeneutics and Functionalism', in Honneth and Joas, *Communicative Action*, pp. 97–118.

12 Habermas's description of steering media is closer to Luhmann's version than to that of Parsons. See N. Luhmann, *The Differentiation of Society*, trans. S. Holmes and C. Larmore, New York: Columbia University Press, 1982, pp. 190–225.

13 Habermas, *Theory of Communicative Action: Volume 2*, pp. 267–273.

14 T. Parsons, *Sociological Theory and Modern Society*, New York: The Free Press, 1967, p. 280.

15 Habermas, *Theory of Communicative Action: Volume 2*, p. 311.

16 Ibid.

17 Honneth, *Critique of Power*, p. 252.

18 Ibid., pp. 302–303.

19 T. Burns and H. Flam, *The Shaping of Social Organization: Social Rule System Theory with Applications*, London: Sage, 1987, p. 233.

20 A. Honneth, 'The Social Dynamics of Disrespect: On the Location of Critical Theory Today', *Constellations*, vol. 1, no. 2, 1994, p. 267.

21 M.L. Kohn, *Class and Conformity: A Study in Values*, Illinois: The Dorsey Press, p. 189. See also M.L. Kohn and K.M. Slomczynski, *Social Structure and Self-Direction: A Comparative Analysis of the United States and Poland*, Cambridge, MA: Basil Blackwell, 1990, pp. 107–170.

22 For further empirical confirmation and discussion of Kohn's work, see L.D. Ritchie, 'Parents' Workplace Experiences and Family Communication Patterns', *Communications Research*, vol. 24, no. 2, April 1997, pp. 175–187.

23 C. Tilly and C. Tilly, *Work Under Capitalism*, Boulder, CO: Westview Press, 1998, p. 234.

24 Feenberg, *Questioning Technology*, p. 80.

25 See J. Habermas, *A Berlin Republic: Writings on Germany*, trans. S. Rendall, Lincoln, NB: University of Nebraska Press, 1997, pp. 135–136. Habermas's earlier views on law mainly dealt with the threats 'juridification' posed for the lifeworld. Then, he thought contesting social actors would need to put the system 'under siege' to exact change. Revising his view, he comments in *A Berlin Republic* that:

> the siege model is too defeatist, at least if you understand the divisions of powers in such a way that administrative and judicial authorities *employing* the law are to have limited access to the grounds mobilized in their full scope by legislative authorities in justifying their decisions. Today, the matters that need regulation are often such that the political legislator is in no position sufficiently to regulate them in advance. In such cases, it is up to administration and judicial authorities to give them concrete form and to continue their legal development, and these require discourses that have to do with grounding rather than with application. . . . [T]o be legitimate . . . a part of democratic will formation must make its way into the administration itself, and the judiciary that creates subsidiary laws must justify itself in the wider forum of a critique of law. In this respect, the sluice model counts on a more far-reaching democratization than the siege model does.
>
> (ibid.)

26 M. Power, 'Habermas and the Counterfactual Imagination', in M. Rosenfeld and A. Arato, *Habermas on Law and Democracy: Critical Exchanges*, Berkeley, CA: University of California Press, 1998, p. 224.

27 J. Habermas, 'The European Nation-State and the Pressures of Globalization',

New Left Review, no. 235, May/June 1999, p. 46. Habermas has increasingly identified the economy with the market system, steered by money. He now argues: 'The market's capacity to steer the economy and bring new information to light is beyond question' (ibid.).

28 J. Habermas, 'A Reply', in Honneth and Joas, *Communicative Action*, p. 261.

29 W. Forbath, 'Short-Circuit: A Critique of Habermas's Understanding of Law, Politics, and Economic Life', in Rosenfeld and Arato, *Habermas on Law and Democracy*, p. 280.

30 Ibid.

31 See J. Habermas, 'The New Obscurity: The Crisis of the Welfare State and the Exhaustion of Utopian Energies', in S. Weber Nicholsen (ed. and trans.), *The New Conservatism: Cultural Criticism and the Historians' Debate*, Cambridge, MA: MIT Press, 1994, pp. 48–70.

32 Touraine's work is also in part a product of the tensions between structuralists and existentialists that dominated post-war French social theory. A number of other social theories attempted to oppose structuralist and functionalist sociology in a similar way. See J. P. Sartre, *The Critique of Dialectical Reason*, A. Sheridan-Smith trans. and J. Rée (ed.), London: Verso, 1991. See also C. Castoriadis, *The Imaginary Institution of Society*, trans. K. Blamey, Cambridge: Polity Press, 1987.

33 A. Touraine, 'An Introduction to the Study of Social Movements', *Social Research*, vol. 52, no. 4, Winter 1985, pp. 784–787.

34 A. Touraine, *The Self-Production of Society*, trans. D. Coltman, Chicago: University of Chicago Press, 1977, p. 62.

35 Ibid., pp. 15–64. Three interrelated concepts convey Touraine's definition of the social field: *historicity*, a *cultural model*, and a *system of historical action*. *Historicity* describes social action that shapes social and cultural practices comprising a mode of accumulation, forms of knowledge and, critically, a cultural model. *The cultural model*, framed by a meta-social warrant, sets parameters for social conduct in a particular system of historical action (or a societal type). The cultural model sets out the legitimate field for both dominant and oppositional contest within a society (ibid., pp. 65–70) and as such is not neutral. It is still connected to the institutions and organisations that comprise society and thereby has some ideological content consistent with dominant interests. *Systems of historical action* define the tentative action structures that give rise to the patterns of order and movement that define societies and give them an observable 'coherence'. This system of action is cemented in a kind of semi-permanent tension between those resources and orientations promoting change (mobilisation, cultural model) and those promoting resources and orientations promoting order (needs and hierarchy) (ibid., pp. 65–115). The struggle over historicity is effectively a struggle over those elements (and counter-elements that *emerge* in struggle) of society where contests take shape – education, technological application, communication systems (ibid., pp. 79–85). Fractures between elements within the system of historical action are the source of potential crisis; the most important crisis, Touraine notes, is the crisis of *historicity* or the crisis between social movements and the organisational system (ibid., pp. 85–87). The events in France of May 1968 – that, according to Touraine, thematised resistance to technocratic control of society – are probably the most obvious example of the kind of crisis he has in mind.

36 Touraine, 'The Study of Social Movements', p. 776.

37 A. Touraine, *The Voice and the Eye: An Analysis of Social Movements*, trans. A. Duff, Cambridge: Cambridge University Press, 1981, pp. 102–138. Here, Touraine provides a comprehensive account of the relationships between social movements and the state.

38 Touraine, 'The Study of Social Movements', p. 787.
39 See D. Bell, *The Coming of Post-Industrial Society: A Venture in Social Fore-casting*, London: Heinemann Educational Books, 1974.
40 A. Touraine *et al.*, *Anti-Nuclear Protest: The Opposition to Nuclear Energy in France*, trans. P. Fawcett, Cambridge: Cambridge University Press, 1983. See also A. Touraine *et al.*, *Solidarity: The Analysis of a Social Movement: Poland, 1980–1981*, trans. D. Denby, Cambridge: Cambridge University Press, 1983.
41 Touraine, *The Voice and the Eye*, p. 213. Here, Touraine offers a detailed description of the intervention methodology (see especially pp. 102–212).
42 See A. Scott, 'Movements of Modernity: Some Questions of Theory, Method and Interpretation', in J. Clark and M. Diani (eds), *Alain Touraine*, London: Falmer, 1996, p. 89. Scott argues that 'Touraine is prevented from fully realizing a non-positivist methodology because of his adherence to a general theory of social development.' As such, it is difficult to be certain whether the detection of the 'highest level of meaning' reflects the prior conception of social development by Touraine or truly reflects the actors' actual self-understanding.
43 The CGT is the Confédération Générale du Travail, the CFDT is the Confédération Française Démocratique du Travail and the FO is Force Ouvrière. The militants were steel, railway, chemical industry, computer-technical, and unskilled workers.
44 A. Touraine, M. Wieviorka and F. Dubet, *The Workers' Movement*, trans. I. Patterson, Cambridge: Cambridge University Press, 1987.
45 S. Mallet, *The New Working Class*, Nottingham: Spokesman Books, 1975. See also A. Gorz, *Strategy for Labor: A Radical Proposal*, Boston: Beacon Press, 1968.
46 Touraine *et al.*, *The Workers' Movement*, pp. 3–17. Touraine and his colleagues highlight the advantages of their social movement/societal type model over alternative models of interpreting labour movement such as the 'community defence', 'proletarian revolt', 'collective bargaining', and 'political representation' approaches.
47 Ibid., pp. 35–36.
48 Ibid., p. 280.
49 Ibid., pp. 206–207. They argue that:

> first, by rejecting industrial culture [the neo-proletariat] has abandoned the whole area of conflict between workers and those who manage production for control over the resources of industrial society. Second, by remaining aloof from disputes over the organization of production it dissociates itself from all skilled or unskilled workers for whom work is the central meaning of their struggle.... And third, without any positive principle to set against the labour market on which it is totally dependent, its political action can only be organized by accepting the leadership of external political or intellectual agents very different from the sort of positive, social appearance presented by the skilled workers who have given the workers' movement a project for society.

50 Ibid., pp. 109–112.
51 A. Touraine, 'Au-delà d'une société du travail et des mouvements sociaux?', *Sociologie et sociétés*, vol. 23, no. 2, Autumn 1991, p. 31. My translation: 'the business is no longer the basic cell of a society that has ceased to be an industrial society.... The success of business no longer depends on its ethics, Protestant or otherwise, but on its strategic capacity and its mobilisation of financial resources and also technical and human resources. It thus creates an immense distance between the two actors of industrial society who are so close to each other that they were almost entirely defined by their relations and con-

flicts, the worker and business. The worker becomes a consumer, and that which was an organisation in the sociological sense of the term becomes truly again a business, defined by its position in the global capital, goods and services markets.'

52 Touraine *et al. The Worker's Movement*, pp. 222–224.

53 Ibid., pp. 275–276

54 J. Alexander and M. Pia Lara, 'Honneth's New Critical Theory of Recognition', *New Left Review*, no. 220, 1996, p. 126 n. 2.

55 Touraine, 'The Study of Social Movements', p. 781.

56 M. Hanagan, 'Social Movements: Incorporation, Disengagement, and Opportunities – A Long View', in M. Giugni, D. McAdam and C. Tilly (eds), *From Contention to Democracy*, Lanham, MD: Rowman & Littlefield, 1998, pp. 25–29.

57 Ibid., pp. 28–29.

58 A. Touraine, 'L'ombre d'un mouvement', in A. Touraine *et al.*, *Le Grand Refus: Réfléxions sur la grève de décembre 1995*, Paris: Fayard, 1995, pp. 11–102.

59 Scott, 'Movements of Modernity', p. 85. Scott notes:

> empirically, new social movements remain, as Touraine is quite aware, stubbornly diverse in their aims, organizational characteristics and strategies. Given this, what warrant can there be for claiming that one level of meaning is 'higher' than the others, and that there is only one potential social movement which can attain it?
>
> (ibid.)

60 Ibid., p. 83.

61 See in particular, C. Offe, 'Full Employment: Asking the Wrong Question?', *Dissent*, Winter, 1995, pp. 77–81. Also J. Keane and J. Owens, *After Full Employment*, London: Hutchinson, 1987; and Habermas, 'The New Obscurity', pp. 48–70. See in addition J. Rifkin, *The End of Work: The Decline of the Global Labor Force and the Dawn of the Post-Market Era*, New York: Jeremy P. Tarcher/Putnam, 1995; and A. Gorz, *Farewell to the Working Class: An Essay on Post-industrial Socialism*, trans. M. Sonenscher, London: Pluto Press, 1982.

62 C. Offe, *Contradictions of the Welfare State*, ed. J. Keane, London: Hutchinson, 1984, p. 153.

63 Other writers, on both the Left and the Right, captured the increasing difficulties of welfare states in managing the economy and social interests alike. These 'crisis of democracy' debates in the 1970s illuminated the problem of legitimacy from competing political perspectives. O'Connor's thesis on the fiscal crisis was of importance in this discussion, linking the problem of generating 'mass loyalty' to the growing fiscal imbalances emerging from social expenditures. See J. O'Connor, *The Fiscal Crisis of the State*, New York: St Martin's Press, 1973, pp. 69–70. O'Connor envisaged the growth of a 'social-industrial' complex as a viable solution to rising social expenditures and slowing productivity where the state creates 'social investment' and new employment for the marginal population, redeeming some of its expenditures through the productivity of a class of (indirectly productive) skilled service workers (ibid., p. 221). On the right, the 'crisis of democracy' theorists argued that grassroots agitation had undermined the proper functioning of democracies. See M. Crozier, S. Huntington, and J. Watanuki, *The Crisis of Democracy: Report on the Governability of Democracies to the Trilateral Commission*, New York: New York University Press, 1975.

64 Pollock's seminal writings on organised capitalism, neatly summarised in 'State

Capitalism: Its Possibilities and Limitations', provide a crucial body of writing on the state, influenced both Habermas and Offe. See F. Pollock, 'State Capitalism: Its Possibilities and Limitations', in A. Arato and E. Gebhardt (eds), *The Essential Frankfurt School Reader*, New York: Urizen Books, 1978, p. 73.

65 Offe, *Contradictions*, p. 139.

66 Ibid.

67 Ibid., p. 39. Offe argues that state intervention in the economy follows the rules of both *positive and negative subordination*. Positive subordination involves orienting the institutional and regulatory framework towards the performance of the capitalist economy; negative subordination involves limiting the potential adverse influences of the institutional framework within the economic system. These forms of subordination create clear structures for accumulation in the form of property law and rights, anti-trust provisions, administrative services and planning as well as social resources for investment. However, the contradictions within economic systems produce an institutional and regulatory build-up that becomes the potential source of interference in commodity production. On the unemployment dilemma, see pp. 198–200.

68 See in particular, Crozier *et al.*, *Crisis of Democracy*; and N. Luhmann, *Political Theory in the Welfare State*, trans. J. Bednarz, Jr., Berlin: Walter de Gruyter, 1990, pp. 35–36. Luhmann bemoans the excessive intervention of politics into the self-sustaining functions of the modern state – echoing 'crisis of democracy' arguments (ibid., pp. 144–145).

69 Offe, *Contradictions*, p. 59.

70 Ibid., p. 140.

71 Ibid., p. 168.

72 Ibid., p. 297.

73 Offe, *Disorganized Capitalism*, pp. 66–71. Offe argues that there are four options open to the state in labour market policy: (i) encouraging *inclusion* on the basis of flexibility and coercion; (ii) industrial 'civil rights'; (iii) encouraging *exclusion* on the basis of supporting excluded populations through welfare; and (iv) expanding work outside the labour market, i.e. in an 'informal' sector (ibid.). Offe argues that the coercive expansion of the labour market only reproduces the 'fiction' of a society based on exchange relationships and that traditional welfare expansion can only work if the needs for social security are relatively limited. The goal of instituting a right to work and broader industrial civil rights would only accelerate trends towards 'jobless growth' by altering strategic calculations of employers (ibid., p. 71). Thus, Offe sees hope in the expansion and institutionalisation of an informal sector.

74 Ibid., p. 6. By 'disorganised' capitalism, Offe means the *failure* of established means of organising interests to mediate between social power and political authority.

75 Ibid., p. 3. Before Offe, Pollock also wrote of a similar scenario, in F. Pollock, *The Economic and Social Consequences of Automation*, trans. W. Henderson and W. Chaloner, Oxford: Basil Blackwell, 1957, pp. 79–92.

76 Offe, *Disorganized Capitalism*, pp. 108–127. Offe elaborates each component of service employment 'supply' and 'demand' in some detail, which I have not attempted to summarise here.

77 Ibid., pp. 120–122. This argument has not proved entirely satisfactory in light of patterns of employment growth in many advanced industrial nations. The growth of service employment (and the conditions for such growth) has implications for the analysis of service work and its place in the occupational class structure more generally. See G. Esping-Andersen, Z. Assimakopoulou, and K. van Kersbergen, 'Trends in Contemporary Class Structuration: A Six-Nation Comparison', in G. Esping-Andersen (ed.), *Changing Classes: Stratifica-*

tion and Mobility in Post-industrial Societies, London: Sage, 1993, pp. 32–57. See also J. Jacobs, 'Careers in the US Service Economy', in Esping-Andersen, *Changing Classes*, pp. 195–224.

78 K. Hinrichs, C. Offe, and H. Wiesenthal, 'The Crisis of the Welfare State and Alternative Modes of Work Redistribution', *Thesis Eleven*, no. 10/11, 1984/85, p. 43.

79 Offe, *Disorganized Capitalism*, pp. 187–188. Offe (with Helmut Wiesenthal) argues:

> for the sake of their power, unions are forced to maintain a precarious balance between mobilization of resources and mobilization of activity, between size and collective identity, and between bureaucracy (which allows them to *accumulate* power) and internal democracy (which allows them to *exercise* power). None of these dilemmas applies with comparable seriousness to business and employers' organizations for the reason that they do not depend on internal democracy, collective identity, or the willingness to engage in solidary action.
>
> (ibid. authors' emphasis)

80 Ibid., p. 218.
81 Ibid., p. 148.
82 Ibid., p. 141; see also Gorz, *Farewell to the Working Class*, pp. 66–75. Gorz develops this argument more polemically, describing the decline of the work ethic and sense of class as the basis for his description of the 'non class of non proletarians'.
83 H. Applebaum, *The American Work Ethic and the Changing Workforce*, Westport, CT: Greenwood, 1998, pp. 215–220. See also S.M Lipset, 'The Work Ethic, Then and Now', *Journal of Labor Research*, vol. 13, no. 1, Winter, 1992, pp. 45–54; and Tilly and Tilly, *Work under Capitalism*, p. 164. The Tillys cite Yankelovich's recent study suggesting that there has been a dramatic upward shift in the number of Americans who identify having a *meaningful* job as being personally important.
84 C. Offe, 'New Social Movements: Challenging the Boundaries of Institutional Politics', *Social Research*, vol. 52, no. 4, Winter 1985, p. 834.
85 Offe, *Modernity and the State*, p. 172. Offe increasingly uses rational choice theory, and not political accounts, to explain the breakdown in support for the welfare state. He argues this breakdown: 'leaves behind ... an interpretive pattern that is deeply mistrustful of social policies as "public goods", and that tends to unravel such policies in terms of gains and losses, exploitation, freeriding ... that is, in individualist "economic man" categories, the behavioural consequences of which are best captured and predicted by rational choice theory.'
86 See M. Gilens, *Why Americans Hate Welfare: Race, Media, and the Politics of Antipoverty Policy*, Chicago: University of Chicago Press, 1999, p. 54. See also R. Jowell *et al.*, *British Social Attitudes: The 12th Report*, Aldershot: Dartmouth Publishing, 1999, p. xv.
87 Offe, *Modernity and the State: East, West*, Cambridge: Polity Press, 1996, pp. 23–24.
88 Ibid., p. 10.
89 Ibid., pp. 135–139. Offe discusses the three 'pure' steering principles of need satisfaction: market, state, and community.
90 Ibid., pp. 208–209.
91 Ibid., p. 214.
92 J. Goul Andersen and J.B. Jensen, *Different Routes to Improved Employment in Europe*, Aalborg: Centre for Comparative Welfare Studies, 2002.

3 Work without limit? Work and welfare in the US model

1 See J. Stiglitz, 'The Roaring Nineties', *The Atlantic Monthly*, October 2002, p. 75. Stiglitz offers a similar definition.
2 G. Hywood, 'The US Battle for Hearts and Minds', *The Sydney Morning Herald*, 4 February 2000, p. 15.
3 'Europe's New Left', *The Economist*, 12–18 Feb. 2000, p. 21.
4 See R. Blank and D. Ellwood, *The Clinton Legacy for America's Poor*, NBER Working Paper Series, Working Paper no. 8437, Cambridge, MA: National Bureau of Economic Research, August 2001, p. 2. See also R.K. Weaver, 'Ending Welfare As We Know It', in M. Weir (ed.), *The Social Divide: Political Parties and the Future of Activist Government*, Washington, DC: Brookings Institution Press, 1998, p. 362.
5 See J. Galbraith 'The Real American Model', 2003, online. Available at www.opendemocracy.org (accessed 23 October 2003). Galbraith rightly criticises the view that the market was the source of America's achievements in the 1990s. He points out that America spent more in its (more) privatised sectors of health care and education, and adopted very expansionary monetary policy, fuelling an expansion in demand.
6 L. Mishel, J. Bernstein, and J. Schmitt, *The State of Working America, 1998–99*, Ithaca, NY: Cornell University Press, 1999, p. 380.
7 See, for example, S.M. Lipset, *Revolution and Counterrevolution: Change and Persistence in Social Structures*, New York: Anchor Books, 1970, p. 150; S.M. Lipset, 'The Work Ethic, Then and Now', *Journal of Labor Research*, vol. 13, no. 1, Winter 1992, pp. 45–54. As Lipset reminds us, understanding American exceptionalism has always been a major preoccupation in the international Left.
8 S.M. Lipset, 'The Decline of Class Ideologies', in T. Nichols Clark and S.M. Lipset (eds), *The Breakdown of Class Politics: A Debate on Post-Industrial Stratification*, Baltimore, MD: Johns Hopkins University Press, 2001, p. 264.
9 Ibid., p. 265.
10 See S. Svallfors, 'Worlds of Welfare and Attitudes to Redistribution: A Comparison of Eight Western Nations', *European Sociological Review*, vol. 13, 1997, pp. 283–304.
11 Ibid., p. 296.
12 V. Hattam, *Labor Visions and State Power; The Origins of Business Unionism in the United States*, Princeton, NJ: Princeton University Press, 1994; and W. Forbath, *Law and the Shaping of the American Labor Movement*, Cambridge, MA: Harvard University Press, 1991. See also J. Currie and J. Ferrie, *Strikes and the Law in the U.S., 1881–1894: New Evidence on the Origins of American Exceptionalism*, NBER Working Paper Series, no. 5368, Cambridge, MA: National Bureau of Economic Research, November 1995, pp. 1–48. Currie and Ferrie claim American labour may have turned to business unionism because earlier (late nineteenth-century) pro-labour legislation did not produce expected gains. This is probably because legal reforms encountered such a layer of business resistance that they were rendered relatively inoperative. See also D. Montgomery, *The Fall of the House of Labor: The Workplace, the State, and American Labor Activism, 1865–1925*, Cambridge: Cambridge University Press, 1987, pp. 5–7.
13 D. Montgomery, *Citizen Worker: The Experience of Workers in the United States with Democracy and the Free Market during the Nineteenth Century*, Cambridge: Cambridge University Press, 1993. In *Citizen Worker*, Montgomery shows that nineteenth-century political and business power in the United States was extraordinarily resistant to the struggles for labour and

social reforms. See also C. Tilly and C. Tilly, *Work under Capitalism*, Boulder, CO: Westview Press, 1998, p. 249.

14 For an account of the challenges to the original Wagner Act during the 1940s, see R. Adams, 'North American Industrial Relations: Divergent Trends in Canada and the U.S.', *International Labour Review*, vol. 128, no. 1, 1989, p. 55.

15 P. Sexton, *The War on Labor and the Left: Understanding America's Unique Conservatism*, Boulder, CO: Westview Press, 1992, pp. 140–161. See also J. Schor, *The Overworked American: The Unexpected Decline of Leisure*, New York: Basic Books, 1990, p. 77. The prevailing view in the labour movement conceded determination of working hours fell within the locus of the 'right to manage': 'although shorter hours had traditionally been a demand for all of labor, it came to be increasingly associated with the left wing' (ibid., p. 77).

16 M. Weir, A.S. Orloff, and T. Skocpol, 'Understanding American Social Politics', in M. Weir, A.S. Orloff, and T. Skocpol (eds), *The Politics of Social Policy in the United States*, Princeton, NJ: Princeton University Press, 1988, p. 21.

17 T. Skocpol, *Social Policy in the United States: Future Possibilities in Historical Perspective*, Princeton, NJ: Princeton University Press, 1995, pp. 246–248.

18 M. Weir, 'The Federal Government and Unemployment: The Frustration of Policy Innovation from the New Deal to the Great Society', in Weir *et al.*, *The Politics of Social Policy in the United States*, pp. 149–190. Weir sums up reformist losses: 'During the New Deal and immediately post-war periods supporters of the administration's employment policy lost four battles: the attempts to reorganize the executive branch, strengthen the National Resources Planning Board, enact the Full Employment Bill, and federalize the Employment Service' (ibid., p. 163).

19 This is not to say American labour has not been an important and effective political lobbyist, especially within the Democrats. See, in particular, T. Dark, *The Unions and the Democrats: An Enduring Alliance*, Ithaca, NY: ILR Press, 1999.

20 G. Esping-Andersen, *The Three Worlds of Welfare Capitalism*, Princeton: Princeton University Press, 1990, pp. 162–190. Gøsta Esping-Andersen points out that the commitment to public sector employment was much greater in Europe (and in other English-speaking nations) than in the United States.

21 Skocpol, *Social Policy in the United States*, pp. 244–245.

22 M. Weir, *Politics and Jobs: The Boundaries of Employment Policy in the United States*, Princeton, NJ: Princeton University Press, 1992, p. 162.

23 Weir, 'The Federal Government and Unemployment', p. 189.

24 R. Brenner, 'The Economics of Global Turbulence: A Special Report on the World Economy, 1950–1998', *New Left Review*, no. 229, May–June 1998, p. 139.

25 OECD, *Employment Outlook*, June, Paris: OECD, 1999, p. 86. See also *The Economist*, 'Working Man's Burden', 6–12 February 1999, p. 88.

26 H.N. Wheeler, 'Industrial Relations in the United States of America', in G. Bamber and R. D. Lansbury, eds, *International and Comparative Relations: A Study of Industrialised Market Economies*, 2nd edition, Sydney: Allen & Unwin, 1993, p. 70.

27 Ibid., p. 78.

28 See Brenner, 'The Economics of Global Turbulence', p. 60. For a first-hand account of the union-busting industry, see M.J. Levitt, *Confessions of a Union Buster*, New York: Crown Publishers, 1993, p. 150. Levitt's comments are insightful:

Union avoidance was the hot topic and the hot business of the decade. Articles promoting anti-union personnel policies appeared by the dozens, in periodicals ranging from *Personnel* and the *Journal of Industrial Relations* to the *Harvard Business Review*. The number of anti-union consulting companies climbed into the hundreds, and labor law firms turned increasingly to the profitable business of counter-organizing. Union-evasion seminars proliferated, some targeting the public sector, where the most aggressive organizing was taking place. As an indication of the acceptance gained by union busters during the 1970s, many seminarists managed to offer their fare on the campuses of colleges and universities, both private and public, quite a step up in respectability and authority from the hotel conference rooms of the past. Some universities – which, let us not forget, are employers as well as schools – actually sponsored the events and granted continuing education credit to program attendees.

(ibid., p. 150)

29 K. Moody, *Workers in a Lean World: Unions in the International Economy*, London: Verso, 1999, pp. 23–34. Moody gives us a sense of the importance of replacement workers during the 1990s in his account of three concurrent strikes in Illinois led by the United Auto Workers against Caterpillar, the Allied Industrial Workers against Staley and United Steelworkers against Bridgestone/Firestone.

30 A glance at the annual research compiled by the international labour movement into violations of union rights hardly inspires optimism. The United States is repeatedly mentioned for its violations. See K. Hodder, *Annual Survey of Violations of Trade Union Rights*, Report of the ICFTU [International Confederation of Free Trade Unions], Section: 'The United States of America', 1999, p. 2 (no page numbers listed). The survey notes that at least one in ten workers campaigning for union representation in the US is fired (ibid., p. 1). There are frequent threats of closure, and actual closure, against workers attempting to organise as well as aggressive anti-union campaigns and surveillance, and widespread use of the law and other methods to avoid bargaining with unions *even when* union recognition is won (ibid., pp. 2–3). And about 40 per cent of American public sector workers are still excluded from collective bargaining. The report further notes: 'an under-funded labour inspectorate and inadequate penalties for employers who violate the law mean that legally established labour standards covering wages and hours, child labour and workplace safety are inadequately enforced' (ibid., p. 5). The report also mentions the increasing incidence of employers provoking strikes in attempts to de-unionise.

31 P. Crampton and J. Tracy, *The Use of Replacement Workers in Union Contract Negotiations: The U.S. Experience, 1980–1989*, NBER Working Paper Series, no. 5106, Cambridge, MA: National Bureau of Economic Research, 1995, p. 4.

32 Ibid., p. 18.

33 Hodder, *Annual Survey of Violations of Trade Union Rights*, p. 4.

34 D. Gordon, 'Underpaid Workers, Bloated Corporations: Two Pieces in the Puzzle of U.S. Economic Decline', *Dissent*, Spring 1996, p. 28. See also Brenner, 'The Economics of Global Turbulence', p. 60. Brenner demonstrates the link between the number of illegal firings of union activists and the profit crisis.

35 D. Gordon, 'Underpaid Workers, Bloated Corporations', p. 32.

36 Ibid., p. 30.

37 Ibid., p. 27.

38 P. Taylor, 'The Dynamics of US Managerialism and the American Corporations', in D. Slater and P. Taylor (eds), *The American Century: Consensus and Coercion in the Projection of American Power*, Oxford: Blackwell, 1999, p. 60.
39 Mishel *et al.*, *The State of Working America*, p. 20.
40 Ibid., p. 21.
41 J. Laabs, 'Has Downsizing Really Missed its Mark?', *Workforce*, April 1999, p. 33.
42 Mishel *et al.*, *The State of Working America*, pp. 236–239.
43 See L. Williams, 'Rethinking Low-Wage Markets and Dependency', *Politics & Society*, vol. 25, no. 4, p. 542.
44 M. Gilens, *Why Americans Hate Welfare: Race, Media, and the Politics of Antipoverty Policy*, Chicago: University of Chicago Press, 1999, pp. 42–59. Gilens points out that specific policies for the poor such as Medicaid, legal aid, and public housing have as much support among wealthy Americans as among the poor.
45 Ibid., p. 172.
46 For some detailed analysis of polling trends on welfare during this period, see Weaver, 'Ending Welfare As We Know It', pp. 372–376.
47 F.F. Piven and R. Cloward, *The Breaking of the American Social Compact*, New York: The Free Press, 1997, pp. 255–256.
48 Blank and Ellwood, *The Clinton Legacy for America's Poor*, p. 10. Blank and Ellwood point out that the two previous Republican administrations had been supportive of the EITC. See also R.K. Weaver, 'Ending Welfare As We Know It', p. 380.
49 Gilens, *Why Americans Hate Welfare*, p. 216.
50 See, for instance, M. Sawicky (ed.), *The End of Welfare?: The Consequences of Federal Devolution for the Nation*, Washington, DC: Economic Policy Institute, 2000.
51 Academic conservatives like Lawrence Mead have been critical of the elite legitimation of social policy. See L. Mead, 'The Rise of Paternalism', in L. Mead (ed.), *The New Paternalism: Supervisory Approaches to Poverty*, Washington, DC: Brookings Institution Press, 1997, p. 24. Mead sums up the new conservative approach as follows:

> Established policy, in short, leaves people free to choose their own course in life. It assumes that the poor, like other people, will conform to the law and the interest of society. But they are free to do otherwise, and if they break the rules, government proceeds against them only after the fact. It seeks to forestall trouble only by threatening *eventual* sanctions. Paternalist social policy changes both emphases. Compared with the traditional approach, paternalist welfare programs become more demanding. Instead of a philosophy of entitlement, they emphasize a social contract, meaning that recipients have to satisfy behavioral requirements, such as working or staying in school, as well as income rules to receive aid. This requires new administrative structures that supervise their activities.

(ibid., p. 24)

See also C. Murray, *Losing Ground: American Social Policy, 1950–1980*, New York: Basic Books, 1995.
52 F.F. Piven and R. Cloward, 'We Should Have Made a Plan!', *Politics & Society*, vol. 25, no. 4, 1997, p. 525.
53 See Weaver, 'Ending Welfare As We Know It', p. 395. Kent Weaver notes that the legislation did meet the demands to put time limits on welfare but it

disappointed conservatives who tried to use welfare reform to (putatively) reduce out-of-wedlock births.

54 For further details of the changes in the Act, see Blank and Ellwood, *The Clinton Legacy for America's Poor*, pp. 15–23. See also D. Eitzen and M. Zinn, 'The Shrinking Welfare State: The New Welfare Legislation and Families', paper presented at the Thematic Session 'The Shrinking State: New Forms of Social Inequality', Annual Meeting of the American Sociological Association, San Francisco, August 1998.

55 R. Scherer, 'From Welfare to … Unions?', *The Christian Science Monitor*, 8 October 1997.

56 C. Cook, 'Plucking Workers: Tyson Foods Looks to the Welfare Rolls for a Captive Labor Force', *The Progressive*, August 1998, pp. 28–31.

57 Ibid., p. 29.

58 Piven and Cloward, *The Breaking of the American Social Compact*, p. 187. Piven and Cloward underline the extent of decommodification (removal of the working-age population from the labour market) that welfare programmes entail.

59 'Nation's Leaders in Welfare to Gather for One America Conference', *Reuters Report*, 3 August 1999.

60 W. Holstein and W. Cohen, 'Ready, Aim, Hire: Corporate America and Workfare as We Know it', *U.S. News and World Report*, 31 March 1997, p. 51.

61 Ibid., p. 49.

62 Eitzen and Zinn, 'The Shrinking Welfare State'.

63 Ibid.

64 See J. Visser and A. Hemerijck, *A Dutch Miracle: Job Growth, Welfare Reform and Corporatism in the Netherlands*, Amsterdam: University of Amsterdam Press, 1997. The number of part-time workers in the workforce in the United States did not increase during the 1990s and has remained quite steady over a longer time period. See OECD, *Employment Outlook 2001*, OECD: Paris, 2002, p. 319.

65 Out of the ten countries surveyed, the United States has a labour force participation rate for workers aged between 55 and 64 exceeded only by Sweden.

66 Other European countries outside our survey, like Norway, have maintained very high employment-to-population ratios, and continue to outperform the United States on this measure.

67 The percentage of the working-age population who are beneficiaries of income support from the state is lower in the United States than in any of the other countries surveyed. Income support to the working-age population includes disability and sickness payments, unemployment benefits, and family payments.

68 Galbraith, 'The Real American Model'.

69 See J. Goul Andersen and J.B. Jensen, *Different Routes to Improved Employment in Europe*, Centre for Comparative Welfare Studies Working Paper, Aalborg University, no. 22, 2002.

70 See F. Scharpf, *The Viability of Advanced Welfare States in the International Economy: Vulnerabilities and Options*, Working Paper 99/9, Cologne: Max Planck Institute for the Study of Societies, 1999, p. 12. Scharpf insightfully observes that 'More surprising is the employment performance of Continental welfare states with intermediate tax burdens: On average, they have as little private sector employment as the Scandinavian countries, and as few public sector jobs as the Anglo-Saxon countries' (ibid.).

71 I would consider the Dutch model to combine elements of the American approach with a European level of social support. The Dutch have increased part-time private sector employment, representing a kind of new compromise

between market employment and state social support. The Netherlands spends the second largest amount of its GDP on income support for its working-age population (expenditure exceeded only by Sweden).

72 Mishel *et al.*, *The State of Working America*, pp. 384–385. See also E. Appelbaum, 'What Explains Employment Developments in the US?', *Economic Policy Institute Briefing Paper*, Washington, DC: Economic Policy Institute, November 2000, p. 5.

73 Mishel *et al.*, *The State of Working America*, p. 385.

74 B. Western and K. Beckett, 'How Unregulated Is the U.S. Labor Market? The Penal System as a Labor Market Institution', *American Journal of Sociology*, vol. 104, 1999, pp. 1030–1060.

75 See *The Economist*, 8 June 1996, pp. 23–25. Crime rates – especially violent crimes against people – are high in the United States because of unusually lenient gun laws, reflecting in part the power of the American firearms lobby. And prisons are increasingly filled with drug dealers and users. *The Economist* notes, 'between 1980 and now, the proportion of those sentenced to prison for non-violent property crimes has remained about the same (two-fifths). The number of those sentenced for drugs has soared (from one-tenth to one-third).'

76 Western and Beckett, 'How Unregulated Is the U.S. Labor Market?', p. 1041.

77 Ibid.

78 Ibid., p. 1052.

79 Ibid., p. 1031.

80 K. Silverstein, 'America's Private Gulag', in D. Burton-Rose, D. Pens, and P. Wright (eds), *The Celling of America: An Inside Look at the U.S. Prison Industry*, Maine: Common Courage Press, 1998, pp. 156–163. Silverstein writes about the growth of private prisons, in particular the U.S. Corrections Corporation, which dominates the industry, and documents corporate interest in prisons:

> private transport companies have lucrative contracts to move prisoners within and across state lines; health care companies supply jails with doctors and nurses; food service firms provide prisoners with meals. High-tech firms are also moving into the field; the Que-Tel Corp hopes for vigorous sales of its new system whereby prisoners are bar-coded and guards carry scanners to monitor their movements. Phone companies such as AT&T chase after the enormously lucrative prison business.
>
> (ibid., p. 162)

81 Mishel *et al.*, *The State of Working America*, pp. 189–190. Minimum wages moved little, even in nominal terms, during the 1980s because of the 'unemployment effect' argument, which enjoyed wide support in Congress.

82 Ibid., p. 139.

83 Ibid.

84 Ibid., pp. 172–173.

85 Ibid., p. 366.

86 See OECD, *Employment Outlook 1996*, Paris: OECD, 1996, p. 72, Table 3.2.

87 See OECD, *Employment Outlook 2001*, Paris: OECD, 2001, p. 108.

88 Mishel *et al.*, *The State of Working America*, p. 362.

89 L. Mishel, J. Bernstein and H. Boushey, *The State of Working America 2002–2003*, Ithaca, NY: Cornell University Press, 2003, Tables 2.7 and 2.8

90 Ibid.

91 B. Western and K. Healy, 'Explaining the OECD Wage Slowdown: Recession or Labour Decline?', *European Sociological Review*, vol. 15, no. 3, 1999, p. 245. See also Michel *et al.*, *The State of Working America*, pp. 183–189.

92 Mishel *et al.*, *The State of Working America*, p. 369.
93 Ibid., p. 388.
94 Bureau of Labor Statistics, *Occupations with the Largest Growth, 1998–2008, MLR: The Editor's Desk*, 29 December 1999, online. Available at: http://www.bls.gov (accessed 23 October 2003).
95 *High Hopes, Little Trust*, 1999, online. Available at: http://www.aflcio.org (accessed 23 October 2003).
96 D. Card and A. Krueger, *Myth and Measurement: The New Economics of the Minimum Wage*, Princeton, NJ: Princeton University Press, 1995.
97 S. Dowrick and J. Quiggan, 'A Survey of the Literature on Minimum Wages', unpublished manuscript, Canberra: The Australian National University, February 2003.
98 J. Schor, *The Overspent American: Upscaling, Downshifting and the New Consumer*, New York: Basic Books, 1998, p. 99.
99 Reserve Bank of Australia, 'Consumer Credit and Household Finances', *Reserve Bank of Australia Bulletin*, June 1999, pp. 15–16.
100 Mishel *et al.*, *The State of Working America*, p. 383.
101 A. Boltho, 'What's Wrong with Europe?', *New Left Review*, no. 22, July–August 2003, p. 10.
102 Blank and Ellwood, *The Clinton Legacy for America's Poor*, p. 2.
103 Piven and Cloward, *The Breaking of the American Social Compact*, p. 256.
104 P. Loprest, 'Families Who Left Welfare: Who are They and How are They Doing?', *Assessing the New Federalism*, Discussion Paper no. 2, Washington, DC: The Urban Institute, 1999, p. 23.
105 Ibid.
106 Blank and Ellwood, *The Clinton Legacy for America's Poor*, p. 54.
107 Ibid.
108. J. Chapman and J. Bernstein, 'Falling through the safety net', EPI Issue Brief, No. 191, 11 April 2003, online. Available at: http://www.epinet.org (accessed 23 October 2003).
109 K. Edin, 'Plenary Address: Work is Not Enough', paper presented at Social Policy Research Centre Conference, Sydney: University of New South Wales, 9–11 July 2003.
110 J. Pixley, *Citizenship and Employment: Investigating Post-industrial Options*, Cambridge: Cambridge University Press, 1994.
111 C. Jencks, L. Perman, and L. Rainwater, 'What is a Good Job?: A New Measure of Labor-Market Success', *American Journal of Sociology*, vol. 93, no. 6, 1988, pp. 1322–1357. Jencks *et al.* argue that control over working hours, training, and the educational requirements of work are non-pay factors that contribute to job satisfaction while repetitive tasks and frequent supervision detract from satisfaction. Long working hours and low skill work thus count towards job dissatisfaction and deeper stresses on social life. A study commissioned by the Australian Council of Trade Unions (ACTU) has documented the aspects of work respondents thought to be unsatisfactory: long working hours or underemployment (indicating a lack of control over working hours) and distress at surveillance and supervision in work were frequent complaints. See Australian Council of Trade Unions, 'Employment Security & Working Hours: A National Survey of Current Workplaces', 1999, online. Available at: http://www.actu.asn.au (accessed 23 October 2003).
112 C. Ross and J. Mirowsky, 'Households, Employment and the Sense of Control', *Social Psychology Quarterly*, vol. 55, no. 3, 1992, p. 230.
113 Ibid.
114 R. Crutchfield and S. Pitchford, 'Work and Crime: The Effects of Labor Strat-

ification', *Social Forces*, vol. 76, no. 1, September 1997, p. 112. In their study of the relationship between work history and crime, Crutchfield and Pitchford provide evidence contradicting the assumption that work, *on any terms*, produces non-criminogenic behaviour. In their analysis of US National Longitudinal Survey of Youth data they suggest:

> most commonsensical interpretations argue that people engage in crime to supplement their material needs or desires, or because of anger and frustration. No doubt this occurs. But our analysis demonstrates, first, that it is not simply the income of work that is important; it is the stability that goes with good work that inhibits criminality. Second, the criminogenic influence of employment patterns operate not simply through the employment status of isolated individuals. The vitality of the local labor market also matters, because the concentration of marginally employed people is itself criminogenic.
>
> (ibid., p. 112)

115 Gabrielle Meagher and I explore the problem of fundamentalist solutions to complex social policy problems in G. Meagher and S. Wilson, 'Complexity and Practical Knowledge in the Social Sciences', *British Journal of Sociology*, vol. 53, no. 4, December 2002, pp. 659–662.

116 J. Mirowsky, C. Ross, and M. van Willigen, 'Instrumentalism in the Land of Opportunity: Socioeconomic Causes and Emotional Consequences', *Social Psychology Quarterly*, vol. 59, no. 4, December 1996, pp. 322–337. Mirowsky and Ross show that socio-economically disadvantaged persons are likely to express values and attitudes consistent with a resigned, 'dog-eat-dog' instrumental world-view.

117 OECD, *A Policy Agenda for Growth: An Overview of the Sources of Economic Growth in OECD Countries*, Paris: OECD, 2003, p. 9.

118 For further discussion of the concept of policy transfer, see D. Dolowitz, 'Policy Transfer: A New Framework of Policy Analysis', in D. Dolowitz with R. Hulme, M. Nellis, and F. O'Neill (eds), *Policy Transfer and British Social Policy: Learning from the USA?*, Buckingham: Open University Press, 2000, pp. 9–37.

119 Ibid., p. 13

120 P. Pierson, *Dismantling the Welfare State? Reagan, Thatcher and the Politics of Retrenchment*, Cambridge: Cambridge University Press, 1994.

121 P. Pierson, 'Increasing Returns, Path Dependence, and the Study of Politics', *American Political Science Review*, vol. 94, no. 2, 2000, p. 252.

122 Ibid.

123 See Svallfors, 'Worlds of Welfare', pp. 283–304. Svallfors finds greater support for redistribution among the European welfare states than among the 'liberal' models of the United States and Canada. This support reflects history and institutions. Policies that increase both employment *and* inequality would be forced to contend with greater oppositional opinion and institutional resistance.

124 D. Dolowitz, 'Policy Transfer: A New Framework of Policy Analysis', in Dolowitz *et al.*, *Policy Transfer and British Social Policy*, p. 26

125 M. Thompson, 'Industrial Relations in Canada', in G. Bamber and R. Lansbury, *International and Comparative Industrial Relations*, Sydney: Allen & Unwin, 1993, pp. 83–99.

126 H. Gospel and G. Palmer, *British Industrial Relations*, 2nd edn, London: Routledge, 1993, pp. 254–256.

127 S. Wilson, 'Union Mobilisation and the 1998 Maritime Dispute', *Journal of Australian Political Economy*, no. 41, June 1998, pp. 23–36.

128 G. Bamber and E. Snape, 'Industrial Relations in Britain', in Bamber and Lansbury, *International and Comparative Industrial Relations*, pp. 40–41.
129 T. Wright, 'PM Paves Way to Cut Wages, Dole', *The Sydney Morning Herald*, 7 July 1997, p. 1. The Australian Prime Minister, John Howard remarked that, 'one of the reasons why America's unemployment level is lower than Australia is that minimum wages in America are much lower than they are in Australia'.
130 C. Crouch, 'A Third Way in Industrial Relations?', in S. White (ed.), *New Labour: The Progressive Future?*, Basingstoke: Palgrave, 2001, pp. 100–102.
131 S. Wilson and N. Turnbull 'Wedge Politics and Welfare Reform in Australia', *Australian Journal of Politics & History*, vol. 47, no. 3, 2001, pp. 384–402.
132 C. Oppenheim, 'Enabling Participation? New Labour's Welfare-to-Work Policies', in White, *New Labour*, pp. 81–82.
133 Crouch, 'A Third Way in Industrial Relations?', p. 107.
134 Galbraith, 'The Real American Model'.

4 The basic income challenge to work and welfare

1 C. Offe, *Contradictions of the Welfare State*, J. Keane (ed.), London: Hutchinson, p. 297.
2 For example, see J. Keane, *Tom Paine: A Political Life*, London: Bloomsbury, 1995, pp. 426–427. Keane draws attention to Paine's support for a citizens' income based on common property rights, which hoped to give individuals genuine independence from the market. See also D. Purdy, 'Citizenship, Basic Income and the State', *New Left Review*, no. 208, November/December 1994, pp. 36–37.
3 D. Purdy, 'Citizenship, Basic Income and the State', pp. 33–37. Libertarian justifications, such as those advocated by Steiner and Carling, generally make reference to (original) common property rights as birthrights that prescribe the forms of 'just taxation' and consider birthright grants as basis for 'just distribution'. For libertarian arguments, see H. Steiner, 'Three Just Taxes', and A. Carling, 'Just Two Just Taxes', in P. van Parijs (ed.), *Arguing for Basic Income: Ethical Foundations for a Radical Reform*, London: Verso, 1992, pp. 81–91 and pp. 93–100, respectively. Communitarians justify basic income in the form of a social dividend, appealing to the ideal that 'all citizens are entitled to share the usufruct of those productive resources which are the common property of society as a whole' (ibid., p. 36). But Purdy points out that both libertarian and communitarian arguments run into trouble either defining the 'social product' or the 'relevant moral community' to whom grants are to be allocated. He says that, 'if the relevant moral community is humanity as a whole, it is impossible to justify the introduction of a universal grant in one state on libertarian or communitarian grounds alone' (ibid., p. 37).
4 Purdy, 'Citizenship, Basic Income, and the State', p. 37.
5 Christopher Bertram discusses the overlap between Rawls's proposals for a just society and the basic income proposal with leading basic income advocate, Philippe van Parijs. See C. Bertram, 'The Need for Basic Income: An Interview with Philippe van Parijs', *Imprints*, vol. 1, no. 3, March 1997, online. Available at: http://www.imprints.org.uk (accessed 23 September 2003).
6 J. Rawls, *A Theory of Justice*, Cambridge, MA: The Belknap Press of Harvard University Press, 1972, p. 92. Rawls claims that 'primary goods ... are things which it is supposed a rational man wants, whatever else he wants' (ibid., p. 92).
7 Ibid., p. 275.

8 See J. Baker, 'An Egalitarian Case for Basic Income', in van Parijs, *Arguing for Basic Income*, p. 125, n4. Baker cites J. Rawls, 'Reply to Alexander and Musgrave', *Quarterly Journal of Economics*, vol. 88, no. 4, 1974, pp. 641–643. Rawls implies that leisure can be considered a primary social good but does not justify entitlement to income.

9 C. Pateman, 'The Patriarchal Welfare State', in A. Gutman (ed.), *Democracy and the Welfare State*, Princeton, NJ: Princeton University Press, 1988, p. 259.

10 P. van Parijs, 'A Basic Income for All', *Boston Review*, October/November 2000, online. Available at: http://bostonreview.net/BR25.5/vanparijs.html (accessed September 2003).

11 L. Wacquant, 'The Rise of Advanced Marginality: Notes on its Nature and Implications', *Acta Sociologica*, vol. 39, no. 2, 1996, pp. 129–130.

12 Ibid., p. 130.

13 B. Jordan, 'Basic Income and The Common Good', in van Parijs, *Arguing for Basic Income*, pp. 155–177.

14 J. Barbalet, *Citizenship: Rights, Struggles and Class Inequality*, Milton Keynes: Open University Press, 1988, p. 28.

15 M. Johnston and R. Jowell, 'Social Capital and the Social Fabric', in R. Jowell *et al.* (eds), *British Social Attitudes: Who Shares New Labour Values?*, Aldershot: Ashgate, 1999, p. 191.

16 See J. Pixley, 'Employment and Social Identity: Theoretical Issues', in M. Roche and R. van Berkel (eds), *European Citizenship and Social Exclusion*, Aldershot: Ashgate, 1997, pp. 119–134.

17 The idea had already found a foothold in the intellectual world in the 1960s. Fromm wrote enthusiastically about the 'psychology of abundance' that a basic income would help produce in releasing human creativities trapped by the dominance of waged-labour. See E. Fromm, 'The Psychological Aspects of the Guaranteed Income', in R. Theobald (ed.), *The Guaranteed Income: Next Step in Economic Evolution?*, New York: Doubleday, 1966, pp. 175–184.

18 See, for example, J. Habermas, *A Berlin Republic: Writings on Germany*, trans. S. Rendall, Lincoln, NB: University of Nebraska Press, 1997, p. 142. Habermas supported a basic income as a way of limiting welfare state 'juridification', and to allow 'citizens' self-respect and political autonomy [to] be made independent of the more or less contingent success of the private individual on the labor market' (ibid., p. 142). See also J. Keane, *Democracy and Civil Society: On the Predicaments of European Socialism, the Prospects for Democracy, and the Problem of Controlling Social and Political Power*, London: Verso, 1988, pp. 69–100. Referring to Norbert Elias's famous phrase, Keane argued in his essay 'Work and the Civilizing Process' that work no longer contributes to the civilising project and uncoupling citizenship claims from work was both inevitable and desirable. See also A. Gorz, *Critique of Economic Reason*, trans. G. Handyside and C. Turner, London: Verso, 1989; A. Gorz, *Reclaiming Work: Beyond a Wage-Based Society*, Oxford: Blackwell, 2000; U. Beck, *The Brave New World of Work*, trans. P. Camiller, Cambridge: Polity Press, 2000; and C. Offe, 'Full Employment: Asking the Wrong Question?', *Dissent*, Winter 1995, pp. 77–81.

19 See Richard Rorty's essay 'Back to Class Politics', in R. Rorty, *Philosophy and Social Hope*, New York: Penguin, 1999, pp. 255–261.

20 Van Parijs, 'A Basic Income for All'.

21 A. Gorz, *Farewell to the Working Class: An Essay on Post-industrial Socialism*, trans. M. Sonenscher, London: Pluto Press, 1982, pp. 66–74.

22 U. Beck, 'Beyond Status and Class: Will There Be an Individualized Class Society?', in V. Meja, D. Misgeld and N. Stehr (eds), *Modern German Sociology*, New York: Columbia University Press, 1987, pp. 340–355. See also U.

Beck, *Risk Society: Towards a New Modernity*, trans. M. Ritter, London: Sage, 1992.

23 C. Offe, *Modernity and the State: East, West*, Cambridge: Polity Press, 1996, p. 198.

24 R. Goodin, 'Towards a Minimally Presumptuous Social Welfare Policy', in van Parijs, *Arguing for Basic Income*, pp. 195–214.

25 R. Goodin, 'Something for Nothing?: A Response to *A Basic Income for All* by Philippe van Parijs', *Boston Review*, October/November 2000, online. Available at http://bostonreview.net/BR25.5/goodin.html (accessed 23 September 2003).

26 A. Gorz, *Paths to Paradise: On the Liberation from Work*, London: Pluto Press, p. 31f.

27 J. Rifkin, *The End of Work: The Decline of the Global Labor Force and the Dawn of the Post-Market Era*, New York: Jeremy P. Tarcher/Putnam, 1995, p. 88.

28 F. Block and J. Manza, 'Could We End Poverty in a Postindustrial Society? The Case for a Progressive Negative Income Tax', *Politics and Society*, vol. 25, no. 4, December 1997, p. 481.

29 Goodin, 'Towards a Minimally Presumptuous Social Welfare Policy', p. 208.

30 E. Anderson, 'Optional Freedoms: A Response to *A Basic Income for All* by Philippe van Parijs', *Boston Review*, October/November 2000, online. Available at: http://bostonreview.net/BR25.5/anderson.html (accessed 23 September 2003).

31 E. Butler, *Hayek: His Contribution to the Political and Economic Thought of Our Time*, New York: Universe Books, 1985, p. 117.

32 See M. Friedman with R. Friedman, *Capitalism and Freedom*, Chicago: Chicago University Press, 1962, pp. 191–195.

33 P. van Parijs, 'The Second Marriage of Justice and Efficiency', in van Parijs, *Arguing for Basic Income*, pp. 216–228. See especially Figures 13.1, 13.2.

34 Ibid., p. 230.

35 Ibid., p. 232.

36 Ibid.

37 A. Alstott, 'Work Versus Freedom: A Liberal Challenge to Employment Subsidies', *Yale Law Journal*, vol. 108, no. 5, 1999, pp. 967–1058.

38 Block and Manza, 'Could We End Poverty in a Postindustrial Society?', p. 484. Polanyi refers to the Speenhamland welfare provisions and the problem of pauperism among workers in late eighteenth-century England. See K. Polanyi, *The Great Transformation*, New York: Farrer & Rinehart, 1944.

39 National Centre for Social Research, *British Social Attitudes Survey*, 2000, online. Available at: http://www.data-archive.ac.uk (accessed 23 October 2003).

40 M. Pusey, *The Middle Australia Project 1996*, [computer file] Kensington: School of Sociology, University of New South Wales, 2000.

41 C. Offe, 'Pathways from Here: A Response to *A Basic Income for All* by Philippe van Parijs', *Boston Review*, October/November, 2000, online. Available at: http://bostonreview.net/BR25.5/offe.html (accessed 23 September 2003).

42 R. Jowell, J. Curtice, A. Park, L. Brook, D. Ahrendt with K. Thomson (eds), *British Social Attitudes: The 12th Report*, Aldershot: Dartmouth Publishing, 1995, p. 243. The questions included in the libertarian–authoritarian scale are (agree/disagree – 5 point scale): Young people don't have enough respect for traditional British values; People who break the law should be given stiffer sentences; For some crimes, the death penalty is the most appropriate sentence; Schools should teach children to obey authority; The law should always be obeyed even if a particular law is wrong; and Censorship of films and magazines is necessary to uphold moral standards.

43 Ibid., p. 244. The questions included in the welfarism scale are (agree/disagree

– 5 point scale): The welfare state makes people nowadays less willing to look after themselves; People receiving social security are made to feel like second-class citizens; The welfare state encourages people to stop helping each other; The government should spend more money on welfare benefits for the poor, even if it leads to higher taxes; Around here, most unemployed people could find a job if they really wanted one; Many people who get social security don't really deserve any help; Most people on the dole are fiddling in one way or another; and If welfare benefits weren't so generous, people would learn to stand on their own two feet.

44 Purdy, 'Citizenship, Basic Income and the State', p. 46. See also K. Widerquist, 'Reciprocity and the Guaranteed Income', *Politics and Society*, vol. 27, no. 3, 1999, pp. 387–402. This problem is also an interesting point of debate among supporters of basic income. White, for instance (discussed in Widerquist), argues that an unconditional basic income represents an exploitation of workers by non-workers. It is doubtful, however, whether work could be represented as a kind of 'pure bad' in order for such an exploitation argument to hold. One might equally argue that an unconditional basic income would systematically deny the disadvantaged access to employment.

45 R. Greenstein and I. Shapiro, *New Research Findings on the Effects of the Earned Income Tax Credit*, Center on Budget and Policy Priorities Paper, 1998, online. Available at: http://www.cbpp.org (accessed 24 September 2003).

46 P. van Parijs, 'Philippe van Parijs Responds', *Boston Review*, October/November 2000, online. Available at: http://bostonreview.net/BR25.5/vanparijs2.html (accessed 23 September 2003).

47 Block and Manza, 'Could We End Poverty in a Postindustrial Society?', pp. 495–497.

48 J. Myles and P. Pierson, 'Friedman's Revenge: "The Reform of "Liberal" Welfare States in Canada and the United States', *Politics & Society*, vol. 25, no. 4, December 1997, p. 466.

49 Ibid., p. 464.

50 Ibid., p. 452. Retrenchment is Pierson's term.

51 Ibid., p. 450.

52 Ibid., p. 464.

53 Greenstein and Shapiro, *New Research Findings*.

54 Ibid., p. 4.

55 D. Ellwood, 'From Welfare to Work', *CEDA Bulletin*, March 1999, p. 5.

56 D. Howell, 'Block and Manza on the Negative Income Tax', *Politics and Society*, vol. 25, no. 4, December 1997, p. 538.

57 I. Watson, 'Proposals for a Wage Freeze and Tax Credits: Will Subsidising Low Wage Jobs Solve Unemployment?', *Parliamentary Library Research Paper 29, 1998–99*, Canberra: Commonwealth of Australia, 1998, online. Available at: http://www.aph.gov.au/library/pubs/rp/1998–99/99rp29.htm (accessed 23 September 2003).

58 P. Dawkins *et al.*, 'Dear John – How to Create More Jobs', *The Australian*, 26 October 1998, p. 13. In Australia, five neo-classical economists mounted the same argument in support of further deregulation of the labour market. Their research shows that for every 2 per cent cut in real wages, there would be a corresponding fall of 1 per cent in unemployment. The economists proposed to abolish 'living wage' adjustments currently administered through the Australian Industrial Relations Commission. This would mean a wages freeze for low-paid workers. Under the proposal, falling real earnings would stimulate jobs and tax credits would compensate workers for lost income.

59 Block and Manza, 'Could We End Poverty in a Postindustrial Society?', pp. 486–493.

60 Ibid., pp. 498–500.
61 Myles and Pierson, 'Friedman's Revenge', p. 466.
62 Ibid.
63 See A.B. Atkinson, 'The Case for a Participation Income', *Political Quarterly*, vol. 67, January–March 1996, pp. 67–70.
64 Goodin, 'Something for Nothing?'.
65 See C. Offe and R. Heinze, *Beyond Employment: Time, Work, and the Informal Economy*, trans. A. Braley, Cambridge: Polity Press, 1992.
66 Rifkin, *The End of Work*, pp. 249–250.
67 B. Frankel, 'Re-Imagining Political Economy', *Arena*, no. 24, August–September 1996, p. 31.
68 Rifkin, *The End of Work*, p. 255.
69 E.S. Phelps, 'Subsidize Wages: A Response to *A Basic Income for All* by Philippe van Parijs', *Boston Review*, October/November 2000, online. Available at: http://bostonreview.net/BR25.5/phelps.html (accessed 23 September 2003).

5 Labour movements and work: exhausted alliances or new challenges?

1 See R. Michels, *Political Parties: A Sociological Study of the Oligarchical Tendencies of Modern Democracy*, trans. E. Paul and C. Paul, New York: Collier Books, 1962. Michels wrote a classic study of the German Social Democratic Party, which pointed to the inevitable trend towards bureaucratisation – the 'iron law of oligarchy'. Party leaderships and functionaries would assume direct control over the mass organisations and movements that brought labour into the political arena. The size, complexity, and demands of an organised movement compel a seemingly rational consolidation of power. He shows that power creates its own momentum, protecting the power-resources of the leadership. See also E. Etzioni-Halevy, *Bureaucracy and Democracy: A Political Dilemma*, London: Routledge and Kegan Paul, 1983, pp. 18–23.
2 K. Moody, *Workers in a Lean World: Unions in the International Economy*, London: Verso Books, 1997, p. 297.
3 S.M. Lipset, M.A. Trow, and J.S. Coleman, *Union Democracy: The Internal Politics of the International Typographical Union*, Glencoe, IL: The Free Press, 1977, pp. 404–406.
4 M. Olson, *The Logic of Collective Action: Public Goods and the Theory of Groups*, Cambridge, MA: Harvard University Press, 1965, p. 96.
5 D. Montgomery, *Citizen Worker: The Experience of Workers in the United States with Democracy and the Free Market during the Nineteenth Century*, Cambridge: Cambridge University Press, 1993, p. 1.
6 S. Cohn, *When Strikes Make Sense – And Why: Lessons from Third Republic French Coal Miners*, New York: Plenum Press, 1993, p. 214.
7 D. Kettler and V. Meja, 'The End of Western Trade Unionism?: Social Progress after the Age of Progressivism', in J. Alexander and P. Sztompka (eds), *Rethinking Progress: Movements, Forces, and Ideas at the End of the Twentieth Century*, Boston: Unwin Hyman, 1990, p. 145.
8 Ibid.
9 G. Seidman, *Manufacturing Militance: Workers' Movements in Brazil and South Africa, 1970–1985*, Berkeley, CA: University of California Press, 1994.
10 International Labour Organisation, *World Labour Report 1997–98: Industrial Relations, Democracy, and Social Stability*, Geneva: International Labour Office, 1997, p. 17.

11 Ibid., p. 81.
12 Ibid., p. 11.
13 Ibid., p. 79.
14 G. Therborn, *Why Some Peoples are More Unemployed than Others*, London: Verso, 1986, p. 111.
15 ILO, *World Labour Report, 1997–98*, p. 10.
16 Ibid., p. 11.
17 For the first two indicators, I have relied on Jelle Visser's recent, comprehensive update: see J. Visser, *Trends in Unionisation and Collective Bargaining*, Geneva: International Labour Office, 2000.
18 B. Western, *Between Class and Market: Postwar Unionization in the Capitalist Democracies*, Princeton, NJ: Princeton University Press, 1997, p. 195.
19 For historical data (1881–1995) on the number of US strikers per 1,000 workers, see C. Tilly and C. Tilly, *Work under Capitalism*, Boulder, CO: Westview Press, 1998, p. 252, Figure 11.3. See also M. Aligasakis, 'Labour Disputes in Western Europe: Typology and Tendencies', *International Labour Review*, vol. 136, no. 1, Spring 1997, pp. 73–99.
20 International Labour Organisation, *World Labour Report 1997–98*, p. 11.
21 Visser, *Trends in Unionisation and Collective Bargaining*, pp. 8, 11.
22 Western, *Between Class and Market*, p. 193.
23 On this point, see B. Ebbinghaus and J. Visser, 'When Institutions Matter: Union Growth and Decline in Western Europe, 1950–1995', *European Sociological Review*, vol. 15, no. 2, June 1999, pp. 135–158. In this detailed evaluation of European union density between 1950 and 1995, Bernhard Ebbinghaus and Jelle Visser list three main influences on union growth and decline. These are *cyclical, structural,* and *configurational* factors. I am indebted to the authors for their clear exposition of this subject – they have helped me organise my own thinking.
24 Ibid., p. 142.
25 D. Peetz, *Unions in a Contrary World: The Future of the Australian Trade Union Movement*, Cambridge: Cambridge University Press, 1998, p. 175.
26 H.S. Farber and A.S. Krueger, *Union Membership in the United States: The Decline Continues*, NBER Working Paper Series, Working Paper No. 4216, Cambridge, MA: National Bureau of Economic Research, November 1992, p. 32.
27 L. Scruggs and P. Lange, 'Where Have all the Members Gone? Globalization, Institutions, and Union Density', *Journal of Politics*, vol. 64, no. 1, February 2002, p. 150.
28 See, again, note 11.
29 Ebbinghaus and Visser, 'When Institutions Matter', p. 154.
30 Peetz, *Unions in a Contrary World*, p. 175.
31 Western, *Between Class and Market*, p. 73.
32 Ebbinghaus and Visser, 'When Institutions Matter', pp. 146–148.
33 Ibid., p. 153. On the Ghent system, see also Western, *Between Class and Market*, pp. 50–65.
34 P. Lange and L. Scruggs, 'Where Have all the Members Gone?: Union Density in the Era of Globalization', unpublished paper, Durham, NC: Duke University, 1998, p. 17. See also L. Scruggs and P. Lange, 'Where Have all the Members Gone?', pp. 126–153.
35 ILO, *World Labour Report 1997–98*, p. 20.
36 Peetz, *Unions in a Contrary World*, p. 180.
37 K. Murphy and C. Martin, 'Unions as a Labor Force', *Australian Financial Review*, 20 March 2000.

38 'Editorial: Class War in the USA', *Multinational Monitor*, vol. 18, no. 3, 1997, online. Available at: http://www.Multinationalmonitor.org (accessed 18 October 2003).

39 The best exposition of this argument is found in A. Touraine, M. Wieviorka, and F. Dubet, *The Workers' Movement*, trans. I. Patterson, Cambridge: Cambridge University Press, 1987.

40 See, for example, G. Evans (ed.), *The End of Class Politics: Class Voting in Comparative Context*, Oxford: Oxford University Press, 1999, pp. 6–7; and G. Evans, 'The Decline of Class Divisions in Britain? Class and Ideological Preferences in Britain in the 1960s and 1980s', *British Journal of Sociology*, no. 44, 1993, pp. 449–471. See also J. Goldthorpe, 'Class and Politics in Advanced Industrial Societies', in T.N. Clark and S.M. Lipset (eds), *The Breakdown of Class Politics: A Debate on Post-Industrial Stratification*, Baltimore, MD: Johns Hopkins University Press, 2001, pp. 105–135.

41 AFL-CIO, 'Americans' Attitudes towards Unions', online. Available at: http://www.aflcio.org, 1999 (accessed 25 October 2003). See also Ebbinghaus and Visser, 'When Institutions Matter', p. 143.

42 D. Biddle *et al.*, *Young People's Attitudes to Trade Unions*, Employment Studies Centre, Newcastle: University of Newcastle, February 2000, p. 5.

43 See Western, *Between Class and Market*, pp. 76–77. Earlier trends were hostile to unions. Western uses Gallup polls to show that support for unions fell between the late 1950s and the late 1970s.

44 W. Galenson, *Trade Union Growth and Decline: An International Study*, Westport, CT: Praeger, 1994, pp. 113–130.

45 See R. Jones, I. McAllister, D. Denemark, and D. Gow, *Australian Election Study 1993*, online. Available at: http//:assda.anu.edu.au (accessed 20 October 2003); C. Bean, D. Gow, and I. McAllister, *Australian Election Study 2001*, online. Available at http//:assda.anu.edu.au (accessed 20 October 2003); A. Heath, R. Jowell, and J.K. Curtice, *British General Election Study 1987*, online. Available at: www.data-archive.ac.uk (accessed 20 October 2003); A. Heath, R. Jowell, J.K. Curtice, and P.N. Norris, *British General Election Study 1997*, online. Available at: www.data-archive.ac.uk (accessed 20 October 2003).

46 The same question about union power (but with different categories) was asked in J. Kelley, R.G. Cushing, and B. Headey, *Australian National Social Science Survey, 1984* (User's guide and data file), Canberra: Social Science Data Archives: The Australian National University, 1987. Then, 82 per cent thought unions had either far too much or a bit too much power. These results suggest that perceptions of union power had already declined considerably before the Australian Election Study 1993.

47 See *Australian Election Study 1993* and *Australian Election Study 2001*.

48 S. Wilson *et al.*, *Australian Survey of Social Attitudes* [computer file], The Australian National University, Canberra: Australian Social Science Data Archive, 2003.

49 J.S. Valenzuela, 'Labour Movements and Political Systems: Some Variations', in M. Regini (ed.), *The Future of Labour Movements*, London: Sage, 1992, pp. 53–101.

50 C. Offe, *Disorganized Capitalism*, J. Keane (ed.), Cambridge: Polity Press, 1985.

51 R. Davies and N. Weiner, 'A Cultural Perspective in the Study of Industrial Relations', in P. Frost *et al.* (eds), *Organizational Culture*, London: Sage, 1985, pp. 355–372.

52 D. McAdam, J. McCarthy, and M. Zald, 'Social Movements', in N. Smelser (ed.), *Handbook of Sociology*, Newbury Park, CA: Sage, 1988, p. 728.
53 C. Wright Mills, *The New Men of Power: America's Labor Leaders*, New York: Augustus M. Kelley, 1971, p. 149.
54 M. Zald and R. Ash, 'Social Movement Organizations: Growth, Decay and Change', *Social Forces*, vol. 44, no. 3, March 1966, p. 340.
55 See B. Valkenburg and R. Zoll, 'Modernization, Individualization, and Solidarity: Two Perspectives on European Trade Unions Today', *European Journal of Industrial Relations*, vol. 1, no. 1, 1995, pp. 126–127.
56 M. Burgmann and V. Burgmann, *Green Bans, Red Union: Environmental Activism and the New South Wales Builders Labourers' Federation*, Sydney: UNSW Press, 1998.
57 Zald and Ash, 'Social Movement Organizations', p. 340. Alvin Gouldner made a similar point in A. Gouldner, 'Metaphysical Pathos and the Study of Bureaucracy', *American Political Science Review*, no. 49, June 1955, pp. 496–507. See also J. Stepan-Norris and Maurice Zeitlin, 'Insurgency, Radicalism, and Democracy in America's Industrial Unions', *Social Forces*, vol. 75, no. 1, 1996, pp. 1–32.
58 J. Stepan-Norris, 'The Making of Union Democracy', *Social Forces*, vol. 76, no. 2, 1997, pp. 475–510.
59 Moody, *Workers in a Lean World*, p. 271.
60 B. Pocock, 'Gender, Strife and Unions' in B. Pocock (ed.), *Strife: Sex and Politics in Labor Unions*, St. Leonards: Allen & Unwin, 1997, pp. 17–18. See also R. Needleman, 'Women Workers: Strategies for Inclusion and Rebuilding', in G. Mantsios (ed.), *A New Labor Movement for the New Century*, New York: Monthly Review Press, 1998, pp. 153–160.
61 W. Higgins, 'The Swedish Municipal Workers' Union – A Study in the New Political Unionism', *Economic and Industrial Democracy*, vol. 17, no. 2, 1996, pp. 167–198.
62 Western, *Between Class and Market*, p. 194.
63 Peetz, *Unions in a Contrary World*, p. 196. Peetz draws on B. Pocock, 'Institutional Sclerosis: The Prospects for Trade Union Transformation', paper presented at the Third International Conference on Emerging Union Structures, The Australian National University, December 1997.
64 G. Ribeill, 'Le conflict des cheminots de novembre–décembre 1995: les avatars politiques d'une grève corporative', *Sociologie du travail*, no. 4, 1997, pp. 425–448.
65 'Labouring over le 35-hour week', *The Guardian*, 11 October 2003.
66 Moody, *Workers in a Lean World*, p. 17. See also D. Howard, 'The French Strikes of 1995: Back to the Future?', *Constellations*, vol. 3, no. 2, 1996, pp. 250–251.
67 Moody, *Workers in a Lean World*, p. 17.
68 P. Bourdieu, *Acts of Resistance: Against the New Myths of Our Time*, Cambridge: Polity Press, 1998, p. 24.
69 Howard, 'The French Strikes of 1995', p. 251.
70 F. Piotet, Les événements de décembre 1995, chroniques d'un conflit', *Sociologie du travail*, no. 4, 1997, 540. Françoise Piotet summarises Touraine's position:

> Ce conflit n'a pas été un véritable mouvement social à défaut pour ses acteurs d'être porteurs d'une vision globale et d'un projet alternatif ou d'une utopie; il a seulement été 'l'ombre d'un mouvement', titre choisi par A. Touraine pour sa contribution au *Grand refus*

> (p. 540)

This conflict hasn't been a real social movement, lacking a global vision and an alternative project or a utopia; it has only been 'the shadow of a movement', the title chosen by Touraine for his contribution to *Grand refus*.

(my translation)

71 M. Wieviorka, 'Le sens d'une lutte', in A. Touraine, F. Dubet, D. Lapeyronnie, F. Khosrokhavar, and M. Wieviorka (eds), *Le Grand Refus: Réfléxions sur la grève de décembre 1995*, Paris: Fayard, 1996, p. 287 and pp. 293–296.
72 Moody, *Workers in a Lean World*, pp. 285–286.
73 A. Gallois, Review of: 'Alain Touraine, François Dubet Lapeyronnie, Farhad Khosrokhavar, and Michel Wieviorka, *Le Grand Refus: Réfléxions sur la grève de décembre 1995* (Fayard, 1996)', *Thesis Eleven*, no. 55, 1998, p. 119.
74 N. Lichtenstein, *The Most Dangerous Man in Detroit: Walter Reuther and the Fate of American Labor*, New York: Basic Books, 1995, p. 333.
75 L. Sustar, 'A New Labor Movement?', *International Socialist Review*, Summer 1997, pp. 20–21.
76 R. Rothstein, 'Union Strength in the United States: Lessons from the UPS Strike', *International Labour Review*, vol. 136, no. 4, 1997, p. 472.
77 D. Moberg, 'Can Labor Change?', *Dissent*, Winter 1996, p. 16. The UMWA is the United Mine Workers of America, AFSCME is the American Federation of State, County, and Municipal Employees and the SEIU is the Service Employees International Union.
78 R. Waldinger *et al.*, 'Justice for Janitors: Organizing in Difficult Times', *Dissent*, Winter 1997, pp. 37–44.
79 A. Banks, 'New Voice, New Internationalism', in Mantsios, *A New Labor Movement*, pp. 286–303.
80 G. Mantsios, 'What Should Labor Stand For?', in Mantsios, *A New Labor Movement*, pp. 49–56.
81 H. Meyerson, 'Rolling the Union On: John Sweeney's Movement Four Years Later', *Dissent*, vol. 47, no. 1, Winter 1999, p. 51. Meyerson, however, notes that the victory was due less to organising and more to the SEIU's growing political clout.
82 Moody, *Workers in a Lean World*, p. 198.
83 Rothstein, 'Union Strength in the United States', pp. 469–492.
84 A. Bernstein, 'Breaking Ranks with the AFL-CIO', 15 September 2003, online. Available at: http://www.businessweek.com (accessed 24 October 2003).
85 AFL-CIO, 'The Union Difference: Political Program for Working Families', online. Available at: http://www.afl-cio.org (accessed 24 October 2003).
86 A. Sneade, 'National Statistics Feature: Trade Union Membership 1999–2000: An Analysis of Data from the Certification Officer and the Labour Force Survey', *Labour Market Trends*, September 2001, London: Government Statistical Service, pp. 433–444.
87 See, for example, an ACTU 'steering document', ACTU, Unions@Work, online. Available at: www.actu.asn.au (accessed 24 October 2003). CUPE is the Canadian Union of Public Employees and CAW is the Canadian Auto Workers.
88 M. Levi, 'Organizing Power: The Prospects for an American Labor Movement', *Perspectives on Politics*, vol. 1, no. 1, March 2003, p. 45.
89 S. Weir, 'The Informal Work Group', in A. Lynd and S. Lynd (eds), *Rank and File: Personal Histories of Working Class Organizers*, Boston: Beacon, 1973, p. 177.
90 McAdam *et al.*, 'Social Movements', p. 716.

91 Ibid., p. 707.
92 Peetz, *Unions in a Contrary World*, pp. 121 and 194.
93 K. Bronfenbrenner and T. Juravich, 'It Takes More than House Calls: Organizing to Win with a Comprehensive Union-Building Strategy', in K. Bronfenbrenner *et al.* (eds), *Organizing to Win: New Research on Union Strategies*, Ithaca, NY: ILR/ Cornell University Press, 1998, pp. 19–36.
94 Ibid., pp. 35–36.
95 Levi, 'Organizing Power', p. 45.
96 Western, *Between Class and Market*, pp. 68–69.
97 Ibid., p. 71. See also T. Dark, *The Unions and the Democrats: An Enduring Alliance*, Ithaca, NY: Cornell University Press, 1999.
98 Western, *Between Class and Market*, pp. 68–69.
99 Ibid., p. 75.
100 See Dark, *The Unions and the Democrats*, pp. 158–189. Dark describes in detail the relationship between Sweeney's AFL-CIO and the Clinton administration, especially appointments to the NLRB, the lack of law reform, and labour's role in defeating the 'fast-track' NAFTA legislation.
101 Levi, 'Organizing Power', p. 59.
102 For a good overview of full employment prospects, see H. Ginsburg *et al.*, 'Special Issue: The Challenge of Full Employment in the Global Economy', *Economic and Industrial Democracy*, vol. 18, no. 1, February 1997, pp. 5–34.
103 See, for example, D. Baker and J. Schmitt, 'The Macroeconomic Roots of High European Unemployment: The Impact of Foreign Growth', conference paper at 'Creating Competitive Capacity: Reassessing the Role of U.S. and German Labor Market Institutions in the New Economy', Washington, DC, 23–25 October 1998.
104 See, for instance, the arguments of Clive Hamilton in C. Hamilton, *Growth Fetish*, Crows Nest: Allen & Unwin, 2003.
105 J. Hunt, *Has Work-Sharing Worked in Germany?*, NBER Working Paper No. W5724, Cambridge, MA: National Bureau of Economic Research, August 1996.
106 G. Schmid, 'Transitional Labour Markets: A New European Employment Strategy', *Discussion Paper FS 98 – 206*, Berlin: Wissenschaftszentrum Berlin für Sozialforschung, October 1998.
107 Ibid., pp. 26–27.
108 Levi, 'Organizing Power', p. 57.
109 See J.B. Judis and R. Teixeira, *The Emerging Democratic Majority*, New York: Scribner, 2002, pp. 62–67. John Judis and Ruy Teixeira discuss the importance of the white working-class vote in contemporary American politics. They do not discuss in any detail the falling numbers of union members among this group. I would suggest that declining unions and stagnant economic prospects among these workers only sharpens the appeal of Republican 'wedge' campaigns. The lack of clear pro-labour policies from the Democrats adds further to this problem.
110 For a comprehensive survey of the policy agenda for women and working-age people in the American context, see T. Skocpol, *The Missing Middle*, New York: W.W. Norton, 2000.
111 On cross-border campaigning, see also Levi, 'Organizing Power', pp. 57–58 and Moody, *Workers in a Lean World*, pp. 227–268.

6 Conclusion

1 See M. Castells, *The Rise of the Network Society*, 2nd edn, Oxford: Blackwell, 2000, p. 276.
2 A. Giddens, *Sociology*, 4th edn, Cambridge: Polity Press, 2003, p. 42.
3 C. Tilly, and C. Tilly, *Work under Capitalism*, Boulder, CO: Westview Press, 1998, p. 264.
4 J. Miller, 'Jobs and Work', in N. Smelser (ed.), *Handbook of Sociology*, Newbury Park, CA: Sage, 1988, pp. 327–359.
5 A. Honneth, *The Fragmented World of the Social: Essays in Social and Political Philosophy*, C. Wright (ed.), Albany, NY: State University of New York Press, 1995, pp. xvii–xix.
6 A. Feenberg, *Questioning Technology*, London: Routledge, 1999.
7 L. Mishel, J. Bernstein, and J. Schmitt, *The State of Working America, 1998–99*, Ithaca, NY: Cornell University Press, 1999, p. 388.
8 See, for example, P.A. Hall and D.W. Soskice, *Varieties of Capitalism: The Institutional Foundations of Comparative Advantage*, Oxford: Oxford University Press, 2001.

Bibliography

Adams, R., 'North American Industrial Relations: Divergent Trends in Canada and the United States', *International Labour Review*, vol. 128, no. 1, 1989, pp. 47–64.

AFL-CIO, 'Americans' Attitudes towards Unions', 1999, online. Available at: http://www.aflcio.org (accessed 25 October 2003).

——, *High Hopes, Little Trust*, 1999, online. Available at: http://www.aflcio.org (accessed 23 October 2003).

——, 'The Union Difference: Political Program for Working Families', online. Available at: http://www.afl-cio.org (accessed 24 October 2003).

Alexander, J., *Theoretical Logic in Sociology: Volume Two: The Antinomies of Classical Thought: Marx and Durkheim*, Los Angeles: University of California Press, 1982.

Alexander, J. and Pia Lara, M., 'Honneth's New Critical Theory of Recognition', *New Left Review*, no. 220, 1996, pp. 126–136.

Aligisakis, M., 'Labour Disputes in Western Europe: Typology and Tendencies', *International Labour Review*, vol. 136, no. 1, Spring 1997, pp. 73–94.

Alstott, A., 'Work Versus Freedom: A Liberal Challenge to Employment Subsidies', *Yale Law Journal*, vol. 108, no. 5, 1999, pp. 967–1058.

Anderson, E., 'Optional Freedoms: A Response to *A Basic Income for All* by Philippe van Parijs', *Boston Review*, October/November 2000, online. Available at: http://bostonreview.net/BR25.5/anderson.html (accessed 23 September 2003).

Appelbaum, E., 'What Explains Employment Developments in the US?', *Economic Policy Institute Briefing Paper*, Washington, DC: Economic Policy Institute, November 2000.

Applebaum, H., *The American Work Ethic and the Changing Workforce*, Westport, CT: Greenwood, 1998.

Arendt, H., *The Human Condition*, Chicago: University of Chicago Press, 1989.

Atkinson, A.B., 'The Case for a Participation Income', *Political Quarterly*, vol. 67, January–March 1996, pp. 67–70.

Australian Council of Trade Unions [ACTU], 'Employment Security & Working Hours – A National Survey of Current Workplaces', 1999, online. Available at: http://www.actu.asn.au (accessed 23 October 2003).

——, *Unions@Work*, online. Available at: www.actu.asn.au (accessed 24 October 2003).

Baker, D. and Schmitt, J. 'The Macroeconomic Roots of High European Unemployment: The Impact of Foreign Growth', conference paper at 'Creating

Competitive Capacity: Reassessing the Role of U.S. and German Labor Market Institutions in the New Economy', Washington, DC, 23–25 October 1998.

Baker, J., 'An Egalitarian Case for Basic Income', in van Parijs, P. (ed.), *Arguing for Basic Income: Ethical Foundations for a Radical Reform*, London: Verso, pp. 101–127.

Bamber, G. and Snape, E., 'Industrial Relations in Britain', in Bamber, G. and Lansbury, R. (eds), *International and Comparative Industrial Relations: A Study of Industrialised Market Economies*, 2nd edn, St Leonards, NSW: Allen & Unwin, pp. 27–54.

Banks, A., 'New Voice, New Internationalism', in Mantsios, G. (ed.), *A New Labor Movement for the New Century*, New York: Monthly Review Press, 1998, pp. 286–303.

Barbalet, J., 'Marx and Weber as Class Theorists and the Relevance of Class Theory Today', in Jennett, C. and Stewart, R. (eds), *Three Worlds of Inequality: Race, Class and Gender*, South Melbourne: Macmillan, 1987, pp. 136–152.

——, *Citizenship: Rights, Struggle, and Class Inequality*, Milton Keynes: Open University Press, 1988.

Bean, C., Gow, D., and McAllister, I., *Australian Election Study 2001*, online. Available at: http//:assda.anu.edu.au (accessed 20 October 2003).

Beck, U., 'Beyond Status and Class: Will There Be an Individualized Class Society?', in Meja, V., Misgeld, D., and Stehr, N. (eds), *Modern German Sociology*, New York: Columbia University Press, 1987, pp. 340–355.

——, *Risk Society: Towards a New Modernity*, trans. M. Ritter, London: Sage, 1992.

——, *The Brave New World of Work*, trans. P. Camiller, Cambridge: Polity Press, 2000.

Bell, D., *The Coming of Post-Industrial Society: A Venture in Social Forecasting*, London: Heinemann Educational Books, 1974.

Berger, J., 'The Linguistification of the Sacred and the Delinguistification of the Economy', in Honneth, A. and Joas, H. (eds), *Communicative Action: Essays on Jürgen Habermas's* The Theory of Communicative Action, Cambridge: Polity Press, 1991, pp. 165–180.

Bernstein, A., 'Breaking Ranks with the AFL-CIO', 15 September 2003, online. Available at: http://www.businessweek.com (accessed 24 October 2003).

Bertram, C., 'The Need for Basic Income: An Interview with Philippe van Parijs', *Imprints*, vol. 1, no. 3, March 1997, online. Available at: http://www.imprints.org.uk (accessed 23 September 2003).

Biddle, D., Croce, N., LeQueux, S., Rowe, D., and Stevenson, D., *Young People's Attitudes to Trade Unions*, Employment Studies Centre, Newcastle: University of Newcastle, February 2000.

Blank, R. and Ellwood, D., *The Clinton Legacy for America's Poor*, NBER Working Paper Series, Working Paper no. 8437, Cambridge, MA: National Bureau of Economic Research, August 2001.

Block, F. and Manza, J., 'Could We End Poverty in a Postindustrial Society?: The Case for a Progressive Negative Income Tax', *Politics & Society*, vol. 25, no. 4, December 1997, pp. 473–511.

Boltho, A., 'What's Wrong with Europe?', *New Left Review*, no. 22, July–August 2003, pp. 5–26.

Bourdieu, P., *Acts of Resistance: Against the New Myths of Our Time*, Cambridge: Polity Press, 1998.

Boyer, R. and Morais, H., *Labor's Untold Story*, New York: United Electrical, Radio and Machine Workers of America, 1972.

Braverman, H., *Labor and Monopoly Capital: The Degradation of Work in the Twentieth Century*, New York: Monthly Review Press, 1974.

Brenner, R., 'The Economics of Global Turbulence: A Special Report on the World Economy, 1950–98', *New Left Review*, no. 229, May–June 1998, pp. 1–265.

Bronfenbrenner, K. and Juravich, T., 'It Takes More than House Calls: Organizing to Win with a Comprehensive Union-Building Strategy', in Bronfenbrenner, K., Friedman, S., Hurd, R.W., Oswald, R.A., and Seeber, R.L. (eds), *Organizing to Win: New Research on Union Strategies*, Ithaca, NY: ILR/Cornell University Press, 1998, pp. 19–36.

Brubaker, R., *The Limits of Rationality: An Essay on the Social and Moral Thought of Max Weber*, London: George Allen & Unwin, 1984.

Bureau of Labor Statistics, *Occupations with the Largest Growth, 1998–2008, MLR: the Editor's Desk*, 29 December 1999, online. Available at: http://www.bls.gov (accessed 23 October 2003).

——, *Comparative Civilian Labour Force Statistics: Ten Countries: 1959–2002*, 2002, online. Available at: http://www.bls.gov (accessed 23 October 2003).

Burgmann, M. and Burgmann, V., *Green Bans, Red Union: Environmental Activism and the New South Wales Builders Labourers' Federation*, Sydney: UNSW Press, 1998.

Burns, T. and Flam, H., *The Shaping of Social Organization: Social Rule System Theory with Applications*, London: Sage, 1987.

Butler, E., *Hayek: His Contribution to the Political and Economic Thought of Our Time*, New York: Universe Books, 1985.

Card, D. and Krueger, A., *Myth and Measurement: The New Economics of the Minimum Wage*, Princeton, NJ: Princeton University Press, 1995.

Carling, A., 'Just Two Just Taxes', in van Parijs, P. (ed.), *Arguing for Basic Income: Ethical Foundations for a Radical Reform*, London: Verso, 1992, pp. 93–98.

Castells, M., *The Rise of the Network Society*, 2nd edn, Oxford: Blackwell, 2000.

Castoriadis, C., *The Imaginary Institution of Society*, trans. K. Blamey, Cambridge: Polity Press, 1987.

Chapman, J. and Bernstein, R., 'Falling Through the Safety Net', EPI Issue Brief, No. 191, 11 April 2003, online. Available at: http://www.epinet.org (accessed 23 October 2003).

Clarke, H., Sanders, D., Stewart, M., and Whiteley, P.F., *British General Election Study 2001*, online. Available at: www.data-archive.ac.uk (accessed 20 October 2003).

Cohn, S., *When Strikes Make Sense – And Why: Lessons from Third Republic French Coal Miners*, New York: Plenum Press, 1993.

Cook, C., 'Plucking Workers: Tyson Foods Looks to the Welfare Rolls for a Captive Labor Force', *The Progressive*, August 1998, pp. 28–31.

Crampton, P. and Tracy, J., *The Use of Replacement Workers in Union Contract Negotiations: The U.S. Experience, 1980–1989*, NBER Working Paper Series, Cambridge, MA: National Bureau of Economic Research, No. 5106, 1995.

Crouch, C., 'A Third Way in Industrial Relations?', in White, S. (ed.) *New Labour: The Progressive Future?*, Basingstoke: Palgrave, 2001, pp. 93–109.

Crozier, M., Huntington, S., and Watanuki, J., *The Crisis of Democracy: Report on the Governability of Democracies to the Trilateral Commission*, New York: New York University Press, 1975.

Crutchfield, R. and Pitchford, S., 'Work and Crime: The Effects of Labor Stratification', *Social Forces*, vol. 76, no. 1, September 1997, pp. 93–118.

Currie, J. and Ferrie, J., *Strikes and the Law in the U.S., 1881–1894: New Evidence on the Origins of American Exceptionalism*, NBER Working Paper Series, Cambridge, MA: National Bureau of Economic Research, No. 5368, November 1995.

Dark, T., *The Unions and the Democrats: An Enduring Alliance*, Ithaca, NY: ILR Press, 1999.

Davies, R. and Weiner, R., 'A Cultural Perspective in the Study of Industrial Relations', in Frost, P. *et al.* (eds), *Organizational Culture*, London: Sage, 1985, pp. 355–372.

Dawkins, P. *et al.*, 'Dear John – How to Create More Jobs', *The Australian*, 26 October 1998, p. 13.

Dolowitz, D., 'Policy Transfer: A New Framework of Policy Analysis', in Dolowitz, D. with Hulme, R., Nellis, M., and O'Neill, F. (eds), *Policy Transfer and British Social Policy: Learning from the USA?*, Buckingham: Open University Press, 2000, pp. 9–37.

Dolowitz, D. with Hulme, R., Nellis, M., and O'Neill, F. (eds), *Policy Transfer and British Social Policy: Learning from the USA?*, Buckingham: Open University Press, 2000.

Dowrick, S. and Quiggan, J., 'A Survey of the Literature on Minimum Wages', unpublished manuscript, Canberra: The Australian National University, February 2003.

Durkheim E., *Socialism and Saint-Simon*, A. Gouldner (ed.), trans. C. Sattler, London: Routledge & Kegan Paul, 1959.

——, *The Division of Labour in Society*, trans. Simpson, G., Glencoe, IL: The Free Press, 1980a.

——, *Emile Durkheim: Contributions to L'Année Sociologique*, Y. Nandan (ed.), trans. J. French, *et al.*, New York: The Free Press, 1980b.

Ebbinghaus, B. and Visser, J., 'When Institutions Matter: Union Growth and Decline in Western Europe, 1950–1995', *European Sociological Review*, vol. 15, no. 2, June 1999, pp. 135–158.

The Economist, 8 June 1996, pp. 23–25.

——, 'Working Man's Burden', 6–12 February 1999, p. 88.

——, Europe's New Left', 12–18 February 2000, p. 21.

Edin, K., 'Plenary Address: Work is Not Enough', Social Policy Research Centre Conference, Sydney: University of New South Wales, 9–11 July 2003.

'Editorial: Class War in the USA', *Multinational Monitor*, vol. 18, no. 3, 1997, online. Available at: http://www. Multinationalmonitor.org (accessed 18 October 2003).

Eitzen, D. and Zinn, M., 'The Shrinking Welfare State: The New Welfare Legislation and Families', paper presented at the Thematic Session 'The Shrinking State: New Forms of Social Inequality', Annual Meeting of the American Sociological Association, San Francisco, August 1998.

Ellwood, D., 'From Welfare to Work', *CEDA Bulletin*, March 1999, 5.

Esping-Andersen, G., *The Three Worlds of Welfare Capitalism*, Princeton, NJ: Princeton University Press, 1990.

Esping-Andersen, G., Assimakopoulou, Z., and van Kersbergen, K., 'Trends in

Contemporary Class Structuration: A Six-Nation Comparison', in Esping-Ander-sen, G. (ed.), *Changing Classes: Stratification and Mobility in Post-industrial Societies*, London, Sage, 1993, pp. 32–57.

Etzioni-Halevy, E., *Bureaucracy and Democracy: A Political Dilemma*, London: Routledge and Kegan Paul, 1983.

Evans, G., 'The Decline of Class Divisions in Britain? Class and Ideological Prefer-ences in Britain in the 1960s and 1980s', *British Journal of Sociology*, vol. 44, no. 3, 1993, pp. 449–471.

—— (ed.), *The End of Class Politics: Class Voting in Comparative Context*, Oxford: Oxford University Press, 1999.

Farber, H.S. and Krueger, A.S., *Union Membership in the United States: the Decline Continues*, NBER Working Paper Series, Working Paper No. 4216, Cambridge, MA: National Bureau of Economic Research, November 1992.

Feenberg, A., *Questioning Technology*, London: Routledge, 1999.

Feher, F., 'The Socialism of Scarcity', *Thesis Eleven*, no. 37, 1994, pp. 98–118.

Forbath, W., *Law and the Shaping of the American Labor Movement*, Cambridge, MA: Harvard University Press, 1991.

——, 'Short-Circuit: A Critique of Habermas's Understanding of Law, Politics, and Economic Life', in Rosenfeld, M. and Arato, A. (eds), *Habermas on Law and Democracy: Critical Exchanges*, Berkeley, CA: University of California Press, 1998, pp. 272–286.

Frankel, B., 'Class, Environmental and Social Movements', in *The Polity Reader in Social Theory*, Cambridge: Polity Press, 1995.

——, 'Re-Imagining Political Economy', *Arena*, no. 24, August–September 1996, 28–33.

Friedman, M. with Friedman, R., *Capitalism and Freedom*, Chicago: University of Chicago Press, 1961.

Friedmann, G., *The Anatomy of Work: The Implications of Specialization*, trans. W. Rawson, London: Heinemann, 1961.

Fromm, E., 'The Psychological Aspects of the Guaranteed Income', in Theobald, R. (ed.), *The Guaranteed Income: Next Step in Economic Evolution?* New York: Doubleday, 1966, pp. 175–184.

Galbraith, J., 'The Real American Model', 2003, online. Available at: www.open-democracy.org (accessed 15 September 2003).

Galenson, W., *Trade Union Growth and Decline: An International Study*, West-port, CT: Praeger, 1994.

Giddens, A., *Capitalism and Modern Social Theory: An Analysis of the Writings of Marx, Durkheim, and Weber*, Cambridge: Cambridge University Press, 1985.

——, *Sociology*, 4th edn, Cambridge: Polity Press, 2003.

Gilens, M., *Why Americans Hate Welfare: Race, Media, and the Politics of Antipoverty Policy*, Chicago: University of Chicago Press, 1999.

Ginsburg, H., Zaccone, J., Schaffner Goldberg, G., Collins, S.D., and Rosen, S.M., 'Special Issue on: The Challenge of Full Employment in the Global Economy: Editorial Introduction', *Economic and Industrial Democracy*, vol. 18, no.1, Feb-ruary 1997, pp. 5–34.

Goldthorpe, J., 'Class and Politics in Advanced Industrial Societies', in Clark, T.N. and Lipset, S.M. (eds), *The Breakdown of Class Politics: A Debate on Post-Industrial Stratification*, Baltimore, MD: Johns Hopkins University Press, 2001, pp. 105–135.

Goodin, R. E., 'Towards a Minimally Presumptuous Social Welfare Policy', in van Parijs, P. (ed.), *Arguing for Basic Income: Ethical Foundations for a Radical Reform*, London, Verso, 1992, pp. 195–214.

——, 'Something for Nothing?: A Response to *A Basic Income for All* by Philippe van Parijs', *Boston Review*, October/November 2000, online. Available at: http://bostonreview.net/BR25.5/goodin.html (accessed 23 September 2003).

Gordon, D., 'Underpaid Workers, Bloated Corporations: Two Pieces in the Puzzle of U.S. Economic Decline', *Dissent*, vol. 43, no. 2, Spring 1996, pp. 23–34.

Gorz, A., *Strategy for Labor: A Radical Proposal*, trans. M.A. Nicolaus and V. Ortiz, Boston: Beacon Press, 1968.

——, *Farewell to the Working Class: An Essay on Post-industrial Socialism*, trans. M. Sonenscher, London: Pluto Press, 1982.

——, *Paths to Paradise: On the Liberation from Work*, London: Pluto Press, 1985.

——, *Critique of Economic Reason*, trans. G. Handyside and C. Turner, London: Verso, 1989.

——, *Reclaiming Work: Beyond a Wage-Based Society*, Oxford: Blackwell, 2000.

Gospel, H. and Palmer, G., *British Industrial Relations*, 2nd edn, London: Routledge, 1993.

Goul Andersen, J. and Jensen, J.B., *Different Routes to Improved Employment in Europe*, Centre for Comparative Welfare Studies Working Paper No. 22, Aalborg University, 2002.

Gouldner, A., 'Metaphysical Pathos and the Study of Bureaucracy', *American Political Science Review*, no. 49, June 1955, pp. 496–507.

——, *The Coming Crisis of Western Sociology*, London: Heinemann Educational Books, 1973.

Greenstein, R. and Shapiro, I., *New Research Findings on the Effects of the Earned Income Tax Credit*, Center on Budget and Policy Priorities Paper, 1998, online. Available at: http://www.cbpp.org (accessed 24 September 2003).

The Guardian, 'Labouring over le 35-hour week', 11 October 2003.

Habermas, J., *Toward a Rational Society: Student Protest, Science and Politics*, trans. J. Shapiro, Boston: Beacon Press, 1970.

——, *Knowledge and Human Interests*, trans. J. Shapiro, London: Heinemann Educational Books, 1972.

——, *The Theory of Communicative Action: Volume 1: Reason and the Rationalization of Society*, trans. T. McCarthy, Boston: Beacon Press, 1984.

——, *The Theory of Communicative Action: Volume 2: System and Lifeworld: A Critique of Functionalist Reason*, trans. T. McCarthy, Cambridge: Polity Press, 1987.

——, *The Philosophical Discourse of Modernity: Twelve Lectures*, trans. F. Lawrence, Cambridge: Polity Press, 1990.

——, 'A Reply', in Honneth, A. and Joas, H. (eds), *Communicative Action: Essays on Jürgen Habermas's* The Theory of Communicative Action, Cambridge: Polity Press, 1991, pp. 214–264.

——, 'The New Obscurity: The Crisis of the Welfare State and the Exhaustion of Utopian Energies', in S. Weber Nicholsen (ed. and trans.), *The New Conservatism: Cultural Criticism and the Historians' Debate*, Cambridge, MA: MIT Press, 1994, pp. 48–70.

——, *A Berlin Republic: Writings on Germany*, trans. S. Rendall, Lincoln, NB: University of Nebraska Press, 1997.

——, 'The European Nation-State and the Pressures of Globalization', *New Left Review*, no. 235, May/June 1999, pp. 46–59.

Hall, P.A. and Soskice, D.W., *Varieties of Capitalism: The Institutional Foundations of Comparative Advantage*, Oxford: Oxford University Press, 2001.

Hamilton, C., *Growth Fetish*, Crows Nest: Allen & Unwin, 2003.

Hanagan, M., 'Social Movements: Incorporation, Disengagement, and Opportunities – A Long View', in Giugni, M., McAdam, D., and Tilly C. (eds), *From Contention to Democracy*, Lanham, MD: Rowman & Littlefield, 1998, pp. 3–30.

Hattam, V., *Labor Visions and State Power: The Origins of Business Unionism in the United States*, Princeton, NJ: Princeton University Press, 1993.

Heath, A., Jowell, R., and Curtice, J.K., *British General Election Study 1987*, online. Available at: www.data-archive.ac.uk (accessed 20 October 2003).

Heath, A., Jowell, R., Curtice, J.K., and Norris, P.N., *British General Election Study 1997*, online. Available at: www.data-archive.ac.uk (accessed 20 October 2003).

Heller, A., *The Theory of Need in Marx*, New York: St. Martin's Press, 1976.

Higgins, W., 'The Swedish Municipal Workers' Union – A Study in the New Political Unionism', *Economic and Industrial Democracy*, vol. 17, no. 2, 1996, pp. 167–198.

Hinrichs, K., Offe, C., and Wiesenthal, H., 'The Crisis of the Welfare State and Alternative Modes of Work Redistribution', *Thesis Eleven*, no. 10/11, 1984/85, pp. 37–55.

Hodder, K., *Annual Survey of Violations of Trade Union Rights*, Report of the ICFTU [International Confederation of Free Trade Unions], Section: 'The United States of America', 1999.

Holstein, W. and Cohen, J., 'Ready, Aim, Hire: Corporate America and Workfare as We Know It', *U.S. News and World Report*, 31 March 1997, p. 51.

Holton, R.J. and Turner, B.S., *Max Weber on Economy and Society*, London: Routledge, 1989.

Honneth, A., *The Critique of Power: Reflective Stages in a Critical Social Theory*, Cambridge, MA: MIT Press, 1991.

——, 'The Social Dynamics of Disrespect: On the Location of Critical Theory Today', *Constellations*, vol. 1, no. 2, 1994, pp. 255–269.

——, *The Fragmented World of the Social: Essays in Social and Political Philosophy*, Wright, C (ed.), Albany, NY: State University of New York Press, 1995.

Howard, D., 'The French Strikes of 1995: Back to the Future?', *Constellations*, vol. 3, no. 2, 1996, pp. 248–260.

Howell, D., 'Block and Manza on the Negative Income Tax', *Politics & Society*, vol. 25, no. 4, December 1997, pp. 533–539.

Howell, D.S. and Wolff, E.N., 'Trends in the Growth and Distribution of Skills in the U.S. Workplace: 1960–1985', *Industrial and Labor Relations Review*, vol. 44, 1991, pp. 486–502.

Hughes, E.C., *On Work, Race, and the Sociological Imagination*, Coser, L. (ed. and intro.), Chicago: University of Chicago Press, 1994.

Hunt, J., *Has Work-Sharing Worked in Germany?*, NBER Working Paper No. W5724, Cambridge, MA: National Bureau of Economic Research, August 1996.

Hywood, G., 'The US Battle for Hearts and Minds', *The Sydney Morning Herald*, 4 February 2000, p. 15.

Ingham, G., 'Some Recent Changes in the Relationship between Economics and

Sociology', *Cambridge Journal of Economics*, vol. 20, no. 2, March 1996, pp. 243–275.

Inglehart, R., *Culture Shift in Advanced Industrial Societies*, Princeton, NJ: Princeton University Press, 1990.

International Labour Organisation, *World Labour Report 1997–98: Industrial Relations, Democracy, and Social Stability*, Geneva: International Labour Office, 1997.

Jacobs, J., 'Careers in the US Service Economy', in Esping-Andersen, G. (ed.), *Changing Classes: Stratification and Mobility in Post-industrial Societies*, London: Sage, 1993, pp. 195–224.

Jencks, C., Perman, L., and Rainwater, L., 'What is a Good Job?: A New Measure of Labor-Market Success', *American Journal of Sociology*, vol. 93, no. 6, 1988, pp. 1322–1357.

Joas, H., 'The Unhappy Marriage of Hermeneutics and Functionalism', in Honneth, A. and Joas, H. (eds), *Communicative Action: Essays on Jürgen Habermas's* The Theory of Communicative Action, Cambridge: Polity Press, 1991, pp. 97–118.

——, *The Creativity of Action*, trans. J. Gaines and P. Keast, Cambridge: Polity Press, 1996.

Johansson, A., 'Taylorism and the Rise of Organised Labour; United States and Sweden', in Gustafsson, B. (ed.), *Power and Economic Institutions: Reinterpretations in Economic History*, Aldershot: Edward Elgar, 1991, pp. 302–336.

Johnston, M. and Jowell, R., 'Social Capital and the Social Fabric', in Jowell, R., Curtice, J., Park, A., Thompson, K. with Jarvis, L, Bromley, C., and Stratford, N. (eds), *British Social Attitudes: Who Shares New Labour Values?*, Aldershot: Ashgate, 1999, pp. 179–200.

Jones, R., McAllister, I., Denemark, D., and Gow, D., *Australian Election Study 1993*, online. Available at: http//:assda.anu.edu.au (accessed 20 October 2003).

Jordan, B., 'Basic Income and The Common Good', in van Parijs, P. (ed.), *Arguing for Basic Income: Ethical Foundations for a Radical Reform*, London: Verso, 1992, pp. 155–177.

Jowell, R., Curtice, J., Park, A., Brook, L., Ahrendt, D. with Thomson, K. (eds), *British Social Attitudes: the 12th Report*, Aldershot: Dartmouth Publishing, 1995.

Judis, J.B. and Teixeira, R., *The Emerging Democratic Majority*, New York: Scribner, 2002.

Keane, J., *Democracy and Civil Society: On the Predicaments of European Socialism, the Prospects for Democracy, and the Problem of Controlling Social and Political Power*, London: Verso, 1988.

——, *Tom Paine: A Political Life*, London: Bloomsbury, 1995.

Keane, J. and Owens, J., *After Full Employment*, London: Hutchinson, 1987.

Kelley, J., Cushing, R.G., and Headey, B., *Australian National Social Science Survey, 1984* (User's guide and data file), Canberra: Social Science Data Archives, The Australian National University, 1987.

Kellner, D., 'Introduction to "On the Philosophical Foundation of the Concept of Labor"', *Telos*, no. 16, 1973, pp. 2–8.

Kettler, D. and Meja, V., 'The End of Western Trade Unionism?: Social Progress after the Age of Progressivism', in Alexander, J. and Sztompka, P. (eds), *Rethinking Progress: Movements, Forces, and Ideas at the End of the Twentieth Century*, Boston: Unwin Hyman, 1990, pp. 123–158.

Kohn, M.L., *Class and Conformity: A Study in Values*, Illinois: The Dorsey Press, 1969.

Kohn, M.L. and Slomczynski, K.M., *Social Structure and Self-Direction: A Comparative Analysis of the United States and Poland*, Cambridge, MA: Basil Blackwell, 1990.

Laabs, J., 'Has Downsizing Really Missed its Mark?', *Workforce*, April 1999, p. 33.

Lange, P. and Scruggs, L., 'Where Have all the Members Gone?: Union Density in the Era of Globalization', unpublished paper, Durham, NC: Duke University, 1998.

Levi, M. 'Organizing Power: The Prospects for an American Labor Movement', *Perspectives on Politics*, vol. 1, no.1, March 2003, pp. 45–68.

Levitt, M.J., *Confessions of a Union Buster*, New York: Crown Publishers, 1993.

Lichtenstein, N., *The Most Dangerous Man in Detroit: Walter Reuther and the Fate of American Labor*, New York: Basic Books, 1995.

Lipset, S.M., *Revolution and Counterrevolution: Change and Persistence in Social Structures*, New York: Anchor Books, 1970.

——, 'The Work Ethic, Then and Now', *Journal of Labor Research*, vol. 13, no. 1, Winter 1992, pp. 45–54.

——, 'The Decline of Class Ideologies', in Nichols Clark, T. and Lipset, S.M. (eds), *The Breakdown of Class Politics: A Debate on Post-Industrial Stratification*, Baltimore, MD: Johns Hopkins University Press, 2001, pp. 249–272.

Lipset, S.M., Trow, M.A., and Coleman, J.S., *Union Democracy: The Internal Politics of the International Typographical Union*, Glencoe, IL: The Free Press, 1977.

Loprest, P., 'Families Who Left Welfare: Who are They and How are They Doing?', *Assessing the New Federalism*, Discussion Paper No. 2, Washington, D.C.: The Urban Institute, 1999.

Löwith, K., *Max Weber and Karl Marx*, Bottomore, T. and Outhwaite, W. (eds), trans. H. Fantel, London: George Allen & Unwin, 1982.

Luhmann, N., *The Differentiation of Society*, trans. S. Holmes and C. Larmore, New York: Columbia University Press, 1982.

——, *Political Theory in the Welfare State*, trans. J. Bednarz Jr., Berlin: Walter de Gruyter, 1990.

Lukes, S., *Emile Durkheim: His Life and Work; A Historical and Critical Study*, London: Penguin, 1973.

McAdam, D., McCarthy, J., and Zald, M., 'Social Movements', in Smelser, N. (ed.), *Handbook of Sociology*, Newbury Park, CA: Sage, 1988.

McCarthy, T., 'Complexity and Democracy: or the Seducements of Systems Theory', in Honneth, A. and Joas, H. (eds), *Communicative Action: Essays on Jürgen Habermas's* The Theory of Communicative Action, Cambridge: Polity Press, 1991, pp. 119–139.

Mallet, S., *The New Working Class*, Nottingham: Spokesman Books, 1975.

Mantsios, G., 'What Should Labor Stand For?', in Mantsios, G. (ed.), *A New Labor Movement for the New Century*, New York: Monthly Review Press, 1998, pp. 44–64.

Marcuse, H., *Reason and Revolution: Hegel and the Rise of Social Theory*, London: Routledge & Kegan Paul, 1968.

——, *Eros and Civilization: A Philosophical Inquiry into Freud*, London: Abacus, 1972.

——, 'On the Philosophical Foundations of the Concept of Labor in Economics', *Telos*, no. 16, 1973, pp. 9–37.

Márkus, G., *Marxism and Anthropology: The Concept of 'Human Essence' in the Philosophy of Marx*, trans. E. de Laczay and G. Markus, Assen: Van Gorcum, 1978.

——, *Language and Production: A Critique of the Paradigms*, Dortrecht: D. Riedel, 1986.

Marx, K., *Capital: A Critique of Political Economy, Volume III, Book III: The Process of Capitalist Production as a Whole*, Engels, F. (ed.), Moscow: Progress Publishers, 1966.

——, *Capital: A Critique of Political Economy: Volume I, Capitalist Production*, trans. S. Moore and E. Aveling, Engels, F. (ed.), London: Lawrence & Wishart, 1970.

——, 'Capital: Selections', in Tucker, R. (ed.), *The Marx–Engels Reader*, New York: W. W. Norton, 1972a, pp. 191–317.

——, 'The German Ideology: Part I', in Tucker, R. (ed.), *The Marx–Engels Reader*, New York: W. W. Norton, 1972b, pp. 110–164.

——, *Grundrisse: Foundations of the Critique of Political Economy (Rough Draft)*, trans. M. Nicolaus, Harmondsworth: Penguin, 1973.

Mayo, E., *The Human Problems of an Industrial Civilization*, New York: Macmillan, 1933.

Mead, L., 'The Rise of Paternalism', in Mead, L. (ed.), *The New Paternalism: Supervisory Approaches to Poverty*, Washington, DC: Brookings Institution Press, 1997, pp. 1–38.

Meagher, G. and Wilson, S., 'Complexity and Practical Knowledge in the Social Sciences', *British Journal of Sociology*, vol. 53, no. 4, December 2002, pp. 659–662.

Meyerson, H., 'Rolling the Union On: John Sweeney's Movement Four Years Later', *Dissent*, Winter 1999, pp. 47–55.

Michels, R., *Political Parties: A Sociological Study of the Oligarchical Tendencies of Modern Democracy*, trans. E. Paul and C. Paul, New York: Collier Books, 1962.

Miller, J., 'Jobs and Work', in Smelser, N. (ed.), *Handbook of Sociology*, Newbury Park, CA: Sage, 1988, pp. 327–359.

Mills, C. Wright, *The New Men of Power: America's Labor Leaders*, New York: Augustus M. Kelley, 1971.

Mirowsky, J., Ross, C., and van Willigen, M., 'Instrumentalism in the Land of Opportunity: Socioeconomic Causes and Emotional Consequences', *Social Psychology Quarterly*, vol. 59, no. 4, December 1996, pp. 322–337.

Mishel, L., Bernstein, J., and Boushey, H., *The State of Working America 2002–2003*, Ithaca, NY: Cornell University Press, 2003.

Mishel, L., Bernstein, J., and Schmitt, J., *The State of Working America, 1998–99*, Ithaca, NY: Cornell University Press, 1999.

Mishel, L. and Schmitt, J., *Beware the US Model: Jobs and Wages in a Deregulated Economy*, Washington, DC: Economic Policy Institute, 1995.

Moberg, D., 'Can Labor Change?', *Dissent*, Winter 1996, pp. 16–21.

Mommsen, W., *Max Weber and German Politics: 1890–1920*, trans. M.S. Steinberg, Chicago: University of Chicago Press, 1984.

Montgomery, D., *Workers' Control in America: Studies in the History of Work, Technology, and Labor Struggles*, Cambridge: Cambridge University Press, 1979.

——, *The Fall of the House of Labor: The Workplace, the State, and American Labor Activism, 1865–1925*, Cambridge: Cambridge University Press, 1987.

——, *Citizen Worker: The Experience of Workers in the United States with Democracy and the Free Market during the Nineteenth Century*, Cambridge: Cambridge University Press, 1993.

Moody, K., *Workers in a Lean World: Unions in the International Economy*, London: Verso, 1997.

Mouzelis, N., *Sociological Theory: What Went Wrong?: Diagnosis and Remedies*, London: Routledge, 1995.

Munch, R. and Smelser, N., 'Relating the Micro and Macro', in Alexander, J., Smelser, N., and Munch, R. (eds), *The Micro-Macro Link*, Berkeley, CA: University of California Press, 1987, pp. 356–373.

Murphy, K. and Martin, C., 'Unions as a Labor Force', *Australian Financial Review*, 20 March 2000.

Murray, C., *Losing Ground: American Social Policy, 1950–1980*, New York: Basic Books, 1995.

Myles, J. and Pierson, P., 'Friedman's Revenge: The Reform of "Liberal" Welfare States in Canada and the United States', *Politics & Society*, vol. 25, no. 4, December 1997, pp. 443–472.

National Centre for Social Research, *British Social Attitudes Survey, 2000*, online. Available at: http://www.data-archive.ac.uk (accessed 23 October 2003).

'Nation's Leaders in Welfare to Gather for One America Conference', *Reuters Report*, 3 August 1999.

Needleman, R., 'Women Workers: Strategies for Inclusion and Rebuilding Unionism', in Mantsios, G. (ed.), *A New Labor Movement for the New Century*, New York: Monthly Review Press, 1998, pp. 151–170.

Oberschall, A., *Social Conflict and Social Movements*, Englewood Cliffs, NJ: Prentice-Hall, 1973.

O'Connor, J., *The Fiscal Crisis of the State*, New York: St. Martin's Press, 1973.

Offe, C., *Contradictions of the Welfare State*, Keane, J. (ed.), London: Hutchinson, 1984.

——, *Disorganized Capitalism: Contemporary Transformations of Work and Politics*, Keane, J. (ed.), Cambridge: Polity Press, 1985a.

——, 'New Social Movements: Challenging the Boundaries of Institutional Politics', *Social Research*, vol. 52, no. 4, Winter 1985b, pp. 817–868.

——, 'Full Employment: Asking the Wrong Question?', *Dissent*, Winter 1995, pp. 77–81.

——, *Modernity and the State: East, West*, Cambridge: Polity Press, 1996.

——, 'Pathways from Here: A Response to *A Basic Income for All* by Philippe van Parijs', *Boston Review*, October/November 2000, online. Available at: http://bostonreview.net/BR25.5/offe.html (accessed 23 September 2003).

Offe, C. and Heinze, R., *Beyond Employment: Time, Work, and the Informal Economy*, trans. A. Braley, Cambridge: Polity Press, 1992.

Olson, M., *The Logic of Collective Action: Public Goods and the Theory of Groups*, Cambridge: Harvard University Press, 1965.

Oppenheim, C., 'Enabling Participation? New Labour's Welfare-to-Work Policies', in White, S. (ed.), *New Labour: The Progressive Future?*, Basingstoke: Palgrave, 2001, pp. 77–92.

Organisation for Economic Co-operation and Development [OECD], *Employment Outlook 1996*, Paris: OECD, 1996.
——, *Employment Outlook 1998*, Paris: OECD, 1998.
——, *Employment Outlook 1999*, Paris: OECD, 1999.
——, *Employment Outlook 2001*, Paris: OECD, 2001.
——, *Education at a Glance 2002*, Paris: OECD, 2002a.
——, *Society at a Glance 2002*, Paris: OECD, 2002b.
——, *A Policy Agenda for Growth: An Overview of the Sources of Economic Growth in OECD Countries*, Paris: OECD, 2003.
Oummen, T., 'Social Movements in a Comparative Perspective: Situating Alain Touraine', in Clark, J. and Diani, M. (eds), *Alain Touraine*, London: Falmer, 1996, pp. 111–125.
Parsons, T., *Sociological Theory and Modern Society*, New York: The Free Press, 1967.
Parsons, T. and Smelser, N., *Economy and Society: A Study in the Integration of Economic and Social Theory*, London: Routledge & Kegan Paul, 1964.
Pateman, C., 'The Patriarchal Welfare State', in Gutman, A. (ed.), *Democracy and the Welfare State*, Princeton, NJ: Princeton University Press, 1988, pp. 231–260.
Peetz, D., *Unions in a Contrary World: The Future of the Australian Trade Union Movement*, Cambridge: Cambridge University Press, 1998.
Perrin, R., 'Emile Durkheim's *Division of Labor* and the Shadow of Herbert Spencer', *The Sociological Quarterly*, vol. 36, no. 4, 1995, pp. 791–808.
Phelps, E. S., 'Subsidize Wages: A Response to *A Basic Income for All* by Philippe van Parijs', *Boston Review*, October/November 2000, online. Available at: http://bostonreview.net/BR25.5/phelps.html (accessed 23 September 2003).
Pierson, P., *Dismantling the Welfare State?: Reagan, Thatcher, and the Politics of Retrenchment*, Cambridge: Cambridge University Press, 1994.
——, 'Increasing Returns, Path Dependence, and the Study of Politics', *American Political Science Review*, vol. 94, no. 2, 2000, pp. 251–267.
Piotet, F., 'Les événements de décémbre 1995, chroniques d'un conflit', *Sociologie du travail*, no. 4, 1997, pp. 523–545.
Piven, F.F. and Cloward, R.A., *The Breaking of the American Social Compact*, New York: The Free Press, 1997a.
——, 'We Should Have Made a Plan!', *Politics & Society*, vol. 25, no. 4, 1997b, pp. 525–532.
Pixley, J., *Citizenship and Employment: Investigating Post-Industrial Options*, Cambridge: Cambridge University Press, 1993.
——, 'Employment and Social Identity: Theoretical Issues', in Roche M. and van Berkel, R. (eds), *European Citizenship and Social Exclusion*, Aldershot: Ashgate, 1997, pp. 119–134.
Pocock, P., 'Gender, Strife and Unions', in Pocock, B. (ed.), *Strife: Sex and Politics in Labor Unions*, St. Leonards, NSW: Allen & Unwin, 1997, pp. 9–25.
Poggi, G., *Calvinism and the Capitalist Spirit: Max Weber's Protestant Ethic*, London: Macmillan, 1983.
——, 'Max Weber's Politics as a Vocation', lecture at the University of New South Wales, School of Sociology, 11 August 1999.
Polanyi, K., *The Great Transformation*, New York: Farrar & Rinehart, 1944.
Pollock, F., *The Economic and Social Consequences of Automation*, trans. W. Henderson and W. Chaloner, Oxford: Basil Blackwell, 1957.

——, 'State Capitalism: Its Possibilities and Limitations', in Arato, A. and Gebhardt, E. (eds), *The Essential Frankfurt School Reader*, New York: Urizen Books, 1978, pp. 71–94.

Postone, M., *Time, Labor, and Social Domination: A Reinterpretation of Marx's Critical Theory*, Cambridge: Cambridge University Press, 1993.

Power, M., 'Habermas and the Counterfactual Imagination', in Rosenfeld, M. and Arato, A. (eds), *Habermas on Law and Democracy: Critical Exchanges*, Berkeley, CA: University of California Press, 1998, pp. 207–225.

Purdy, D., 'Citizenship, Basic Income and the State', *New Left Review*, no. 208, November/December 1994, pp. 30–48.

Pusey, M., *The Middle Australia Project 1996*, [computer file] Kensington: School of Sociology, University of New South Wales, 2000.

Radin, M., *Contested Commodities*, Cambridge, MA: Harvard University Press, 1996.

Rawls, J., *A Theory of Justice*, Cambridge, MA: The Belknap Press of Harvard University Press, 1972.

——, 'Reply to Alexander and Musgrave', *Quarterly Journal of Economics*, vol. 88, no. 4, November 1974, pp. 633–655.

Reserve Bank of Australia, 'Consumer Credit and Household Finances', *Reserve Bank of Australia Bulletin*, Sydney: RBA, June 1999, pp. 11–17.

Ribeill, G., 'Le conflict des cheminots de novembre–décembre 1995: les avatars politiques d'une grève corporative', *Sociologie du travail*, no. 4, 1997, pp. 425–448.

Rifkin, J., *The End of Work: The Decline of the Global Labor Force and the Dawn of the Post-Market Era*, New York: Jeremy P. Tarcher/Putnam, 1995.

Ritchie, L. D., 'Parents' Workplace Experiences and Family Communication Patterns', *Communications Research*, vol. 24, no. 2, April 1997, pp. 175–187.

Rocher, G., *Talcott Parsons and American Sociology*, trans. B. Mennell and S. Mennell, London: Nelson, 1974.

Rorty, R., *Philosophy and Social Hope*, New York: Penguin, 1999.

Ross, C. and Mirowsky, J., 'Households, Employment and the Sense of Control', *Social Psychology Quarterly*, vol. 55, no. 3, 1992, pp. 217–235.

Rothstein, R., 'Union Strength in the United States: Lessons from the UPS Strike', *International Labour Review*, vol. 136, no. 4, 1997, pp. 469–492.

Rueschemeyer, D., *Power and the Division of Labour*, Cambridge: Polity Press, 1986.

Runciman, W.G., 'Ideology: Introduction', in Runciman, W.G. (ed.), *Max Weber: Selections in Translation*, trans. E. Matthews, Cambridge: Cambridge University Press, 1985, pp. 135–137.

Sartre, J. P., *The Critique of Dialectical Reason*, trans. A. Sheridan-Smith, Rée, J. (ed.), London: Verso, 1991.

Sawicky, M. (ed.), *The End of Welfare?: Consequences of Federal Devolution for the Nation*, Washington, DC: Economic Policy Institute, 1999.

Scharpf, F., *The Viability of Advanced Welfare States in the International Economy: Vulnerabilities and Options*, Working Paper No. 99/9, Cologne: Max Planck Institute for the Study of Societies, 1999.

Scherer, R., 'From Welfare to ... Unions?', *The Christian Science Monitor*, 8 October 1997.

Schmid, G., 'Transitional Labour Markets: A New European Employment Strategy', *Discussion Paper FS 98–206*, Berlin: Wissenschaftenszentrum Berlin für Sozialforschung, October 1998.

Schor, J.B., *The Overworked American: The Unexpected Decline of Leisure*, New York: Basic Books, 1991.

——, *The Overspent American: Upscaling, Downshifting and the New Consumer*, New York: Basic Books, 1998.

Scott, A., 'Movements of Modernity: Some Questions of Theory, Method and Interpretation', in Clark, J. and Diani, M. (eds), *Alain Touraine*, London: Falmer, 1996, pp. 77–92.

Scruggs, L. and Lange, P., 'Where Have all the Members Gone? Globalization, Institutions, and Union Density', *Journal of Politics*, vol. 64, no. 1, February 2002, pp. 126–153.

Seidman, G., *Manufacturing Militance: Workers' Movements in Brazil and South Africa, 1970–1985*, Berkeley, CA: University of California Press, 1994.

Sexton, P., *The War on Labor and the Left: Understanding America's Unique Conservatism*, Boulder, CO: Westview Press, 1992.

Silverstein, K., 'America's Private Gulag', in Burton-Rose, D., Pens, D., and Wright, P. (eds), *The Celling of America: An Inside Look at the U.S. Prison Industry*, Monroe, Maine: Common Courage Press, 1998, pp. 156–163.

Skocpol, T., *Social Policy in the United States: Future Possibilities in Historical Perspective*, Princeton, NJ: Princeton University Press, 1995.

——, *The Missing Middle*, New York: W.W. Norton, 2000.

Sneade, A., 'National Statistics Feature: Trade Union Membership 1999–2000: An Analysis of Data from the Certification Officer and the Labour Force Survey', *Labour Market Trends*, September 2001, London: Government Statistical Service, pp. 433–444.

Steiner, H., 'Three Just Taxes', in van Parijs, P. (ed.), *Arguing for Basic Income: Ethical Foundations for a Radical Reform*, London: Verso, 1992, pp. 81–92.

Stepan-Norris, J., 'The Making of Union Democracy', *Social Forces*, vol. 76, no. 2, 1997, pp. 475–510.

Stepan-Norris, J. and Zeitlin, M., 'Insurgency, Radicalism, and Democracy in America's Industrial Unions', *Social Forces*, vol. 75, no. 1, 1996, pp. 1–32.

Stiglitz, J., 'The Roaring Nineties', *The Atlantic Monthly*, October 2002, pp. 75–89.

Sustar, L., 'A New Labor Movement?', *International Socialist Review*, Summer 1997, pp. 19–26.

Svallfors, S., 'Worlds of Welfare and Attitudes to Redistribution: A Comparison of Eight Western Nations', *European Sociological Review*, vol. 13, 1997, pp. 283–304.

Sweezy, P., *The Theory of Capitalist Development: Principles of Marxian Political Economy*, New York: Monthly Review Press, 1970.

Taylor, M., 'The Dynamics of US Managerialism and the American Corporations', in Slater, D. and Taylor, P. (eds), *The American Century: Consensus and Coercion in the Projection of American Power*, Oxford: Blackwell, 1999, pp. 51–66.

Therborn, G., *Science, Class and Society: On the Formation of Sociology and Historical Materialism*, London: New Left Books, 1976.

——, *Why Some Peoples are More Unemployed than Others*, London: Verso, 1986.

Thompson, K., *Emile Durkheim*, New York: Tavistock, 1982.

Thompson, M., 'Industrial Relations in Canada', in Bamber, G. and Lansbury, R. (eds), *International and Comparative Industrial Relations: A Study of Industrialised Market Economies*, 2nd edn, Sydney: Allen & Unwin, 1993, pp. 83–99.

Tilly, C. and Tilly, C., *Work under Capitalism*, Boulder, CO: Westview Press, 1998.

Touraine, A., *The Self-Production of Society*, trans. D. Coltman, Chicago: University of Chicago Press, 1977.

——, *The Voice and the Eye: An Analysis of Social Movements*, trans. A. Duff, Cambridge: Cambridge University Press, 1981.

——, 'An Introduction to the Study of Social Movements', *Social Research*, vol. 52, no. 4, Winter 1985, pp. 749–787.

——, 'Au-delà d'une société du travail et des mouvements sociaux?', *Sociologie et sociétés*, vol. 23, no. 2, Autumn 1991, pp. 30–41.

——, *Critique of Modernity*, trans. D. Macey, Cambridge, MA: Blackwell, 1995.

——, 'L'ombre d'un mouvement', in Touraine, A., Dubet, F., Lapeyronnie, D., Khosrokhavar, F., and Wieviorka, M., *Le Grand Refus: Réfléxions sur la grève de décembre 1995*, Paris: Fayard, 1996, pp. 11–102.

Touraine, A., Dubet, F., Wieviorka, M., and Strzelecki, J., *Solidarity: The Analysis of a Social Movement: Poland, 1980–1981*, trans. D. Denby, Cambridge: Cambridge University Press, 1983.

Touraine, A., Hegedus, Z., Dubet, F., and Wieviorka, M., *Anti-Nuclear Protest: The Opposition to Nuclear Energy in France*, trans. P. Fawcett, Cambridge: Cambridge University Press, 1983.

Touraine, A., Wieviorka, M., and Dubet, F., *The Workers' Movement*, trans. I. Patterson, Cambridge: Cambridge University Press, 1987.

US News and World Report, 'World-class Workaholics: Are Crazy Hours and Takeout the Elixir of America's Success?', 20 December 1999.

Valenzuela, J.S., 'Labour Movements and Political Systems: Some Variations', in Regini, M. (ed.), *The Future of Labour Movements*, London: Sage, 1992, pp. 53–101.

Valkenburg, B. and Zoll, R., 'Modernization, Individualization, and Solidarity: Two Perspectives on European Trade Unions Today', *European Journal of Industrial Relations*, vol. 1, no. 1, 1995, pp. 114–144.

van Parijs, P., 'The Second Marriage of Justice and Efficiency', in van Parijs, P. (ed.), *Arguing for Basic Income: Ethical Foundations for a Radical Reform*, London: Verso, 1992, pp. 215–240.

——, 'A Basic Income for All', *Boston Review*, October/November 2000a, online. Available at: http://bostonreview.net/BR25.5/vanparijs.html (accessed September 2003).

——, 'Philippe van Parijs Responds', *Boston Review*, October/November 2000b, online. Available at: http://bostonreview.net/BR25.5/vanparijs2.html (accessed 23 September 2003).

Visser, J., *Trends in Unionisation and Collective Bargaining*, Geneva: International Labour Office, 2000.

Visser, J. and Hemerijck, A., *A Dutch Miracle: Job Growth, Welfare Reform and Corporatism in the Netherlands*, Amsterdam: University of Amsterdam Press, 1997.

Wacquant, L., 'The Rise of Advanced Marginality: Notes on its Nature and Implications', *Acta Sociologica*, vol. 39, no. 2, 1996, pp. 121–139.

Waldinger, R. *et al.*, 'Justice for Janitors: Organizing in Difficult Times', *Dissent*, Winter 1997, pp. 37–44.

Watson, I., 'Proposals for a Wage Freeze and Tax Credits: Will Subsidising Low Wage Jobs Solve Unemployment?', *Parliamentary Library Research Paper 29, 1998–99*, Canberra: Commonwealth of Australia, 1998, online. Available at: http://www.aph.gov.au/library/pubs/rp/1998-99/99rp29.htm (accessed 23 September 2003).

Weaver, R.K., 'Ending Welfare As We Know It', in Weir, M. (ed.), *The Social Divide: Political Parties and the Future of Activist Government*, Washington, DC: Brookings Institution Press, 1998, pp. 361–416.

Weber, M., *The Protestant Ethic and the Spirit of Capitalism*, trans. T. Parsons, London: Allen & Unwin, 1930.

——, *The Theory of Social and Economic Organization*, trans. A. Henderson and T. Parsons, Parsons, T. (ed.), New York: The Free Press, 1968.

——, 'Class, Status, Party', in Gerth, H.H. and Mills, C. Wright (eds), *From Max Weber: Essays in Sociology*, London: Routledge & Kegan Paul, 1974, pp. 181–195.

——, 'The Origins of Industrial Capitalism in Europe' in Runciman, W.G. (ed.), *Max Weber: Selections in Translation*, trans. E. Matthews, Cambridge: Cambridge University Press, 1985, pp. 331–340.

Weir, M., 'The Federal Government and Unemployment: The Frustration of Policy Innovation from the New Deal to the Great Society', in Weir, M., Orloff, A.S., and Skocpol, T. (eds), *The Politics of Social Policy in the United States*, Princeton, NJ: Princeton University Press, 1988, pp. 149–190.

——, *Politics and Jobs: The Boundaries of Employment Policy in the United States*, Princeton, NJ: Princeton University Press, 1992.

Weir, M., Orloff, A.S., and Skocpol, T., 'Introduction: Understanding American Social Politics', in Weir, M., Orloff, A.S., and Skocpol, T. (eds), *The Politics of Social Policy in the United States*, Princeton, NJ: Princeton University Press, 1988, pp. 3–27.

Weir, S., 'The Informal Work Group', in Lynd, A. and Lynd, S. (eds), *Rank and File: Personal Histories of Working Class Organizers*, Boston: Beacon, 1973, pp. 177–179.

Western, B., *Between Class and Market: Postwar Unionization in the Capitalist Democracies*, Princeton, NJ: Princeton University Press, 1997.

Western, B. and Beckett, K., 'How Unregulated Is the U.S. Labor Market? The Penal System as a Labor Market Institution', *American Journal of Sociology*, vol. 104, no. 4, 1999, pp. 1030–1060.

Western, B. and Healy, K., 'Explaining the OECD Wage Slowdown: Recession or Labour Decline?', *European Sociological Review*, vol. 15, no. 3, 1999, pp. 233–249.

Wheeler, H.N., 'Industrial Relations in the United States of America', in Bamber, G. and Lansbury, R. (eds), *International and Comparative Relations: A Study of Industrialised Market Economies*, 2nd edn, Sydney: Allen & Unwin, 1993, pp. 55–82.

Widerquist, K., 'Reciprocity and the Guaranteed Income', *Politics & Society*, vol. 27, no. 3, 1999, pp. 387–402.

Wieviorka, M., 'Le sens d'une lutte', in Touraine, A., Dubet, F., Lapeyronnie, D., Khosrokhavar, F., and Wieviorka, M., *Le Grand Refus: Réfléxions sur la grève de décembre 1995*, Paris: Fayard, 1995, pp. 247–296.

Williams, L., 'Rethinking Low-Wage Markets and Dependency', *Politics & Society*, vol. 25, no. 4, 1997, pp. 541–550.

Wilson, S., 'Union Mobilisation and the 1998 Maritime Dispute', *Journal of Australian Political Economy*, no. 41, June 1998, pp. 23–36.

——, *Australian Survey of Social Attitudes [draft computer file]*, The Australian National University, Canberra: Australian Social Science Data Archive, 2003.

Wilson, S. and Turnbull, N., 'Wedge Politics and Welfare Reform in Australia', *Australian Journal of Politics & History*, vol. 47, no. 3, 2001, pp. 384–402.

Wright, T., 'PM Paves Way to Cut Wages, Dole', *The Sydney Morning Herald*, 7 July 1997.

Zald, M. and Ash, R., 'Social Movement Organizations: Growth, Decay and Change', *Social Forces*, vol. 44, no. 3, March 1966.

Index

bureaucracy 42; communication 45; democratisation 44; end of work 2–3, 162–3; identity 43–4; lifeworld 9, 40, 41, 42, 177n10; Marcuse 23; 'Science and Technology as "Ideology"' 40; social change 41, 165; social rationalisation 40–1, 177n10; social theory 43–4; systems theory 44–5; technical rationalisation 42–3; *The Theory of Communicative Action* 41, 44; work 3, 9, 37–40
Hanagan, Michael 49–50
Hawke government 148
Hayek, Friedrich von 110
health care 157, 184n5
health insurance 87, 157
Healy, K. 86
Hegel, G.W.F. 14, 15, 17, 18, 172n5
Heidegger, Martin 174n34
Heinze, R. 120
Heller, Agnes 15–16, 19–20, 172–3n17
Hinrichs, K. 53
hiring and firing 71
Hispanic Americans 84
historicity 179n35
Hoffa, James Jr 145, 146
Holton, Robert 25
Honneth, Axel 9, 39, 41–4, 165
household debt 89
Howard government 95, 96, 97–8, 135, 148
Howell, David 118
Hughes, Everett 9–10
human relations, workplace 28, 32–3, 175–6n56
Hunt, Jennifer 156

incarceration 82–3, 189n75, n80
income support 80; Britain 97; downsizing 91–2; EU 116; low-wages 7; US 80, 188n67; welfare 67–8
individualism 66
industrial relations 32, 71, 72, 95, 136–7
industrial society 30, 180–1n51
informal sector 56, 121
Ingham, G. 174n37
institutions 13–14, 25, 36, 104–5, 132
International Confederation of Free Trade Unions 71–2
International Labour Organisation 127, 133; *World Labour Report* 127, 131
International Typographical Union 125

Iraq war 147
Italy: collective bargaining 130; education 82; EPR 57, 58; income support 80; low-wages 88; productivity 89; strikes 129; trade union membership 128; unemployment 78, 79, 82; working hours 88

Japan: collective bargaining 130; education 82; GDP/welfare 165; income support 80; low-wages 88; strikes 129; trade union membership 128; unemployment 78, 79, 82; working hours 88
Jensen, Jan Bendix 59
Joas, Hans 16–17
job creation: basic income 102, 123; deregulation 66; labour market 119; negative income tax 102; public sector 157; quality jobs 121–2, 160
job insecurity 72–3
job satisfaction 190n110
jobs with equality 7–8, 124, 169–70
jobs with inquality 6, 166–7
Johansson, A. 28
Jordan, Bill 105
Jospin, Lionel 142, 143
Judis, John 201n109
Juppé government 142
Juravich, Tom 149
'Justice for Janitors' 50, 144

Keane, John 107, 192n2
Keating government 148
Kellner, Douglas 23, 174n34
Kennedy government 70
Kettler, David 28–9, 126–7
Khosrokhavar, Farhad 143
Kohn, Melvin 44
Korea, South 127
Krueger, Alan 87, 131

labour: capitalism 34, 173n20; cheap 75–6; EU 68; marginalised 18; production 39; social movements 46; socially useful 56, 102, 116; technological change 17–18; Third World 160; *see also* employment; work
labour, division of: anomic 31; Durkheim 29, 30–1, 34, 176n64; forced 31; Marx 29; solidarity 176n64
labour laws 45, 71, 93–4

For Product Safety Concerns and Information please contact our EU
representative GPSR@taylorandfrancis.com
Taylor & Francis Verlag GmbH, Kaufingerstraße 24, 80331 München, Germany

www.ingramcontent.com/pod-product-compliance
Ingram Content Group UK Ltd.
Pitfield, Milton Keynes, MK11 3LW, UK
UKHW040927180425
457613UK00004B/44